Finding favour
in the sight of God

NEW STUDIES IN BIBLICAL THEOLOGY 46

Series editor: D. A. Carson

Finding favour
in the sight of God

A THEOLOGY OF WISDOM LITERATURE

Richard P. Belcher Jr

APOLLOS

IVP Academic
An imprint of InterVarsity Press
Downers Grove, Illinois

APOLLOS (an imprint of Inter-Varsity Press)
36 Causton Street
London SW1P 4ST, England
ivpbooks.com
ivp@ivpbooks.com

InterVarsity Press, USA
P.O. Box 1400
Downers Grove, IL 60515, USA
ivpress.com
email@ivpress.com

InterVarsity Press® is the book-publishing division of InterVarsity Christian Fellowship/USA®, a movement of students and faculty active on campus at hundreds of universities, colleges, and schools of nursing in the United States of America, and a member movement of the International Fellowship of Evangelical Students. For information about local and regional activities, visit intervarsity.org.

Inter-Varsity Press, England, originated within the Inter-Varsity Fellowship, now the Universities and Colleges Christian Fellowship, a student movement connecting Christian Unions in universities and colleges throughout Great Britain, and a member movement of the International Fellowship of Evangelical Students. That historic association is maintained, and all senior IVP staff and committee members subscribe to the UCCF Basis of Faith. Website: www.uccf.org.uk.

Unless otherwise indicated, Scripture quotations are from the ESV Bible (The Holy Bible, English Standard Version), copyright © 2001 by Crossway, a publishing ministry of Good News Publishers. Used by permission. All rights reserved.

Scripture quotations marked NASB are from the New American Standard Bible®, Copyright © 1960, 1962, 1963, 1968, 1971, 1972, 1973, 1975, 1977, 1995 by The Lockman Foundation. Used by permission.

In the chapters on the book of Ecclesiastes, the author's own translation of the biblical text is used.

First published 2018

Set in Monotype Times New Roman
Typeset in Great Britain by CRB Associates, Potterhanworth, Lincolnshire
Printed in Canada

USA ISBN 978-0-8308-2647-6 (print)
USA ISBN 978-0-8308-7213-8 (digital)

UK ISBN 978-1-78359-714-7 (print)
UK ISBN 978-1-78359-715-4 (digital)

InterVarsity Press is committed to ecological stewardship and to the conservation of natural resources in all our operations. This book was printed using sustainably sourced paper.

British Library Cataloguing-in-Publication Data
A catalogue record for this book is available from the British Library.

Library of Congress Cataloging-in-Publication Data
Names: Belcher, Richard P., 1934- author.
Title: Finding favour in the sight of God : a theology of wisdom literature /
  Richard P. Belcher, Jr.
Description: Downers Grove, IL, USA : InterVarsity Press, [2018] | Series:
  New studies in biblical theology ; 46 | Includes bibliographical
  references and index.
Identifiers: LCCN 2018017718 (print) | LCCN 2018025086 (ebook) | ISBN
  9780830872138 (eBook) | ISBN 9780830826476 (pbk. : alk. paper)
Subjects: LCSH: Wisdom--Biblical teaching. | Wisdom literature. | Bible.
  Proverbs--Criticism, interpretation, etc. | Bible. Job--Criticism,
  interpretation, etc. | Bible. Ecclesiastes--Criticism, interpretation, etc.
Classification: LCC BS1199.W57 (ebook) | LCC BS1199.W57 B45 2018 (print) |
  DDC 223/.06--dc23
LC record available at https://lccn.loc.gov/2018017718

P	19	18	17	16	15	14	13	12	11	10	9	8	7	6	5	4	3	2	1
Y	34	33	32	31	30	29	28	27	26	25	24	23	22	21	20	19	18			

This book is dedicated to five wonderful grandchildren

Lewellyn Grace Dixon
Boston Cole Dixon
Christopher Stephen Sewell
Caleb Paul Sewell
MacKenzie Joy Sewell

May you increase in wisdom and in stature
and in favour with God and man

Contents

Series preface

New Studies in Biblical Theology is a series of monographs that address key issues in the discipline of biblical theology. Contributions to the series focus on one or more of three areas: (1) the nature and status of biblical theology, including its relations with other disciplines (e.g. historical theology, exegesis, systematic theology, historical criticism, narrative theology); (2) the articulation and exposition of the structure of thought of a particular biblical writer or corpus; and (3) the delineation of a biblical theme across all or part of the biblical corpora.

Above all, these monographs are creative attempts to help thinking Christians understand their Bibles better. The series aims simultaneously to instruct and to edify, to interact with the current literature, and to point the way ahead. In God's universe, mind and heart should not be divorced: in this series we will try not to separate what God has joined together. While the notes interact with the best of scholarly literature, the text is uncluttered with untransliterated Greek and Hebrew, and tries to avoid too much technical jargon. The volumes are written within the framework of confessional evangelicalism, but there is always an attempt at thoughtful engagement with the sweep of the relevant literature.

One of the commitments of biblical theology is to study and delineate the contours of collections of biblical books, of books belonging to one genre – and no genre feels more out of step with the rest of the Bible than the wisdom literature. Here there is little emphasis on salvation history, no focus on the covenant, no prophetic oratory or apocalyptic imagery, relatively little that would be understood as prediction, and no extended legal codes. All sides acknowledge the wisdom genre is difficult to define, and not easy to integrate with the rest of the Bible; yet all sides acknowledge that wisdom's influence spills over into other genres: for example, Psalm 1 is rightly thought of as a wisdom psalm, while the polarities with which Jesus ends the Sermon on the Mount are rightly understood to be superlative examples of wisdom preaching.

For long periods of time, wisdom literature was periodically neglected by Old Testament scholars – and then, as has happened during the last few decades, there is a flurry of renewed interest in it. The NSBT series has previously offered two volumes that bear on the topic: the helpful study of Proverbs 1 – 9 by Daniel J. Estes, *Hear, My Son* (vol. 4), and the delightful mixed genre volume by Barry G. Webb, *Five Festal Garments* (vol. 10). In the present volume Richard Belcher carefully sifts recent approaches to Old Testament wisdom, and learns much from all of them, but comes away insisting that, while wisdom is richly human, it is not humanistic: it is deeply God-centred, and properly grounded in creation. Moreover, he carefully tests his theses and emphases by devoting two or three chapters each to three quite different examples of wisdom literature: Proverbs, Job and Ecclesiastes.

This thoughtful book, like the wisdom it seeks to explore, will open up fresh horizons of reflection, and, please God, make its readers wiser than they were before.

D. A. Carson
Trinity Evangelical Divinity School

Author's preface

Wisdom literature is no longer the 'orphan child' it was in the distant past. There has been an explosion in the interest in wisdom, so that now many works are available to explain it. There is every opportunity for people to 'Get wisdom; get insight' (Prov. 4:5), but if one pays close attention to the world of the twenty-first century, it seems apparent that the practical sensibilities that come from wisdom are found in very few places, which means that wisdom literature is needed now more than ever. The book of Proverbs lays the proper foundation for the education of the next generation. It gives parents practical guidelines for helping their children walk the way of wisdom grounded in the fear of the Lord. Of course, Proverbs also helps the wise to increase in learning. The book of Job wrestles with suffering and the sovereignty of God. It reminds us that we are not in control of this world, or even of our own lives, so we must trust in a sovereign God to work out his purposes. The book of Ecclesiastes wrestles with the meaning of life in a world that seems to be falling apart, much like the world in which we live. Each of these books points us backward to the foundational principles of how to live life in a fallen world and forward to the need for Christ and the gospel of good news.

I would like to thank Dr Carson for the opportunity to write on this topic for this series. I have fond memories of eating ribs at a restaurant when he came to teach for Reformed Theological Seminary (RTS) in Charlotte, North Carolina. I would like to thank Philip Duce for his patience in answering my questions along the way and for giving good guidance. Thanks also to Eldo Barkhuizen for his detailed and timely copy-editing of the electronic files. Others have assisted me in this project. It has been a privilege to teach at RTS Charlotte for over twenty years. I would like to thank Dr Ligon Duncan, the Chancellor of RTS, and Dr Mike Kruger, the president of the Charlotte campus, for making RTS a faculty-friendly place to work that encourages teaching and research. I would like to thank Jessica Hudson at the RTS Charlotte library for her help in getting resources, some of them quickly at the last minute. I have had very good teaching assistants over the years, including Mark James, Brittain Brewer and Robert Hertha, who have helped in a variety of ways on this project. Also, Michael Bauer went beyond the call of duty by reading through the manuscript and offering helpful suggestions. I would like to thank Peter Hastie, the principal of Presbyterian Theological College in Melbourne, Australia, for the opportunity to teach this material in August 2016. My family has always been a great source of blessing. Many thanks to my wife, Lu, for her invaluable support: let her works praise her in the gates (Prov. 31:31). Our three daughters are now grown (Nikki, Danielle and Alisha), and each of them is walking the path of wisdom, for which we are so thankful. We are the happy grandparents of five grandchildren, to whom we dedicate this book. Our prayer is that each of you finds wisdom and learns to walk in the path of righteousness

So you will find favour and good success
in the sight of God and man.
(Prov. 3:4)

Richard P. Belcher Jr

Abbreviations

AB	Anchor Bible
ANE	ancient Near East(ern)
ANET	*Ancient Near Eastern Texts Relating to the Old Testament*, ed. J. B. Pritchard, 3rd ed. with Supplement, Princeton: Princeton University Press, 1969
BBR	*Bulletin of Biblical Research*
BI	*Biblical Interpretation*
Bib	*Biblica*
BK	*Bibel und Kirche*
BKAT	Biblischer Kommentar, Altes Testament
BSac	*Bibliotheca sacra*
BST	The Bible Speaks Today
DBSJ	*Detroit Baptist Seminary Journal*
DOTWPW	*Dictionary of the Old Testament: Wisdom, Poetry, & Writings*, ed. T. Longman III and P. Enns, Downers Grove: InterVarsity Press; Nottingham: Inter-Varsity Press, 2008
EBC	Expositor's Bible Commentary
ESV	English Standard Version (2011)
EvQ	*Evangelical Quarterly*
HS	*Hebrew Studies*
HUCA	*Hebrew Union College Annual*
IBS	*Irish Biblical Studies*
ICC	International Critical Commentary
Int	*Interpretation*
ITC	International Theological Commentary
JBL	*Journal of Biblical Literature*
JSOT	*Journal for the Study of the Old Testament*
LXX	Septuagint
NAC	New American Commentary
NASB	New American Standard Bible (1977)
NCBC	New Century Bible Commentary

NIB	*The New Interpreter's Bible*, ed. L. Keck, 10 vols., Nashville: Abingdon, 2015
NIBC	New International Biblical Commentary
NICNT	New International Commentary on the New Testament
NICOT	New International Commentary on the Old Testament
NIDOTTE	*New International Dictionary of Old Testament Theology and Exegesis*, ed. W. A. VanGemeren, 5 vols., Grand Rapids: Zondervan, 1997
NIGTC	New International Greek Testament Commentary
NIV	New International Version (2011)
NIVAC	The NIV Application Commentary
NKJV	New King James Version (1982)
NS	New Series
NSBT	New Studies in Biblical Theology
NT	New Testament
NTC	New Testament Commentary
OT	Old Testament
OTL	Old Testament Library
PNTC	Pillar New Testament Commentary
PTW	Preaching the Word
QR	*Quarterly Review*
RSV	Revised Standard Version (1952)
SBLDS	Society of Biblical Literature Dissertation Series
SJT	*Scottish Journal of Theology*
Syr	Syriac
Tg(s)	Targum(s); Targumic
Them	*Themelios*
THOTC	Two Horizons Old Testament Commentary
TJ	*Trinity Journal*
TOTC	Tyndale Old Testament Commentaries
TWOT	*Theological Wordbook of the Old Testament*, ed. R. Laird Harris, G. L. Archer Jr and B. K. Waltke, 2 vols., Chicago: Moody, 1980
TynB	*Tyndale Bulletin*
Vg	Vulgate
VT	*Vetus Testamentum*
VTSup	Supplements to Vetus Testamentum
WBC	Word Biblical Commentary
WTJ	*Westminster Theological Journal*
ZTK	*Zeitschrift für Theologie und Kirche*

Chapter One

The problem of wisdom literature in Old Testament theology

Wisdom literature has emerged recently from the shadow of salvation history to become a discipline in its own right in OT studies. This emergence has not occurred without its own problems, including the definition of wisdom, the relationship of wisdom literature to the rest of the OT, and the relationship of Israel's wisdom literature to that of the ANE. These problems are important because they have an impact on the understanding of the theology of Proverbs, Job and Ecclesiastes.

Wisdom literature: an orphan in Old Testament theology

OT scholars have not always known what to do with wisdom literature. Many ignored it in their development of OT theology, or, worse, saw it as an aberrant offshoot of Israel's religion, more like an errant child.[1] Murphy called wisdom literature an orphan.[2] Wright wrote a biblical theology that emphasized theology as a proclamation of the acts of God. The difficulty with wisdom literature is that its narrow focus does not allow it to include a recital of God's action in history. It also does not fit into the type of faith exhibited in the historical and prophetic literatures.[3]

Eichrodt wrote *Theology of the Old Testament* (originally published in German in 1933), which centres on the concept of the covenant.[4]

---

[1] Clements 1995: 269, 271.

[2] Murphy 1969: 289.

[3] Wright 1952: 103–104.

[4] Eichrodt 1967: 1.36. The covenant is the concept in Israelite thought that 'gave definitive expression to the binding of the people to God and by means of which they established firmly from the start the particularity of their knowledge of him'. For Eichrodt's general approach see Hayes and Prussner 1985: 179–184. They call Eichrodt's work one of the most significant works of its genre published in the twentieth century.

He rejected two common approaches to OT theology. One was the attempt to organize biblical materials according to the outlines of dogmatic theology and the other was the pure historical approach that did not emphasize theology. He wanted to present a comprehensive survey and a systematic ordering of the material as a self-contained entity, exhibiting a constant basic character in spite of ever-changing historical conditions.[5] He devoted ten pages in the second volume of his OT theology to a discussion of the wisdom of God. For a long time the wisdom of God made no contribution to Israel's religious understanding because it was perceived to have a strong secular flavour.[6] The gnomic wisdom in Solomonic circles was concerned primarily with skill in practical affairs and rules for success in daily life. The secular nature of wisdom literature was also due to its dependence on Egyptian literature. This connection made it clear that Israelite wisdom literature could not give a central place to the national religion of Yahweh, with the latter's emphasis on the cult, the covenant and messianic hopes.[7] Wisdom was bound to the outlook of humanity in general and to guidance in practical affairs. This early wisdom remained too dependent on foreign models. Only later in the Persian period did wisdom expand its horizon to examine the purpose and order of the cosmos in Proverbs 1 – 9, Job, Ecclesiastes, and the apocryphal writings of Ecclesiasticus, Baruch and the Wisdom of Solomon.[8]

G. von Rad also wrote a magisterial OT theology (published in 1957). He argued against the organization of OT theology around central topics or systematic theological categories. He believed these approaches imposed an alien structure on the OT. The focus of attention should be Israel's own explicit assertions about Yahweh formulated as creedal confessions.[9] One way that Israel responded to the saving acts of Yahweh was to write creedal confessions. A more personal response to the saving acts of Yahweh was to offer praise to him, to ask him questions and even to complain to him about her sufferings. The psalms and the wisdom literature are the answer that Israel makes to Yahweh's saving acts. In this response a theological

[5] Hayes and Prussner 1985: 180.
[6] Preuss 1987: 114–136. He argues that wisdom is marginal to Israel's faith and that the God of wisdom is not Yahweh (see also Bartholomew 2016: 11).
[7] Hayes and Prussner 1985: 184.
[8] Eichrodt 1967: 2.80–83.
[9] Hayes and Prussner 1985: 233–234.

doctrine of humanity becomes clear. The way Israel saw herself before God is worth the highest attention theologically.[10]

The difficult nature of wisdom literature

Scholars had trouble fitting wisdom literature into the rest of the OT because this literature was different from other parts of the OT.[11] Wisdom literature has little emphasis on key concepts that dominate the rest of the OT. Scholars were so immersed in the study of salvation history and God's acts in history that they did not know how to approach literature that did not have that emphasis. Wisdom literature does not emphasize the covenant or the other major traditions of the OT, such as the revelation of God at Mount Sinai or the concept of Israel as God's special people. Instead, the emphasis is on observation rather than revelation and on the individual rather than the nation. The sages did not understand history as the arena in which God worked to accomplish his plans for his covenant people. They were more concerned with the individual than the nation, so that redemptive historical events did not play a role in their thoughts.[12] A distinction between wisdom and Yahwism developed so that they were understood as two totally different approaches to God. Some even argued that wisdom was not a genuine expression of Israelite faith. Wisdom literature was seen as an alien body in the OT and the attempt of Israel to shape herself in the image of her neighbours.[13]

Two factors were working against wisdom literature. It not only stressed different things than the rest of the OT but also looked very much like the wisdom literature of the ANE. These two factors led many to draw the conclusion that Israel's wisdom literature was secular and patterned after the literature of the ANE. There are similarities between Israel's wisdom literature and the wisdom literature of the ANE, particularly Egyptian wisdom literature. Similarities in content are evident because they share many of the same themes. Both speak of riches that fly away (Prov. 23:5; *ANET*, 422).[14] Both speak of the importance of justice and not oppressing the poor or

---

[10] Von Rad 1962: 1.355–356.
[11] For a perceptive analysis of the development of wisdom around several turns (historical, literary, postmodern and theological) see Bartholomew 2016: 3–36.
[12] Crenshaw 1974: 23–55.
[13] Murphy 1975: 117. Murphy gives examples of those who see wisdom as an alien body, but argues that wisdom and Yahwism go together.
[14] These examples are found in Kidner 1985: 126.

the widow (Prov. 15:25; 31:9; *ANET*, 415). Both speak of treating the enemy kindly by giving him food to eat (Prov. 25:21; *ANET*, 422). Both speak of disciplining a child with a rod (Prov. 23:13–14) or a beating (Ahikar 2.22).[15] Similarities were also seen between the Egyptian work *The Instruction of Amenemope* and Proverbs 22:17 – 24:22 (see chapter 4). The book of Job has been compared to Mesopotamian works that deal with similar themes, such as *A Man and His God*, *The Babylonian Theodicy* and *I Will Praise the Lord of Wisdom* (also called *The Babylonian Job*). Although there are significant differences between Job and these works, the similarities caused scholars to view the wisdom literature of Israel as different from the rest of the OT and an attempt to shape Israel in the image of other nations.

A new foundation for wisdom literature: creation

In the older works of OT theology the place of both creation and wisdom was determined by the role of the historical traditions of election, covenant and redemption. Von Rad's statement 'The Yahwistic faith of the Old Testament is a faith based on the notion of election and therefore primarily concerned with redemption' shows the problem of fitting the doctrine of creation into OT history. How can creation be related to the problem of redemption that dominates the whole OT?[16] He argued that certain statements in Deutero-Isaiah show that the doctrine of creation had been incorporated into salvation history and put into the service of redemption. Creation was brought into direct contact with redemption in Isaiah 43:1 and 44:24, showing that the doctrine of creation does not belong in a separate category from the redemption at the Red Sea. These two distinct acts are part of the same act of the universal redemptive purpose of God. The doctrine of creation, however, still does not stand on its own but is swallowed up in the doctrine of redemption.[17]

Both creation and wisdom were understood to stand outside the mainstream of the historical traditions. Only later in Israel's history were these ideas brought into harmony with the historical traditions of Israel when the faith of Israel was confronted with new ideas, and

---

[15] Kidner 1985: 131.
[16] Von Rad 1968: 131.
[17] Ibid. 136, 138.

interest in the traditions of salvation history had grown weak.[18] In this way creation faith became part of the central faith of salvation history.[19]

G. von Rad also addressed wisdom in a later book, *Wisdom in Israel*, where he explored how the experiential knowledge in wisdom came to expression and what made up the fundamentals of its understanding of the world. He wanted to examine wisdom on its own terms. The discovery of the wisdom literature from the ANE showed that the post-exilic dating of the wisdom material was mistaken because wisdom was an earlier phenomenon common to the ANE. It also raised the question of the relationship of wisdom to Yahwistic faith that was seen as more exclusive. A work was needed that started with the wisdom texts themselves to understand the thinking and values of the wise men.[20]

Wisdom is concerned with the order in creation to help human beings acquire knowledge of their environment to achieve mastery over life. The creation order communicates truth that Israel seeks to express. In wisdom a wise man was in search of himself and took things into his own hands without appeal to a specific, divine commission. This approach is different from the approach of the theologians of history, who present Israel's historical experience. The initiative in the former lay with human beings and in the latter with Yahweh. These two groups use a different language and set of concepts. The thinking of the wise men was not stimulated by divine activity in history but by human existence. Salvation was not brought about by Yahweh's activity in history or by any kind of human agency (Moses or David), but by specific factors inherent in creation itself. In this way wisdom was a phenomenon that stood on its own and was in theological tension with traditional Yahwism.[21] This is a distinctive Israelite concept, for the idea of a testimony emanating from creation is attested only in Israel.[22]

Other scholars began to argue for an independent basis and structure for creation. Zimmerli argued that wisdom had no relationship to the history between God and Israel but operated

---

[18] Von Rad 1962: 1.449–452. Von Rad notes that internal conditions, such as freeing herself from the archaic forms of faith, were conditions that led to new ideas. Part of these new ideas in wisdom literature included the cosmic wisdom of Prov. 8.

[19] Reventlow 1985: 139–140.

[20] Von Rad 1972: 6–10.

[21] Ibid. 289–291, 307, 314.

[22] Reventlow 1985: 177.

within its own theological framework of creation. Wisdom seeks to order life and to build the rules of life based on observation of the world. It recommends the blessing that human beings can obtain by following the rules of its teaching and warns against the harm that comes to the one who disregards them.[23] In developing the theological framework for wisdom Zimmerli highlighted the dichotomies between wisdom and OT theology. Proverbs speaks about people, never the people as the elect of Yahweh. The king is never identified as the anointed king of Israel or the son of David. God is also never identified as the God of Israel or as God of the Fathers. Although wisdom may borrow from other parts of the OT, such as inhabiting the land (Prov. 2:22–23), there is not a clear reference to the history of Israel. There is also a difference between the authority of the law and the authority of wisdom. The admonition of the wise man remains in the framework of counselling. Counsel allows a certain amount of liberty for people: they can either follow or not follow the advice. It has the authority of insight, but that is different from the authority of the Lord in the law. And yet God authorizes human beings to go out into the world to investigate it, to draw conclusions concerning behaviour that leads to blessing, and behaviour that leads to negative consequences.[24]

Schmid sought to end the silence concerning creation theology and to address the perception that creation theology is secondary to Christian theology by giving it a central theological significance as the broad horizon of biblical theology. He acknowledges that creation takes second place because it is viewed as late in Israel's history. If one looks at how creation is handled in the ANE, several things become apparent. Creation did not just deal with the origin of the world but with the concept of order. This order manifests itself in a political order over against chaos and in a legal order manifested in justice. The connection between the cosmic, political and social orders that find their unity in creation is manifested in wisdom, as in the Egyptian concept of Ma'at, in the integral concept of the role of the king, and in the connection between act and consequence. Schmid found this approach in the pre-exilic prophets, where they criticize the people based on the order found in interpersonal relationships that is also connected in creation faith to law and wisdom. The concept of righteousness in the exilic and post-exilic prophets was not understood narrowly as a legal matter but as a

---

[23] Zimmerli 1964: 146–158.
[24] Ibid. 152–153.

universal world order in a comprehensive salvation. These views are also found in the Deuteronomistic and Primeval Histories. In other words, history is understood as the implementation of the order of creation. God's creation of the world order and his sustaining of it provide the framework for history.[25]

The influence of wisdom in the Old Testament

As wisdom became more prominent as an independent discipline, scholars began to find wisdom ideas and themes in many places of the OT. Crenshaw comments that von Rad's study of the influence of wisdom on the Joseph narrative led to similar claims of wisdom's influence upon Esther and the 'succession narrative' (2 Sam. 9 – 2 Kgs 2). In addition, discoveries of new wisdom texts from Mesopotamia, Ugarit and Egypt spurred the trend to unprecedented heights.[26] In fact, wisdom became so prominent in OT studies that a book devoted to wisdom in ancient Israel finds wisdom influence in OT narrative traditions, in Solomonic historiography, Amos, Hosea, Isaiah, Jeremiah, Daniel and the psalms.[27] Crenshaw warned that the excitement of this new direction in scholarship led to 'exaggerated claims supported by dubious arguments and assumptions' so that a study of methodology to determine wisdom influence was needed.[28] If wisdom's influence is everywhere, then wisdom's influence is nowhere, because the definition of wisdom is too broad.

Crenshaw argues that wisdom speech does not mean wisdom influence. Wisdom can be defined as 'the quest for self-understanding in terms of relationships with things, people, and the Creator' that moves on three levels. Nature wisdom tries to master things for human survival and well-being by studying natural phenomena as they relate to people and nature. Juridical and practical wisdom examine human relationships in an ordered society, and theological wisdom deals with issues of theodicy. Wisdom influence can be proved only by a stylistic or ideological peculiarity found primarily in wisdom. Just the use of wisdom terms, topics or common words such as 'hear, know, keep, law, teach, etc.' does not mean wisdom influence.[29] The history of

---

[25] Schmid 1984: 102–108.
[26] Crenshaw 1995: 312. He lists wisdom's influence on Gen. 1 – 11, 37, 39 – 50; Exod. 34; Deuteronomy; 2 Sam. 9 – 20; 2 Kgs 1 – 2; Amos, Habakkuk, Isaiah and Jonah.
[27] Day et al. 1995.
[28] Crenshaw 1995: 313.
[29] Ibid. 313–316.

wisdom is also important when it is possible to determine its structural development, geographic spread and ideological formulation.[30] Crenshaw concludes that the Joseph story, the succession narrative and the book of Esther are lacking in the characteristics that would prove wisdom influence. Some of the problems he sees are the use of common topics that are in wisdom but not peculiar to wisdom and the use of numerous non-wisdom themes.[31] His conclusions concerning wisdom influence are beneficial, but he sees wisdom as an entity separated from other streams of the OT that has its own peculiar ideological emphases.[32]

The definition of wisdom

The definition of wisdom is important in trying to determine its influence on other parts of the OT and in trying to define wisdom literature. Crenshaw notes that no single definition is sufficient because of the variety of phenomena covered by the Hebrew word.[33] There are three things generally associated with wisdom: the use of wisdom forms, the occurrence of certain themes or subject matter, and an emphasis on creation. The use of wisdom forms includes the use of the word 'blessed', various forms of proverbs (antithetical proverbs, better-than sayings), acrostics, numerical sayings, parables, riddles and fables.[34] The use of certain themes is also associated with wisdom. These themes include divine retribution (the deed–consequence relationship),[35] theodicy, marriage, raising children, creation order, human experience, and the two ways.[36] The development of creation as the basis of wisdom gave wisdom an independent status over

---

[30] Crenshaw (ibid. 317) calls the change in wisdom in apocryphal works the 'most striking observation'.

[31] Ibid. 318–325.

[32] Sneed 2015: 53–54. He argues against the approach to wisdom represented by Crenshaw.

[33] Crenshaw 1981: 16–17.

[34] See chapter 2 for definitions of words associated with wisdom.

[35] Retribution can be defined as the conviction that the righteous will prosper and the wicked will suffer in proportion to their respective righteousness and wickedness (Walton 2008: 647). Righteous deeds should lead to blessing, and wicked deeds should lead to negative consequences. A better phrase to describe this might be 'character–consequence' because it is the attitudes and resulting lifestyles that are in focus (Boström 2016: 139). This work will use the phrase 'deed–consequence' to highlight the mechanical view of this relationship that can develop, as in the book of Job.

[36] Perdue 1994b: 34–48. He lists many of these themes in discussing approaches to wisdom theology. Crenshaw (1981: 18) speaks of a particular world view and common topics, such as the dangers of adultery, the perils of the tongue, undeserved suffering, etc.

against the emphasis on history, covenant and law. Wisdom emphasizes interaction with creation based on observation, reflection and drawing conclusions (Prov. 24:30–34), a different approach from receiving revelation from God.

The different emphasis in wisdom literature over against salvation history has led some to characterize it as humanistic,[37] where its foundation and goals are distinct from Yahwism. Crenshaw's definition of wisdom as 'the reasoned search for specific ways to assure well-being and the implementation of those discoveries in daily existence' is good as far as it goes. The problem is that he characterizes the distinctive wisdom ethic as people trying to secure their well-being apart from the need or expectation of divine assistance.[38] This view goes against clear statements in Proverbs (1:7; 3:5–7) and does not account for the fact that when Job struggles with his suffering, he seeks to hear from God. Crenshaw highlights that 'wisdom addresses natural, human, and theological dimensions of reality, and it constitutes an attitude toward life, a living tradition, and a literary corpus'.[39]

More recently, Kynes argues that wisdom as a category is 'plagued by definitional deficiency, amorphous social location, and haemorrhaging influence, among other maladies'.[40] It is a modern scholarly construct created in the mid-nineteenth century. Wisdom as a genre category and as a movement with its own social location and world view distinct from the rest of the OT should be abandoned. An emphasis on experience does not need to be set against revelation, and creation does not need to be separated from history. A better approach would be to explore connections between texts normally associated with wisdom and other biblical texts (intertextuality) to see what these books have in common.[41] He is willing to use the title 'wisdom literature' for Proverbs, Ecclesiastes and Job, in agreement with Weeks, who states 'so long as this is taken simply as a description of subject-matter, and not of form or origin'.[42] A comparison of these

---

[37] The more wisdom, with its own method and foundation, is viewed as separate from the rest of the OT the more it will be understood as secular humanistic or secular. This includes a view like that of Preuss (1972: 117–145), who argued at one point that the God of wisdom is more like the god of the ANE than the God of the rest of the OT. Wisdom is focused on human effort for salvation. But even Crenshaw (1990: 216) affirms that the sages believed in their own ability to cope in the face of adversity.

[38] Crenshaw 1981: 24.

[39] Ibid. 24–25.

[40] Kynes 2015: 11.

[41] Ibid. 32.

[42] Weeks 1999: 27.

three wisdom books demonstrates certain similarities that help in the interpretation of each other, but these three books should also be compared with other texts that will bring to light common ideas and themes.[43]

Kynes and Sneed have raised legitimate concerns about the 'traditional' approach to wisdom represented by Crenshaw, and advocate a unified relationship between wisdom and the rest of the OT. Longman appreciates their concerns and concludes that Kynes's advocacy of intertextuality as the key for studying wisdom books achieves much the same results as his genre-based approach.[44] Bartholomew also sees intertextuality as a way to move the discussion forward concerning the relationship between Proverbs, Job and Ecclesiastes, the relationship between these wisdom books and the rest of the OT, the relationship between OT wisdom and the NT, and the reception history of OT wisdom.[45] These approaches have led to a more nuanced discussion of wisdom and its relationship to the rest of the OT. Just because Judges 9 uses a fable does not mean it is wisdom literature. Just because a text deals with marriage does not mean it is wisdom literature (Mal. 2:10–16). Just because a text describes the investigation and organization of God's creation does not mean it is wisdom literature (Gen. 2:19–20). It is appropriate, however, to explore these common themes that are found in the wisdom books and other books of the OT.[46] Although there is room for discussion whether some parts of the OT should be characterized as wisdom literature,[47] it should be clear that Proverbs, Job and Ecclesiastes are the main wisdom books.

[43] Kynes 2015: 31. Kynes has a forthcoming work (see the bibliography) that continues this argument. Longman (2017: 276–282) agrees with many of Kynes's concerns but believes that his criticisms are effective against a wooden (and outdated) view of genre. Longman argues the case for wisdom literature as a genre category based on a fluid understanding of genre (there are multiple levels of abstraction in texts).

[44] Longman 2017: 282.

[45] Bartholomew 2016: 23–24.

[46] For recent treatments of wisdom in other parts of the OT along these lines see Firth and Wilson 2016. Chapters in this book not only cover Proverbs, Job, Ecclesiastes and the Song of Solomon, but also include the analysis of wisdom themes in Ruth, OT narrative and Psalms, as well as chapters on the themes of retribution and biblical theology. Longman 2017 also has chapters that cover Deuteronomy, Psalms, Song of Songs and Prophecy as well as a chapter on Joseph and Daniel and a chapter on Adam and Solomon.

[47] There is debate about whether the Song of Solomon and certain psalms should be classified as wisdom. For recent discussions that see wisdom themes in the Song see Clarke 2016: 100–112 and Longman 2017: 75–77. For analysis of wisdom in the psalms see Stocks 2016: 194–201 and Longman 2017: 66–69.

The development of wisdom in biblical theology

There is a general consensus in critical scholarship that a development in wisdom literature took place over several centuries. The impetus for the wisdom movement does not necessarily come from Solomon, as presented in 1 Kings 4, but from the loss of the monarchy in the fall of Jerusalem to Babylon. The era of wisdom's fullest literary development occurs in the post-exilic period. Israel transitioned from a nation state to a scattered people among many nations. This change led to an international outlook that was more universal.[48] The corporate perspective on life that allowed the individual emphasis reflected in wisdom literature to develop was lost. Proverbs combined older wisdom before the exile (Prov. 10:1 – 22:21) with later wisdom after the exile, and then wisdom literature as late as the Hellenistic period was added (Prov. 1 – 9). The book of Job comes from the Persian period because it no longer treats disease as the concern of cultic purity and holiness. Ecclesiastes comes from the late third century as it reveals the influence of Greek philosophy on Jewish life.[49] The progress of wisdom is explained in a number of ways. Some speak of a crisis of wisdom, where wisdom became hardened and not open to new observations. A mechanical view of the deed–consequence relationship developed. Job and Ecclesiastes are a response to this crisis.[50] Others stress that the changing times in which Israel lived in the Persian period produced a crisis of social stress that older ways of thinking were not able to combat. The response in Proverbs was an emphasis on the family to preserve the community's ideals. Ecclesiastes is a salvage operation for coping with the crisis of changes in socio-economics, politics and epistemology (a distinctly sapiential focus).[51] Crenshaw speaks of a process of theologization that took place over time in three stages that culminated in the identification of wisdom with Torah in Sirach.[52] Wisdom developed as a response to the changing social conditions in Israel after the exile.

A major reason that the post-exilic period is viewed as the impetus for the development of wisdom literature is that the account of Solomon in 1 Kings 4 is considered to be unreliable legend and

---

[48] Clements 1992: 22, 25.
[49] Ibid. 33–34.
[50] Schmid 1966: 162–164.
[51] Brown 2014: 39–40, 139–142.
[52] Crenshaw 1976: 24–25.

folklore.[53] Assumptions concerning the dating of books make a difference in how one perceives the development of wisdom and how it relates to OT theology. In discussing what texts should be used to establish creation theology, Hermission argues that Genesis 1 is not the place to start because it is a late, mature product of Israelite creation theology.[54] The critical reconstruction of Israel's history that Wellhausen popularized is still common even if source criticism and the way he presented Israel's history are not followed. Scripture clearly presents a flowering of wisdom under Solomon; and if one accepts that account, then a different view of the development of wisdom is possible.[55] Without denying the differences between salvation history and wisdom literature, there are many reasons to see areas of similarity and common concern that lead to a more unified approach to creation, wisdom and salvation history. First, wisdom must already have been in existence before the reign of Solomon for there to have been an emergence of wisdom during his reign.[56] The fact that Solomon as king was not only wise but that he was to enforce the law of God makes connections between Proverbs and Deuteronomy understandable (Prov. 6:20–22 and Deut. 6:7–9).[57]

Second, the early chapters of Genesis contain key elements from both creation and salvation history. Genesis 1 begins with creation as a world of order as God transforms the earth from being uninhabitable for life (formless and void) to a place habitable for plants, animals and people. God establishes the order of evening and morning and

[53] Crenshaw 1981: 42–54. Not all scholars follow Crenshaw. Clements (1992) argues that wisdom had a close association with the monarchy. Brueggemann (1972) attempts to reclaim wisdom ethics by focusing on David's role 'as a man of faith in a world come of age', showing that people are able to choose wisely and decide responsibly.

[54] Hermission 1978: 47.

[55] Schultz 1997: 277–278. He argues against a historical development or crisis in wisdom and sees the relationship between Proverbs, Job and Ecclesiastes as an inner dialogue, not a contradiction. The 'crisis' view arose partly because differences between Proverbs and Ecclesiastes were no longer explained in terms of Solomon's biography. There is a basic unity between these three wisdom books in that neither Job nor Ecclesiastes rejects the traditional wisdom of Proverbs. I agree with this assessment except that the first-person autobiography of Qohelet does conflict with Proverbs, but the epilogue agrees with Proverbs. The debate is an inner dialogue that can take place in a person who has experienced the blessings of God (Proverbs) but has also experienced suffering so that there is a wrestling with the issues of life (Job and Ecclesiastes).

[56] Crenshaw 1981: 57. He recognizes that most canonical proverbs, except Prov. 1 – 9, existed before the rise of the monarchical state, but views the account in 1 Kgs 4 as legend and fable.

[57] Hubbard 1966: 12–13. He discusses the establishment of the monarchy and the rise of the wisdom movement with the implication that links between the wisdom movement and Israel's covenant faith are not as late as many argue.

the creation of vegetables and animals according to their kind. Human beings are given the highest place in creation in order to rule over God's creation, under his authority, and to care for creation. In Genesis 2 Adam is placed in the garden to work it. He has to learn how to care for the plants in the garden. He also names the animals in the garden, an activity of exercising dominion in organizing and cataloguing things in God's creation. Adam is also given a law to obey (Gen. 2:16) and, some would argue, a covenant to keep.[58] The serpent in Genesis 3 is called 'crafty' ('ārûm), a term that is common in Proverbs where the positive meaning of 'prudent' dominates (Prov. 12:6, 23; 14:8, 15). Occurrences outside Proverbs generally convey the negative meaning of getting what you want in a deceptive, dishonest way (Job 5:12; 15:5; Exod. 21:14).[59] The disobedience of Adam and Eve to God's command disrupts relationships and brings the disorder of the curse of sin into God's creation (Gen. 3:16–19). God's response to deliver human beings from the curse of sin (Gen. 3:15) is the beginning of salvation history, which has the goal to restore order in creation. The rest of the OT tells this story and points to the fulfilment of God's purposes in Jesus Christ. The God of creation is the God of salvation history. Genesis 1 – 3 contains all the elements of order, disorder, covenant, law and the beginnings of salvation history.[60] These facts do not prove that Genesis 1 – 3 is wisdom literature, but it is important that these ideas are closely associated with each other in this foundational text.[61]

Third, the account of Solomon in 1 Kings makes allusions to Adam in the garden so that Solomon functions as a second Adam.[62] Solomon is acclaimed king at Gihon (1 Kgs 1:33, 38, 45), a water source on the slope below Jerusalem that bears the same name as one of the primeval rivers of Genesis 2:13. Solomon is urged to become a 'man' ('îš) and 'keep' (šāmar) the charge of Yahweh (1 Kgs 2:2–3) just as the first one to be called a 'man' is charged with keeping the garden (Gen. 2:15). Solomon exercises dominion over God's creation by his

---
[58] Frame 2013: 62–66.
[59] Luc 1997: 539–540.
[60] See also Schultz 1997: 303–305. He argues that Gen. 1 – 3 is foundational for wisdom literature.
[61] This approach is very similar to Kynes's emphasis of pursuing common themes in wisdom and other parts of the OT. Bartholomew (Bartholomew 2016: 25–26) also sees a connection between the ordering of creation in Gen. 1 – 2 and wisdom. Wisdom and law share an underlying assumption of a 'carved' creation order.
[62] Many of the connections between Solomon and Adam come from Davies 2011: 39–57; see also Longman 2017: 94–108.

understanding of animals and plants (1 Kgs 4:33), just as Adam did in the garden (Gen. 2:19–20). What is different for Solomon is that God gave Solomon great wisdom in order to administer justice in the kingdom (1 Kgs 3:9, 28). Also, the prospect of life is held out to Solomon, conditional on his obedience to the divine command (1 Kgs 9:1–9) just as it was to Adam (Gen. 2:16–17). Solomon's kingdom was only a partial restoration of dominion lost at the fall because it failed to restore order in God's creation. He was only a precursor of the coming king, the Second Adam, who would destroy the power of the curse of sin and restore creation by freeing it from corruption (Rom. 8:19–23). The powers of the age to come have broken into history in the kingdom of Christ, but the fullness of deliverance and restoration awaits his second coming. Until then, wisdom literature helps God's people successfully navigate the pitfalls of life.

The plan of the book

The following chapters focus on Proverbs, Job and Ecclesiastes, with three chapters given to each book. Some attention is given to introductory questions, but the focus is on the message and theology of each book. Proverbs sets forth, over against the way of folly, the way of wisdom that is founded in God's creation order and in the fear of Yahweh. God as Creator has set an order in the world that cannot be fully understood apart from special revelation and is an expression of his justice. Proverbs recognizes that people cannot fully comprehend God's ways in the world because of the freedom of God and the finiteness and fallen nature of people. Job wrestles with the disorder of suffering and its relationship to piety. The friends of Job operate with a mechanical view of divine retribution, so that if Job is suffering he must have sinned. This is a distortion of the view of Proverbs but it causes Job to wrestle with God's justice and how he should respond to suffering even though he is innocent. The mystery and sovereignty of God is emphasized in God's response to Job, showing that people understand little about God's ways in the world concerning individual suffering and that the proper response is to fear Yahweh. Qohelet wrestles with the disorder in the world concerning the breakdown of the deed–consequence relationship as he examines labour, wisdom and God's justice in a world that does not make sense. The epilogue of the book clearly points to the solution of the proper response: fear God and keep his commandments. Finally, the relationship of Christ to wisdom is explored in terms of his teaching ministry and his person and work. He is the wisdom of God (1 Cor. 1:24), 'in whom are hidden all the treasures of wisdom and knowledge' (Col. 2:3).[63]

---

[63] Several English translations are used throughout this book; but if the English translation is not identified, then it is the ESV, except for the chapters on Ecclesiastes, where I use my own translation of the text.

Chapter Two

The message
of Proverbs 1 – 9

A brief introduction to the book

The name Solomon is closely associated with the book of Proverbs. It occurs in several titles that introduce sections of the book (1:1; 10:1; 25:1). Proverbs 1:1 serves as a title for the whole book as it is grammatically connected to the prologue (1:2–7). Also, the motto of the book (the fear of Yahweh in v. 7) is repeated in 31:30.[1] Thus the prologue introduces the whole book. But Solomon is not the only name connected with the book. The name Agur occurs in the title to 30:1 and King Lemuel occurs in the title to 31:1. Little information is available to identify these individuals. The Hebrew word *maśśā'* (30:1; 31:1) is the word for 'oracle', but with a slight emendation it could also be a geographical reference to a tribe in Arabia.[2] Even if one rejects the geographical reference, these two individuals are likely non-Israelites. Agur grew up apart from the knowledge of God (30:3) and Lemuel is a king of unknown origin. Job and his friends are also non-Israelites who worship the God of Israel.

There is debate whether Agur is the author or source of all of Proverbs 30 and whether Lemuel (or his mother) is the author or source of all of Proverbs 31. In other words, are the numerical sayings (Prov. 30:10–33) from Agur and is the poem to the virtuous woman (Prov. 31:10–31) from Lemuel? Waltke argues that Proverbs 30 is a unit that comes from Agur and if Proverbs 31:10–31 stands alone without a superscription it is a unique orphan in Proverbs.[3] Many others argue that the numerical sayings and the poem to the virtuous woman are independent sections because of their distinct

---

[1] Lucas 2015: 49. The title of 1:1 is connected to the prologue by a series of purpose clauses composed of infinitive construct verbs.

[2] Longman (2006: 518) argues for the geographical reference and Waltke (2004: 454) and Steinmann (2009: 586) argue for 'oracle'.

[3] Waltke 2004: 27.

form and structure.[4] Two other headings identify 'the words of the wise' (22:17 – 24:22) and 'the sayings of the wise' (24:23–34).

The book of Proverbs is composed of several collections of proverbs and wisdom sayings associated with Solomon. This association fits the biblical account of Solomon's kingship that his wisdom surpassed the wisdom of the people of the east and the wisdom of Egypt (1 Kgs 4:30), and that he was very involved with the production of proverbs (1 Kgs 4:32). A flowering of wisdom occurred under Solomon's reign. Many scholars do not accept this view because they believe the account of Solomon is late and legendary.[5] The connection to Hezekiah (Prov. 25:1) is more plausible in their view because by that time an organized literary wisdom movement could have arisen,[6] but the other titles connecting the proverbs to Solomon are later than Hezekiah's time period of 700 BC.[7] Kitchen, on the other hand, argues that the four sections of the book of Proverbs conform to the literature of the ANE that predates the time of Solomon. Proverbs 1 – 24 follows a Type B form and Proverbs 25 – 29 and 30 and 31 follow a Type A form.[8] He argues that Proverbs 1 – 24 dates to Solomon's time (950 BC), Proverbs 25 – 29 comes from Hezekiah's time, and Proverbs 30 – 31 follows shortly thereafter.[9] Other views of the final form of the book by evangelical scholars include the period of Ezra in the mid-400s,[10] the Persian period from 540 to 332[11] and the 300s following the adoption of the standard Hebrew text.[12] Solomon had a major role in either writing or collecting most of the proverbial sayings in Proverbs 1 – 29.[13]

[4] Lucas 2015: 3; Kidner 1964: 183. The different structure is based on the LXX, which has a different order in these chapters. On this basis Longman (2006: 518) takes Agur's words to include 30:1–14.
[5] See Scott 1976: 84–101; Crenshaw 1981: 49–54.
[6] Scott 1976: 95.
[7] Crenshaw 1981: 45.
[8] Kitchen 2008: 552. Type A has an authorial title followed directly by the main text. Type B is more complex, with a title (Prov. 1:1) followed by a preamble (1:1–7), and then a long prologue (1:8 – 9:18) followed by a subtitle (10:1) introducing the main text (Prov. 10 – 24).
[9] Ibid. The later date is due in part to the different structure of the LXX Proverbs.
[10] Steinmann 2009: 18.
[11] Waltke 2005: 37.
[12] Longman 2006: 25. The later date is due in part to the different structure of the LXX Proverbs.
[13] Wilson (2017: 2) comments that 'as a book it claims to be substantially, but not entirely, Solomonic'.

The preamble (1:1–7): key concepts and people

The preamble sets forth the purpose of the book, the audience of the book and the epistemological foundation of the book. The purpose of the book is set forth in four infinitives (vv. 2–4):

'To know wisdom and instruction'
'to understand words of insight'
'to receive instruction in wise dealing, in righteousness,
    justice, and equity'
'to give prudence to the simple, knowledge and discretion
    to the youth'

The basic purpose of the book is to know wisdom and instruction. The word 'wisdom' (*hokmâ*) is a keyword and has a variety of meanings. It can refer to the technical skill of those who made the garments for the priesthood (Exod. 28:3) and who built the tabernacle (Exod. 31:3, 6). It includes the ability to render judgment (1 Kgs 3:28; Isa. 11:1–6) and to lead people (Deut. 34:9).[14] Wisdom can be summarized as the ability to understand how life works in order to respond appropriately.[15] It allows someone to develop skilfulness in living a wise life by being able to navigate life in order to achieve success. Understanding the character of different kinds of people is necessary in order to know how to respond to them. Wisdom also includes understanding the way the world that God has created works because God has built wisdom into his creation (Prov. 3:19). Certain actions or attitudes may lead to certain results. These results are not amoral but reflect God's justice because the divine order of the world derives from the righteous character of Yahweh.[16] The better one understands the way the world works the better decisions a person will be able to make in seeking the path of wisdom.

Coupled with wisdom is the word 'instruction' (*mûsār*). This word could be translated 'discipline', as it refers to a chastening lesson that shapes character and corrects moral faults. It has a wide variety of uses. Positively, it is used to encourage correct behaviour (Prov. 15:5; 19:20). Negatively, it is used to reprove wrong behaviour and can even be used of corporal punishment (Prov. 13:24; 22:15; 23:13).

---

[14] Most of the references come from Goldberg 1980: 1.283.
[15] Waltke 2004: 76–77.
[16] Estes 1997: 27.

The knowledge that comes from wisdom and instruction is not a theoretical knowledge but is a practical knowledge that is learned through a variety of experiences of life. This aspect of wisdom is highlighted in the phrase 'to receive instruction in wise dealing'. The instruction of discipline shapes people's character to help them grasp the implications of a situation in order to make beneficial decisions.[17] The right decisions lead to righteousness, justice and equity.[18]

One group that will particularly benefit from the teaching of wisdom is the 'simple' or the 'naive' (*pĕtî*). They can easily be led astray because they are open to all kinds of enticements to go the wrong way. They have not developed the ability to discern right from wrong. The word 'youth' is used in parallel with the simple and describes a stage of life that everyone experiences. Although the word for 'youth' (*na'ar*) can cover a wide range of age groups,[19] it primarily refers to the period of youth from infancy to just before marriage. The emphasis is on someone who is chronologically young, an adolescent and unmarried person who is typically immature.[20] Young people lack wisdom because they lack experience in life. They have not yet developed the wisdom to discern the right from the wrong way. Part of the purpose of Proverbs is to give prudence, knowledge and discretion to them. 'Prudence' (*'ormâ*) and 'discretion' (*mĕzimmâ*) refer to the ability to plan in order to reach goals. Both are used with the negative sense of cunning or scheming to achieve one's desires,[21] but here the positive sense of using good judgment to achieve the desired goal is in view.[22] The ability to plan needs knowledge in order to succeed. The purpose of wisdom in Proverbs is to help a young person have the right goals in life so he or she can appropriately plan to reach those goals.[23]

---

[17] Waltke 2004: 94.

[18] Lucas (2015: 50) notes that righteousness, justice and equity are moral qualities intended to indicate the way 'wise dealing' is to be practised.

[19] The word is used of an unborn child (Judg. 13:5, 7), a child just born (1 Sam. 4:21), a three-month-old child (Exod. 2:6), a child not yet weaned (1 Sam. 1:22), a child recently weaned (1 Sam. 1:24), a seventeen-year-old (Gen. 37:2) and a thirty-year-old (Gen. 41:12). Hamilton (1997: 3.126) notes that in these usages the young person is not married. Fisher (1980: 2: 585–586) also points out that *na'ar* (plural) is used to refer to 'servants' (2 Kgs 19:6) and 'soldiers' (1 Kgs 20:15).

[20] Longman 2006: 97.

[21] Negative uses of prudence are rare in Proverbs but Gen. 3:1 is a negative use of a related word (*'ārûm*). Negative uses of discretion include 12:2; 14:17.

[22] Positive uses of prudence include 12:23; 13:16; 22:3; 27:12; and positive uses of discretion include 2:11–12; 3:21.

[23] Koptak (2003: 60) comments that the placing of 'the wise' (1:5) between the simple/youth (1:4) and the fools (1:7) shows that the simple must make a decision to follow

Becoming a wise person also includes understanding words of insight (1:6). In other words, a wise person understands life situations and words that are perceptively written. Wisdom is embedded in God's creation and is embedded in texts that are faithful to God. Even the wise will benefit from wisdom (1:5–6). The wise and the naive represent the two poles on the spectrum of wisdom. Certain forms of wisdom teaching are emphasized in relation to the wise in verse 6. The more wisdom one has the more one is able to understand wisdom teaching. The first word (*māšāl*) is typically translated 'proverb' but has a wider range of meanings, including different types of sayings,[24] didactic poems (Isa. 14:4–10), wisdom psalms (Pss 49:4; 78:2) and parables (Ezek. 17:2; 21:5). The word 'saying' (*mĕlîṣâ*) is from the verb 'scorn' (*lîṣ*) and likely refers to a satire or mocking poem. The 'words of the wise' likely refers to written wisdom collections.[25] A 'riddle' (*ḥîdâ*) is an enigmatic saying, question or story whose meaning must be determined by the audience (Judg. 14:14). A wise person will be able to comprehend the wisdom contained in such sayings.

And yet 'to know wisdom and instruction' is not just learned through experience but also requires the proper foundation: 'The fear of the LORD is the beginning of knowledge' (1:7). The fear of the LORD refers primarily to a subjective response of humility, love and trust in God so that a person is willing to submit his or her life to the ways of God. It is a God-centred view of life that includes a reverence for God. As the beginning of knowledge, the fear of the LORD is the first and controlling principle of a person's life.[26] Without it wisdom, as defined by God, is not attainable. The fear of the Lord is not used as often in the NT as in the OT (Acts 9:31; Phil. 2:12; Col. 3:22; Rev. 19:5), but is associated with those who follow God's way of repentance and faith.

Fools, on the other hand, despise wisdom and instruction. Fools reject the wisdom and discipline exhibited in Proverbs and express it in the way they live their lives. They are basically unteachable. Different kinds of fools are described in Proverbs.[27] One type of 'fool'

the way of wisdom lest they end up being fools. See Estes 1997 for a discussion of the virtues and goals of wisdom that come from the world view of Proverbs.
[24] Longman 2006: 99. Longman includes the proverb (Prov. 21:12, 25, 31), the comparison (Prov. 10:26; 11:22), the beatitude (Prov. 8:32, 34), the 'better' saying (Prov. 15:16–17) and the numerical saying (Prov. 30:15–16, 18–19, 21–23, 24–28).
[25] Ibid. 2006: 100.
[26] Kidner 1964: 59. For the distribution of this phrase throughout the book of Proverbs, showing that it is a central idea in the book, see Wilson 2017: 22.
[27] For a discussion of different character types in Proverbs see Lucas 2015: 219–230.

(*kĕsîl*) is the dull or thick-headed person who has a tendency to make wrong decisions because he will not listen to other people. Instead, he loves to hear himself talk (Prov. 18:2, 6–7) and is not able to deal with the present (Prov. 17:24). Another word for a 'fool' (*'ĕwîl*) stresses moral deficiency, a lack of self-control as displayed in words or temper (Prov. 12:16). This fool thinks he has all the answers (Prov. 12:15). Another type of 'fool' (*nabal*) is a disgraceful person who does not have respect for anything or anyone (Prov. 17:7, 21; 30:22), much like the person named Nabal (1 Sam. 25:17). Wisdom's goal is to keep a young person from developing into a fool by choosing the way of wisdom.

Proverbs 1:8 – 9:18: a choice between two ways

Two types of material make up this section. The main type of writing is a longer discourse called an 'instruction'. It generally follows the form of a direct address, 'Hear, my son' (Prov. 1:8), an exhortation, 'and forsake not your mother's teaching' (Prov. 1:8), a motivation, 'for they are a graceful wreath' (Prov. 1:9), the lesson proper (Prov. 1:10–18) and a conclusion (Prov. 1:19). Each of the instructions is addressed to a son (or sons) and originates from the father, although the teaching of the mother is also mentioned (1:8; 6:20).[28] The primary setting of these instructions is the home, where the parents have the responsibility to guide the young person to choose the way of wisdom. Some of the proverbs later in the book could have originated in the court to train those who would serve at the court. Although the son is the one addressed in the instructions, it is clear that the daughters are also taught wisdom because the mother is very capable of teaching the son.[29] These instructions are also called 'lectures' to differentiate them from the wider genre of instruction and to identify their precise nature of a father teaching a son about wisdom.[30] The other type of material in Proverbs 1 – 9 is addresses given by wisdom personified

[28] The recognition of the teaching of the mother is very unusual in ancient wisdom literature (Longman 2006: 105).
[29] The father–son relationship should not be understood as a teacher–pupil relationship, although implications for the teacher–pupil relationship can be drawn from the father–son relationship. Crenshaw (1998) has shown that the evidence for professional education in Israel is inferential and that not until the second century BC does an extant text refer to a school. Thus the primary teachers were parents, but over time the teaching at home was complemented by special guilds set up to teach certain skills, including training for those who would serve the royal court.
[30] Fox 2000: 45.

as a woman designated as Lady Wisdom. She exhorts the simple to follow her ways because of the blessings and benefits that she brings to life. These addresses are called 'Interludes'[31] but 'Lady Wisdom's Teaching' fits the content of the material. The father instructs the son in the home and Lady Wisdom calls out to the simple in the streets and the marketplace. Both teach the benefits of the way of wisdom and the dangers of the way of folly. Proverbs 1 – 9 clearly sets forth two ways of life. After setting out the blessings and benefits of the way of wisdom and the destructive consequences of the way of folly, a choice is called for in Proverbs 9.

The structure of Proverbs 1 – 9

There are eleven lectures and four teachings of Lady Wisdom. The following structure is fairly common but there may be a few differences among commentators on some divisions:

Lecture 1: A warning against joining the wicked to make easy
    money (1:8–19)
Lady Wisdom's teaching: Warning the simple of the dangers
    of rejecting wisdom (1:20–33)
Lecture 2: The benefit of wisdom to protect against different
    kinds of wicked people (2:1–22)
Lecture 3: Wisdom encourages trust in Yahweh (3:1–12)
Lady Wisdom's teaching: The benefits of wisdom (3:13–20)[32]
Lecture 4: The value of wisdom in living a life of integrity
    (3:21–35)
Lecture 5: The importance of obtaining wisdom (4:1–9)
Lecture 6: Stay on the path of wisdom and avoid the path
    of the wicked (4:10–19)
Lecture 7: The beneficial impact of wisdom that reaches the
    heart (4:20–27)
Lecture 8: The folly of adultery versus the wisdom of marriage
    (5:1–23)
Lecture 9: Navigating difficult situations and difficult people
    in life (6:1–19)
Lecture 10: The false promises of adultery (6:20–35)
Lecture 11: The destructive consequences of adultery (7:1–27)

[31] Ibid. 47.
[32] Waltke (2005: 250) includes 3:13–20 as part of Lecture 4 (3:13–35), but Fox (2000: 44) makes it a separate section as part of Wisdom's teaching.

Lady Wisdom's teaching: Wisdom's close association with
   God (8:1–31)
Lady Wisdom's final teaching: The contrasts between Lady
   Wisdom and Lady Folly (8:32 – 9:18)

The message of Proverbs 1 – 9

The father's instruction highlights two broad themes. Certain people
and situations in life, associated with the way of foolishness, must be
avoided because they cause ruin. Wisdom will help a person understand these situations and avoid them. The father's instruction also
teaches the benefits of wisdom. The way of wisdom not only helps a
person avoid the problems of life, but also brings great blessings into
a person's life. These two themes are interwoven throughout the
father's instruction, but will each be emphasized separately to
highlight the message of the instructions.

Avoiding the obstacles of life

Certain situations and people in life must be avoided because they
bring irreparable harm to the son's life. The situations to avoid include
the pressure to join the wicked to make easy money (1:8–19), crooked,
devious men (2:12–14; 3:31–32; 4:14–18; 6:12–18), the adulterous
woman (2:16–19; 5:1–23; 6:20–35; 7:1–27), putting up security (6:1–5),
and laziness (6:6–11). Parental instruction teaches a young person
different ways to avoid difficult situations and people. First, a young
person must understand the false allurement that accompanies the
offer to walk the path of wickedness or folly. This understanding is
particularly evident in the two main temptations facing the young
person: easy money and easy sex. The allurement of easy money
comes from peer pressure by sinners who entice the son to join the
gang (1:8–14). The verb 'entice' (*pth*) is related to the word for 'simple'
(*pĕtî*) and expresses persuasion through seduction or deception. The
offer is to acquire a lot of money by lying in wait for blood and
ambushing the innocent without cause. In other words, the plan is to
make easy money by robbing others. It is imperative for the young
person to understand the false offer of wealth and to see the true
outcome of this way of life (1:15–19). People who are quick to do evil
are setting a trap for their own lives because they are not able to see
the true outcome of their ways. Those greedy for unjust gain will
ultimately lose their lives. A young person must be able to see the true
outcome of such a life in order to resist the false allurement of easy
money.

Another major temptation facing the son is the allurement of easy sex apart from commitment. The importance of this temptation is seen in how many times it is addressed in Proverbs 1 – 9. This temptation comes in the form of the adulterous woman who is first introduced in 2:16 as 'the forbidden woman' and 'the adulteress'. The word 'forbidden' is the Hebrew word for 'strange' (*zār*), and the word 'adulteress' is the Hebrew word for someone who is 'foreign' (*nokrî*). She is strange or foreign in the sense that she is not the legitimate wife of the son. In fact, she is described as one who has abandoned the covenant of marriage (2:17). She is not faithful to the 'companion of her youth' and forgets the covenant of marriage made in the presence of God. This woman is best described as the adulterous woman. She offers the easy pleasures of a sexual relationship without the cost of commitment.

The son must be able to see beyond the powerful, captivating allurement of such a relationship to understand the devastating, ruinous results that will destroy his life. The adulterous woman is briefly introduced in 2:16–19, where her character is defined and the results of a relationship with her are briefly described. Further instructions concerning this woman highlight the allurement and the true end of the relationship. She entices the young man with her flattering words. Her lips drip honey and her speech is smoother than oil (5:3; 6:24; 7:21). She uses seductive charm and deceitful flattery to lure the young man into her trap.[33] She is not shy in making known her desires. She is seductively dressed, boisterous, and brazenly seizes him, kisses him and makes an offer that is hard to refuse (7:10–21). She offers a night of sexual pleasure, including food from the sacrificial payment of her vows, erotic accompaniments, and the relaxed safety of not having to worry about her husband interrupting their tryst. This is a powerful, overwhelming temptation that requires wisdom to handle properly.

The wisdom of the father's instruction emphasizes several things. A young man must take preventative measures in order to avoid such a temptation. He must be willing to listen to and receive the father's teaching by incorporating it into his life (7:1–3). He must also embrace wisdom as 'my sister' and be committed to avoid situations and places where the adulterous woman would have opportunity to make her seductive plea. He must not go near her corner, or take the road to her house, or be found there in the twilight of the evening (5:9; 7:8–9).

---

[33] Waltke 2004: 308. He notes that 'smoother than oil' is a metaphor for deceitful flattery (Prov. 2:16; 29:5; Ps. 55:21).

He must flee immorality. A more positive preventative measure is found in the beauty of marriage and the satisfaction that it provides (5:15–20). Security is found in the exclusive relationship of marriage as well as in the physical delight of the intoxicating nature of love in marriage. A healthy marriage helps a person avoid the adulterous woman. In fact, at the end of the section on the joys of marriage the following question is asked:

> Why should you be intoxicated, my son,
>   with a forbidden woman,
> and embrace the bosom of an adulteress?

Wisdom enables a person to see beyond the captivating allurement of the pleasures of such a relationship to see the disastrous consequences that will plague the rest of a person's life. The supposed freedom of a sexual relationship apart from commitment turns into slavery (5:22). A young person's honour, strength and labours are not enjoyed because they go to others who are identified as strangers and foreigners (5:8–11). There is both social ruin in the loss of reputation and economic ruin that can lead to poverty. These consequences may come about because of the jealousy of the husband who will exact continuous revenge without being satisfied by any compensation (6:33–35). Spiritual consequences also result from sexual immorality, including departure from the path of life that can become irreversible (2:19). This path is a bitter and painful path (5:4) with death mentioned several times as the result (2:18; 5:5; 7:27). Life and death hang in the balance and the young person will have to choose whether to walk the path of sexual promiscuity or the path of sexual fidelity. Ultimately, this is a choice between whether to follow Lady Folly or Lady Wisdom, a choice that will come to a climax in Proverbs 9.

The benefits of wisdom

The benefits of wisdom are the second general theme of the father's instructions. A close association exists between the father's teaching, the law of God and wisdom. Several terms used to refer to the father's instruction are commonly associated with the law. The regular word for 'law' (*tôrâ*) is used for both the mother's teaching (1:8; 6:20) and the father's teaching (3:1; 4:2; 7:2).[34] The words 'commandment'

---

[34] The word *tôrâ* can mean 'instruction', but to call it a secular word that has no allusion to the divine law (Fox 2000: 79) seems to be a forced dichotomy in the light

(*miṣwâ*) and 'wisdom' (*ḥokmâ*) are also used for the father's teaching (2:1; 3:1; 5:1; 6:20; 7:1–2). Exhortations to keep the father's commandments and not to turn away from them are identified with the exhortation to get wisdom. The father's teaching is the means by which the son obtains wisdom (4:4–6). Both the father's instruction (1:9) and wisdom (3:21–22; 4:9) are described as attractive adornments, like jewellery, that are worn on the head or neck as a way to signify the honour and life that come from both.[35] The beneficial results of the father's instruction and wisdom are the same. Both bring the blessings of life (3:2; 3:16), give guidance in life (3:23; 6:22–23) and offer protection from the way of foolishness (2:11–14; 4:6), especially the adulterous woman (5:1–3; 6:24; 7:4–5). The law is foundational and wisdom helps a person live out the law more specifically in everyday life.[36] Wisdom and law are communicated to the next generation by the parents. Their teaching in Proverbs has the same authority as the law because it agrees with the law and helps a young person understand the law. Parents should take seriously their responsibility to bring children up in the fear and admonition of the Lord because their teaching has a significant role in shaping their lives.

Wisdom provides both tangible, physical blessings and spiritual blessings. It is difficult to separate completely the physical benefits of wisdom from the spiritual. The teaching of Proverbs will help a person find favour and good success in the sight of God and man (3:4). The word 'favour' (*ḥēn*) describes 'beneficent actions that are freely offered or received and contribute to the well-being of another or to the health of a relationship'. Such actions go beyond what is necessary or customary.[37] When used of God's relationship with human beings, favour takes on the connotation of grace (Gen. 6:8; Exod. 33:12; Prov. 3:34), but it can also refer to the bestowal of blessings by God on a person's life with an emphasis on the evidence of that blessing being seen by others ('in the sight of'). This is the meaning when the father's teaching, closely identified with the law of God and wisdom, is called 'adornment [*ḥēn*] for your neck' (Prov. 3:22; see also 1:9). The word 'success' (*śēkel*) in the phrase 'good

of the general parallels between Proverbs and Deuteronomy. Longman (2017: 169–174) discusses the relationship between covenant, wisdom and law.
[35] In Prov. 3:22 life and adornment parallel each other.
[36] The relationship between law and wisdom is mentioned in Deut. 4:6, where keeping the law 'will be your wisdom'. The law gives wisdom but wisdom also translates the law into instructions for everyday life. In other words, proverbs help apply the law to life situations (Kline 1972: 62–64).
[37] Fretheim 1997: 2.204.

success' also highlights that others see the beneficial results of prudence, insight or understanding in the life of the son.[38]

The benefits of wisdom are set forth as an incentive to follow the way of wisdom. Benefits include the physical blessings that wisdom provides, but these blessings cannot be limited to material blessings. One of the blessings of wisdom is long life that results from living a wise life (Prov. 3:2; 4:10; 9:11). Generally speaking, the more one can avoid the dangers of wickedness the better opportunity there is to live a long life (Prov. 3:25; 9:11). The fear of Yahweh is not only the beginning of wisdom, but is also associated with long life (Prov. 9:11; 10:27). God is the author of life in all of its dimensions, so that life should not be limited to this earth. Life that comes from God cannot be destroyed by death (see chapter 4).

Wisdom also brings peace into a person's life (3:2). The Hebrew word for 'peace' (šālôm) expresses more than just the absence of strife, but includes the full-orbed blessings that a person can expect from wisdom, including health (Ps. 38:3 [4]), prosperity (Ps. 73:3), security (Ps. 122:7–8), well-being (Job 5:24), contentment (Ps. 4:8) and good relationships with people (Ps. 34:13–14) and with God (Ps. 85:8). Although the word 'peace' is not used very often in Proverbs,[39] these same blessings also come to the wise in Proverbs: health (4:22), prosperity (3:16), security (3:23), well-being (4:18), contentment (3:24), good relations with people (3:27) and with God (2:6–8). The security that comes from wisdom is presented as walking on the right path without stumbling. Life lived without the fear of sudden terror or the ruin of the wicked allows a person to sleep peacefully. The source of this security is confidence in Yahweh, who keeps a person's foot from slipping (Prov. 3:21–26). Walking in the way of the good and keeping the paths of the righteous also leads to living in the land that God has given his people without fear of being driven from it (Prov. 2:20–22). In other words, the way of wisdom is a sure way to receive the inheritance that God has promised to his people. These ideas cannot be separated from the covenant blessing of living in the land securely (Deut. 28:11) and the covenant judgment of exile from the land because of disobedience (Deut. 28:63–64).[40]

[38] Fox 2000: 147. He comments that normally this word refers to the ability of a person to understand a situation in order to respond appropriately, but in 3:4 the perception is how others see the person who has 'success'.
[39] The word 'peace' occurs only in Prov. 3:2, 17; 12:20.
[40] Longman (2006: 125) notes that the verb nsḥ is used in Prov. 2:22 and Deut. 28:63 to refer to being removed from the land.

The material blessings of wisdom cannot be separated from a person's spiritual life. If a person seeks after wisdom like one seeks after silver, he or she will find the knowledge of God and understand the fear of Yahweh. In turn, Yahweh, who is the source of wisdom, is the one who gives wisdom. The result is that a person's life is protected (Prov. 2:4–7) by an outer protection that comes from Yahweh, who is a shield to those who walk in integrity, and an inner protection that comes from wisdom within the heart (Prov. 2:10). Wisdom leads to discretion that guards the life of a wise person and keeps one from the way of evil (Prov. 2:11–12). Thus wise conduct comes from the heart, defined as the centre of a person's existence, the totality of the inner person,[41] or the core of a person's life. It is the control centre that gives direction to the other faculties of a person's life.[42] A wise person guards the heart because the springs of life flow from it (Prov. 4:23). Guarding the heart means that people also give attention to what they say, what they look at and where they walk (Prov. 4:24–27). Wisdom keeps a person from crooked speech, wandering eyes and wayward feet. Wisdom is valuable because it offers a person the full blessings of life, both material and spiritual.

The personification of wisdom
There are several passages, identified as Lady Wisdom's Teaching, that personify wisdom as a way to encourage the young and the naive to follow her teaching. Wisdom is a street preacher (1:20–33) who stations herself in the public arena calling aloud in the markets and the noisy streets to those who are identified as the simple, the scoffers and fools who hate knowledge. She reminds them that if they would turn to follow her, they would receive her spirit and her words. She offers them a spiritual change and a new way of understanding life.[43] They have refused to listen to Lady Wisdom and will experience the results of such refusal. Terror and calamity will overtake them like a storm (1:27). It will be too late then to seek wisdom because she will not answer when they call her. They have chosen their way and

---

[41] Longman 2006: 119.
[42] For a full discussion of the meaning and function of the heart see Waltke 2004: 90–92.
[43] The ESV translates *rûaḥ* as 'spirit', referring to the essence of wisdom. Some translations translate it as 'thoughts' in parallel with the next clause of the verse, 'I will make my words known to you' (1:23b). Wisdom is seeking to shape the simple person by her ideas through her words (Wilson 2017: 69; Waltke 2004: 199). Longman (2006: 112) argues that the close association between wisdom and spirit in the OT is missed if *rûaḥ* is translated 'thoughts'.

will experience the fruit of their own devices (1:31). Wisdom will laugh at their calamity and mock them when terror strikes. It is very serious to refuse the way of wisdom and to choose the path of foolishness. Such a choice has life and death consequences. Those who listen to wisdom will dwell secure without dread of disaster (1:33).

Wisdom is presented in ways that parallel what is said about God in other parts of the OT. Wisdom proclaims, 'I will pour out my spirit to you' (Prov. 1:23), and God declares, 'I will pour my Spirit upon your offspring' (Isa. 44:3; see also Joel 2:28). Wisdom stretches out her hand to those who will not listen, just as God does in Isaiah 65:2: 'I spread out my hands all the day to a rebellious people'. Wisdom laughs at the calamity of the fool who rejects her just as God laughs at those who seek to throw off his authority (Ps. 2:4). If fools continue to reject Wisdom, there will come a time when they will seek her but not be able to find her (Prov. 1:28). As part of the judgment against his people God promises a time when they will seek him but not be able to find him (Hos. 5:6–7). These parallels show that Wisdom is closely associated with God and the purposes of God.

Proverbs 8 is an important chapter that focuses on Lady Wisdom and her teaching. Wisdom sets forth the reasons her teachings should be followed. The character of her teachings, the benefits of her teachings and the close association she has to God even before the creation of the world are emphasized. These are reasons why Wisdom should be followed. Wisdom is again presented as a street preacher in 8:1–5. Proverbs 8 also expands on the role of Wisdom. She speaks the truth (8:6–11), positively identified with words that are right and straight and negatively avoiding words that are twisted or crooked. Truth is a precious commodity that has more value than silver or gold. Wisdom also gives knowledge and insight that enables someone to exercise 'prudence' and 'discretion' (8:12–21). These two words emphasize the ability to plan in order to reach proper goals. Wisdom is so valuable that kings and rulers use her to govern in the right way. Such governing cannot be separated from the fear of Yahweh that produces hatred of pride, arrogance and the way of evil. Those who love wisdom find a reciprocating partner (8:17) and experience the blessings of wisdom that are better than gold. Wisdom produces an enduring wealth and righteousness that include a blessed inheritance. The contrast of gold with an enduring wealth suggests that there is a wealth that is not fleeting but endures even beyond a person's life.

The relationship of Wisdom to Yahweh goes back to creation itself (8:22–31). Beginning with verse 22 Wisdom's status is defined in relationship to Yahweh and his actions, as he is the subject of the verbs in verses 22–29.[44] The precise relationship of Wisdom to Yahweh has been a matter of debate and has theological and Christological implications. The meaning of the verb *qānâ* is important (8:22) in understanding this relationship. The basic lexical meaning is 'acquire', but something can be acquired in different ways. Many times the verb means to buy something (Gen. 47:20). Another way to acquire something is to create it.[45] The Greek OT, along with the Tg and Syr, translates this verb as 'create' (*ktizō*). Psalm 139:13 and Deuteronomy 32:6 are appealed to for this meaning. During the Arian controversies of the early church when the primary Bible used by the church was the Greek OT, the Arians appealed to this passage to argue that Christ was a created being. The clarity of the NT concerning the person of Christ as God won the day, but Proverbs 8:22 was significant in the debates.[46]

Two other options are possible for the meaning of the verb *qānâ*. Waltke argues for the meaning of procreation, which works well in passages such as Psalm 139:13, Deuteronomy 32:6 and Genesis 4:1. Proverbs 8:24–25 expresses this idea with the use of the verb *ḥîl*, translated Yahweh 'brought me forth'. Wisdom was 'brought forth' before there were springs of water, mountains or the earth with its fields. Wisdom was there when God created the world by establishing the heavens above, assigning the waters their boundaries and laying the foundations of the earth (vv. 27–29). The second option for the meaning of this verb is 'to possess' (ESV, NASB, NKJV). Fox argues against this meaning because the verbs in 8:22–26 describe a one-time action, not a continuous possession. This excludes prior possession because wisdom was acquired as the first of his deeds.[47] Steinmann, on the other hand, argues that 8:22 does not refer to the beginning of Wisdom but to the beginning of God's creative work.[48] Wisdom existed before the created order and so is outside that order. Yahweh took possession of a wisdom that he then used in his work of creation.[49] Wisdom was already something that God possessed

---

[44] Lucas 2015: 80–81.
[45] Fox 2000: 279.
[46] For an interesting account of how Athanasius understood Prov. 8:22 based on the LXX's translation 'create' see Robertson 2017: 59–63; for a broader discussion of the role of Prov. 8 in the Arian controversy in the early church see Steinmann 2009: 219–229 and Emerson 2017: 47–56.
[47] Fox 2000: 279.
[48] Steinmann 2009: 207.
[49] Vawter 1980: 213, 215. He comments that wisdom existed before the created order and then became instrumental in the production of the created order.

'before his works of old' (NASB). It is difficult to choose between these two options. Both of them allow Wisdom to exist before the creation of the world and to become part of creation (see below). If the main point of Proverbs 8:22–31 is not the process of the acquisition of wisdom, whether by a new act of creation or by acquiring an existing entity, but that God has wisdom and has used it to create the world, then 'possess' is the better translation because it draws attention to the outcome rather than the process.[50]

The role of Wisdom is further defined by verses 30–31 when Wisdom declares:

> then I was beside him, like a master workman,
> and I was daily his delight,
> rejoicing before him always,
> rejoicing in his inhabited world
> and delighting in the children of man.

The meaning of 'master workman' (*'āmôn*) has been the subject of much debate. Different vowels could supply different meanings leading to different views of the word.[51] Some, based on understanding the word as a passive particle (*'āmûn*) meaning 'nursed, brought up', understand it to refer to Wisdom as a little child. This meaning is supposed to fit the context of Wisdom being born and playing beside God as a witness to creation.[52] The problem is that Wisdom's presentation of herself as a little child does not make her serious claim to authority as a rationale for following her very credible.[53] The predominant view is that this word means 'master workman', with support from the ancient versions (LXX, Syr and Vg), and has possible attestation in the reference to 'artisans' in Jeremiah 52:15.[54] There are several difficulties with this view. Jeremiah 52:15 is not a strong attestation of this word, because the LXX omits the word and the parallel text of 2 Kings 25:11 reads 'multitude'. Most translations of Proverbs 8:30 supply the word 'like' to produce the phrase 'like a master workman', but there is no word for 'like' in the Hebrew. There are also questions as to whether 'master workman' fits the

---

[50] Wilson 2017: 128.
[51] See Scott 1960 for a review of the history of the interpretation of this word.
[52] Fox 2000: 287.
[53] Waltke 2005: 419.
[54] Kidner 1964: 80–81; Steinmann 2009: 212.

context, because the acts of creation are performed by God.[55] There is no clear statement that Wisdom was a participant or some kind of mediator in creating the world; rather, Wisdom is consistently presented as at God's side during the events of creation.[56]

This word (*'mn*) could also be understood as meaning 'faithful', which is the way Symmachus, Theodotion and the Tgs understand its meaning.[57] This fits the context that presents Wisdom as constantly beside God during the process of creation. Waltke draws a parallel between the clauses in the following way:

and I was	beside him	faithfully
and I was	delighting	daily
	celebrating before him	at all times[58]

Wisdom should be followed because she was there from the beginning of creation and served as a witness to creation.[59]

Wisdom is closely associated with God's creation. If Wisdom is an instrument that God uses to create the world (Prov. 3:19), then creation should show evidence of wisdom. The whole world is depicted as Wisdom's province (vv. 27–29, 31). God orders creation by 'drawing' (*ḥāqaq*) a circle on the face of the deep, by 'marking out' (*ḥāqaq*) the foundations of the earth and by setting a 'limit' (*ḥōq*) to the sea. The use of this verb and noun emphasizes the order that God established in creation. Jeremiah 31:35–37 uses similar terms to refer to the stability of the order of creation as a standard for God's covenant promises. Thus in Proverbs 8 wisdom is used by God to establish cosmic order (8:27–29) and is used by kings to bring order

---

[55] Scott 1960: 216–217. He comments that the idea of Wisdom as a hypostasis is associated with the view of Wisdom as a master workman; however, not all who argue for 'master workman' understand Wisdom as a hypostasis (Kidner 1964: 80–81; Longman 2006: 203, 212).

[56] Wilson (2017: 131) states that the emphasis of Prov. 8:22–31 is on the presence of Wisdom with God from the very beginning. He writes, 'If anything, wisdom is being used by God, woven into the fabric of the world, rather than herself being active.'

[57] This would understand *'āmôn* to be the qal infinitive absolute of *'mn* (Waltke 2004: 420).

[58] Ibid.

[59] There is a difference in nuance between procreation and creation, between Wisdom being brought forth for a purpose and Wisdom being created for a purpose. It is hard to conceive of Wisdom being created by God as if Wisdom did not exist before that moment if Wisdom is an attribute of God. Even if Wisdom is the personification of God's revelation, the complexity between general revelation, special revelation and Christ as revelation makes the meaning 'create' difficult.

in society when kings rule by 'decreeing' (*ḥāqaq*) what is just (8:15).[60] It is clear that there is an order to creation and society that is associated with Wisdom.[61]

Wisdom is personified in Proverbs as a street preacher (Prov. 1:20–33) and a banquet hostess (Prov. 9:1–6). This pattern means that Wisdom in Proverbs 8 should also be understood as the personification of a concept and not as a hypostasis. We conclude from Proverbs 8 that God is the source of Wisdom, that Wisdom was at God's side during creation, that Wisdom is associated with the order of creation and that Wisdom delights in creation. The association of Wisdom with the order of creation led von Rad to identify Wisdom as the personification of the world order that is in reality the self-revelation of creation.[62] This identification has merit, for when the sages investigate the order of creation they are not investigating an autonomous order but something God himself has established in creation. And yet the origins and authority of Wisdom suggest more than a personified order of creation. Lady Wisdom is the voice of Yahweh, the divine summons issued in and through creation heard on the level of human experience.[63]

Lady Wisdom is also personified in Proverbs 9 as a banquet hostess. The significance of Proverbs 9 is that Lady Wisdom is contrasted with Lady Folly in order to highlight the choice between them. Proverbs 9 has three sections. The first and third sections (9:1–6; 9:13–18) contrast Lady Wisdom and Lady Folly, and the middle second section (9:7–12) shows the implications of the choice by contrasting the character and outcome of the wicked person with the wise person. The wicked person, identified as a scoffer, does not listen to reproof, but a wise person sees the benefit of reproof as a way to increase in

[60] This discussion depends on the comments in Van Leeuwen 2015: 3.811.

[61] The fact that Wisdom is both an instrument used by God to create the world (Prov. 3:19) and a personification with God before creation (Prov. 8:22–26) is not a problem. Qohelet will use wisdom as an instrument to investigate life and as an object of his investigation.

[62] Von Rad 1972: 151–157. Von Rad sees a general connection with the Egyptian concept of 'order', *ma'at*, but also argues that Israel's concept is completely different.

[63] Murphy 2002: 138. Wisdom is associated with both special revelation and general revelation. Waltke (2004: 86–87) argues that Wisdom in Prov. 1 – 9 personifies only Solomon's inspired wisdom represented in the proverbs of Solomon and the sayings of the wise (see the parallel in Prov. 4:5). Waltke discounts the view that Wisdom represents the created order that Israel learned to interpret through the latter's experience, because it lacks exegetical support in Proverbs. This discussion has tried to show some association between Wisdom and the order of creation; but, as will be argued in chapter 4, special revelation is the foundation upon which general revelation is to be investigated.

learning. The key difference between the wicked and the wise is the fear of Yahweh as the beginning of wisdom (1:7; 9:10). Lady Wisdom and Lady Folly participate in similar activities. Both give their speeches from the highest point of the city (vv. 3, 14), speak to the same audience of the simple (vv. 4, 16), offer food (vv. 5, 17) and make promises (vv. 5–6, 17). But there are also significant differences between the two. Lady Wisdom is presented as a banquet hostess who has built a stable house, has prepared a substantial feast and has sent out the invitation to the simple to come to the feast that she has prepared (9:1–6). In contrast, Lady Folly is inactive (sitting at the door of her house), loud and ignorant, who offers the meagre food of water and bread, with the allure that it is stolen and eaten in secret (9:13–18). There are clear associations between Lady Folly and the adulteress. Both are loud and without knowledge (7:11–13; 9:13). Both present the message that stolen water is sweet (implied in the seductive invitation of 7:16–20; 9:17). Both try to entice their victim through seduction (7:10–13, 21; 9:13) and the result of both is destruction and death (7:27; 9:18).

The way to avoid the adulterous woman and Lady Folly is to pursue the joys and benefits of marriage and the substantial blessings of Lady Wisdom. The personification of Wisdom as a woman allows the father to exhort the son to seek wisdom and to embrace her. She offers blessings associated with the joys of life and her characteristics are exemplified in the wise and virtuous wife described in Proverbs 31:10–31.[64] The picture presented of this wife is, on the one hand, an ideal picture. She is described, with the use of an acrostic, as a complete woman. She is involved in a variety of activities because she has different interests and abilities. She excels in every area of life for the benefit of her family. The different activities she participates in include real estate (v. 16), agriculture (v. 16), clothing (v. 24) and ministry to the poor (v. 20). She surpasses all women (v. 29). And yet, on the other hand, this woman is a concrete example of a woman who fears Yahweh.[65] She is called an 'excellent' (ḥayil) wife, a word that can refer to the strength of a warrior (2 Kgs 24:14, 16) or the social standing

---

[64] Wilson (2017: 319) lists several parallels between Lady Wisdom and the woman described in Prov. 31:10–31. Lucas (2016: 50) describes their relationship this way: 'Rather, while Woman Wisdom *personifies* wisdom, the Strong Woman *typifies* wisdom by *incarnating* some of its characteristics' (emphases original).

[65] Waltke 2005: 517–520. He argues persuasively that the wife is not symbolic but represents a real woman who is a role model in the wisdom she embodies (see also Fox 2009: 891, 910–912).

of a wealthy man (Ruth 2:2).[66] The wife in Proverbs 31 is called a
woman of strength (vv. 17, 25) because she displays strength in her
energetic activity[67] and in her character rooted in the fear of Yahweh
(v. 30). She generates trust in her husband who gives her the freedom
to develop her gifts and interests.[68] The words for 'strength' used in
this passage have military connotations,[69] including the description
of the husband as having 'no lack of gain' (v. 11). This description refers to the plunder brought back from the spoils of war. This
wife is engaged in the battle of life as she fights on behalf of her
family.[70] Her works are on display for all to see (v. 31) and her children
and husband recognize her worth in their praise of her (v. 28).
Although no wife should feel a failure if she does not meet this ideal,
the characteristics of this wife are set forth as an example.[71] The
Hebrew order of books in the third section of the canon, called
the Writings, brings together three women of strength: the wife of
Proverbs 31, followed by Ruth as the living reality of such a woman
(Ruth 3:11), followed by the woman of the Song of Solomon who
describes herself as a mature woman (Song 8:6–7, 10).[72] Proverbs
31:10–31 is the capstone to the book of Proverbs, a fitting conclusion to a book directed to the son who should not only seek Lady
Wisdom but should seek a wife who exemplifies the characteristics
of wisdom.

The choice that confronts the simple (Prov. 9:4) is life or death. The
way of foolishness, represented by Lady Folly, produces heartache
and destruction. The way of wisdom, represented by Lady Wisdom,
produces joy and blessing. Both Lady Wisdom and Lady Folly are
associated with the highest places of the city (9:3, 14), where temples
were normally built. Such an association confirms that the choice is

---

[66] Fox 2009: 891. He defines this concept as strength in wealth, physical power,
military might, practical competencies or character.

[67] Wolters 2001: 11. He comments that the focus is not on inner feelings or the
physical appearance of the woman but on her mighty feats of valour. It is a portrait
of verbs. These characterizations fit his identification of Prov. 31:10–31 as heroic poetry.
Such a portrait is a contrast to the typical ANE emphasis on the physical charms of a
woman from an erotic point of view (13). His identification of the genre of this passage
as a hymn is disputed by Waltke (2005: 516) and Fox (2009: 902).

[68] All the activities of the wife are for the sake of her home, which is her base of
operations in her communal life (Fox 2009: 890).

[69] Wolters 2001: 10.

[70] Longman 2006: 543.

[71] Ps. 112 by the use of an acrostic sets forth the ideal of a man who fears Yahweh,
and so parallels Prov. 31:10–31 to some degree.

[72] Prov. 31:10 and Ruth 3:11 use the word ḥayil, but Song of Solomon does not.

a religious choice.[73] Lady Wisdom is calling people to follow God's way that begins with the fear of Yahweh. Lady Folly is calling people to reject God's way to follow the way of foolishness and wickedness. Her meagre fare of bread and water hints that she offers little beyond the allure of great promises that cannot be fulfilled. To choose her leads to death, but to choose Lady Wisdom leads to life that comes only from God.

Christological implications of Lady Wisdom

The personification of Lady Wisdom in Proverbs 8 raises a number of questions. The ancient character of Lady Wisdom leads many to ask whether Israel has borrowed this concept from other nations. Several suggestions include Egyptian Isis, Canaanite Astarte or Mesopotamian Inanna.[74] Von Rad associated Wisdom's relationship to creation, and the order of creation, with the Egyptian concept of *ma'at*, but recognized that the Israelite idea is completely different from the Egyptian view.[75]

Some argue that Wisdom is not the personification of a concept but is a divine hypostasis, an independent entity existing alongside God.[76] Feminist scholars see the development of Sophia Christology out of the Jewish Wisdom tradition that was inherited by the NT writers to describe the pre-existence of Jesus. They understand Sophia as a divine hypostasis who is co-eternal with God and an agent of creation.[77] Sophia is even seen by some as a female goddess figure who is a rival to Yahweh's power, with demands for people to follow her and her promise of salvation for those who do.[78]

Others argue that Lady Wisdom in Proverbs 8 is a divine hypostasis that has direct connections to Jesus Christ. Steinmann argues that Proverbs 8:22–26 refers unambiguously to the pre-existence of divine

[73] Longman 2006: 222. Estes (2010) clearly shows that Prov. 1 – 9 is not just the tale of two women but the tale of two ethical systems.
[74] Hadley 1995: 235 and Lucas 2016: 44–47. Waltke comments that in Prov. 8 there is no mythological reality expressed, because Yahweh has no spouse (2004: 412).
[75] Von Rad 1972: 151–157.
[76] Not all who use the term 'hypostasis' define it the same way. For different definitions of hypostasis see Scott 1970: 42.
[77] Schroer 2000: 124; see also Fiorenza 1994; Spencer 1995.
[78] Cole et al. 2016: 15–30. There was a Reimagining Conference in 1993 where the Lord's Supper was celebrated with milk and honey and a prayer to 'Our Maker Sophia'. The book *Wisdom's Feast*, recently reprinted, provides the theological basis for the worship of Sophia, including Bible studies, sermons and liturgies. An analysis of this view occurs in chapter 11.

Wisdom as a hypostasis of the eternal Trinity. More specifically, this passage speaks of Christ's eternal divine nature and his eternal generation from the Father.[79] It is difficult from an OT standpoint to argue that Lady Wisdom in Proverbs 8 is a divine hypostasis of Christ's eternal divine nature. Lady Wisdom is consistently presented in Proverbs 1 – 9 as a personification of wisdom. There are too many differences between Lady Wisdom and Christ to identify them, but the similarities are significant for later connections to Christ. Both Wisdom and Christ are presented as instruments of creation (Prov. 3:19, 'by wisdom'; John 1:3, 'through him'; and Col. 1:16, 'by him' and 'through him'), but Christ plays a much greater role in creation as creation is 'for him' (Col. 1:16) and he restores creation to its intended order (Mark 1:40–45) by reconciling all things to himself (Col. 1:20). And yet the personification of Wisdom lays a foundation for a typological relationship with Christ, where the differences are not a problem because the anti-type is always a greater fulfilment than the type.[80] Connections to Christ can be made not just with Proverbs 8, but with how Wisdom is personified as a street preacher and a banquet hostess.[81] Both Wisdom and Christ are street preachers proclaiming their message in public places, calling people to follow them, and warning of the dangers if people reject their message. Both Wisdom and Christ are like banquet hostesses sending forth messengers, inviting people to a banquet of substantial food, experiencing opposition from sinners and promising life to those who come to the banquet. Both Wisdom and Christ existed with God before all things, descended from heaven, offered blessings in the symbols of food and drink, sent out invitations for people to join them and were rejected by the masses. But Christ is greater than Wisdom because he is specifically identified as the Son (John 1:18), equal with God his Father (John 10:30), the image of the invisible God (Col. 1:15), the one who will reconcile all things to himself (Col. 1:20).

---

[79] Steinmann 2009: 210, 214.

[80] Emerson (2017: 44–66) discusses the role of Prov. 8 in the context of eternal generation and argues that the difference between those who affirm it and those who do not relates to their theological and hermeneutical approach. His goal is to show that there are legitimate theological and interpretive rationales for using Prov. 8 as a basis for teaching eternal generation. In my approach, what is said about Wisdom in Prov. 8 will be fulfilled in Christ in a greater way. The personification of Wisdom allows both the differences with Christ to be affirmed and the similarities with Christ to be acknowledged.

[81] For similarities and differences between Wisdom and Christ see Waltke 2004: 130–131.

Chapter Three

The hermeneutics of Proverbs

Proverbs 1 – 9 clearly lays out the benefits of following Wisdom, and the negative consequences of choosing Folly are clearly laid out through longer discourses called instructions. Proverbs 10 changes genre from longer instructions to shorter individual sayings called proverbs. Certain difficulties must be addressed in understanding proverbs in order to avoid inappropriate conclusions. This chapter will examine those difficulties to lay a foundation for how to interpret proverbs.

The genre of a proverb

Collections of individual proverbs begin in Proverbs 10. It is difficult to read these chapters because they cannot be read as a unified composition. For example, the proverbs in Proverbs 20 cover a variety of topics. Verse 1 is a saying about wine, verse 2 is a saying about the king's wrath, verse 3 is about avoiding strife, verse 4 is about a lazy person, and so forth. Proverbs 20 is difficult to read because the sayings appear unconnected to each other. A person must stop with each verse to think about what it is communicating; each proverb could stand on its own apart from what the proverb in the next verse says. This fits the original purpose of the proverbs to be used in different situations. As one reads through Proverbs 20, not only does verse 2 deal with the king but so do verses 8 and 26; not only does verse 4 deal with the lazy person but so does verse 13. Both verses 10 and 23 talk about differing weights and measures. Proverbs 20 is not meant to be read as a unified composition, such as a psalm or a narrative.

The form of a proverb adds to this problem. A simple definition of a proverb is a short, pithy saying in common use.[1] The word 'pithy' means 'full of meaning' so that a proverb is a short saying that is full

---

[1] VanGemeren (2016: 377) offers a similar definition: 'a short, pithy statement that transmits an intergenerational observation cast in a fixed literary form free in poetic variation'.

of meaning.[2] The fact that proverbs are brief, are meant to stand on their own and seem to be gathered in a haphazard fashion raises several problems of interpretation. The problems will be stated first and then will be addressed.

The lack of literary context

A basic hermeneutical principle is that the meaning of a word is determined by how that word is used in context. Words have more than one nuance and it is the literary context that is the most reliable guide for determining the meaning of words.[3] The book of Proverbs seems to have little or no literary context to understand the individual sayings.[4] A good example is the familiar Proverbs 22:6, translated by the NASB as

> Train up a child in the way he should go,
> Even when he is old he will not depart from it.

The phrase 'in the way he should go' could be translated 'according to his way' and is ambiguous in meaning because it is not clear whose way is in view. The lack of a literary context leads to different views concerning the meaning of the phrase 'according to his way'. The traditional view is that 'his way' refers to God's way and that if a child is brought up in the way of God this will provide a foundation from which a child will live his or her life even when reaching old age. This gives hope to parents who have wayward children that they will come back to the foundation of God's way. Stuart argues that this phrase should be understood as 'according to his (own) way'. If a child is allowed to be selfish and do what he or she wants when young, then that child will have selfish tendencies later in life.[5] Others argue that 'according to his way' refers to the child's way, or the child's nature, so that the education of the child should be geared toward the degree of mental and bodily development of the

---

[2] For a discussion of the broad usage of the Hebrew word *māšāl* see the previous chapter. The meaning of *māšāl* includes the individual sayings that are in view in this discussion.

[3] Klein et al. 1993: 156–158.

[4] McKane (1970: 413) states that 'there is no context, for each sentence is an entity in itself and the collection amounts to no more than the gathering together of a large number of independent sentences . . .'

[5] Stuart 2009: 41.

child.[6] The training of the child should fit the character of the child.[7] The point is that it is hard to know what 'his way' means when there is little context to define the phrase. The lack of a literary context does not mean that the proverbs cannot be understood. There is support for the traditional view.[8] The word 'train' (*ḥānak*) has the sense of starting a young person off with a strong commitment to a certain course of action. In Proverbs this refers to religious and moral direction to counteract the foolish way. The fact that discipline is needed shows that it takes work to encourage a young person to start in the right direction. The consequence of this strong spiritual initiative is that the youth will not depart from the original initiative. This proverb should not be understood as a guarantee that a child who starts off in the right direction will automatically continue in that direction. Early moral initiative has a positive impact on a person for good, but that is not the whole truth about the training of a child and the development of a child's character.[9]

Secular or religious meaning?

Many proverbs seem like common-sense adages that can be found in an advice column of the newspaper or in a fortune cookie. This raises the question whether the proverbs are religious or secular in meaning. One commentator states, 'the content . . . is closer to life in the secular world, and to the day-to-day problems of the ordinary man who is content to leave traditional theology to the experts'.[10] Some proverbs seem to have little connection to a religious view of life. For example, 'Wealth brings many new friends, / but a poor man is deserted by his friend' (Prov. 19:4); 'The light of the eyes rejoices the heart, / and good news refreshes the bones' (Prov. 15:30); or 'Desire without knowledge is not good, / and whoever makes haste with his feet misses his way' (Prov. 19:2). These proverbs seem to fall into the category of good

---

[6] Delitzsch 1978b: 86–87; Kidner 1964: 147. The possible problem with this view is that the image of 'way' does not predicate human nature but a lifestyle that is learned and chosen (Schwab 2009: 7.590).

[7] Garrett (1993: 188) understands the verse to mean not that the instruction should be tailor-made for each individual child but that one should begin instructing a child in elementary principles of right and wrong as soon as possible. This view is close to the traditional view.

[8] Commentaries that support the traditional view include Waltke, Longman, Fox, J. A. Kitchen, Wilson and Ross.

[9] Wilson (2017: 7) comments that 'parental training has a strong impact, not that it bears sole responsibility'.

[10] Scott 1965: xvi.

advice with no obvious connection to theology or a religious under-standing of life.

The view that proverbs are secular advice is supported by two factors. First, Proverbs does not mention the foundational subjects of the covenant, the law and the temple that are prominent in the rest of Scripture. The offices of prophet and priest are also absent from the book. Second, Proverbs draws conclusions based on observa-tions and reflections concerning life experiences. For example, in Proverbs 24:30–34 someone passes by the vineyard of a sluggard and observes that the field is overgrown with thorns and the stone wall is broken down. The process is described in verse 32:

> Then I saw and considered it;
> I looked and received instruction.

This person perceives the condition of the field of the lazy person, considers what he sees, and then receives instruction based on what he has observed. The instruction gleaned from this experience is that a little slumber or sleep can lead to poverty (vv. 33–34). Something is observed, reflections are made on that observation and then lessons are drawn. This method has led some to question the authority of Proverbs. God speaks to Moses face to face. The prophets identify the source of their knowledge with 'Thus says the LORD'. But God does not speak to anyone directly in Proverbs, nor is there an appeal to the law as a basis for what is being said. The priest and prophet clearly speak with divine authority, but it is not clear that those who speak wisdom also speak with divine authority.[11] Zimmerli states, 'Certainly we cannot say that counsel has no authority. It has the authority of insight. But that is quite different from the authority of the Lord, who decrees.'[12] The authority of proverbs is placed on a different level than the authority of the prophets or the law. If something is only counsel or advice, then people have the freedom to heed the advice or to ignore it.

Are the proverbs absolute statements?

The understanding of the intent of a proverb is important. Is a proverb a promise from God that will always come true? Is a proverb

---

[11] Scott 1961: 3.
[12] Zimmerli 1976b: 321.

more limited in its scope, giving only a slice of life? What is the best way to understand the intent of a proverb? Some want to universalize a proverb so that it applies to every situation. The popular form of this approach leads to the health and wealth gospel. For example, Proverbs 12:21 states:

No harm befalls the righteous,
But the wicked are filled with trouble.
(NASB)

How do you know whether you are righteous? You are righteous if you are not experiencing any trouble, because the wicked experience trouble. Or Proverbs 10:22 states:

The blessing of the LORD makes rich,
and he adds no sorrow with it.

How do you measure the blessing of Yahweh in your life? This verse states that the measure of God's blessing is the amount of your wealth. You know you are blessed by God if you are wealthy. A mechanical relationship develops between a person's situation in life and his or her relationship with God. If you are wealthy, you are blessed by God; but if not, then you are lacking God's blessing. If there is trouble in your life, then you must be wicked or have done something wrong. If you experience negative consequences, then you must have done something wrong to bring about those negative consequences (the deed–consequence relationship). If you are suffering, then you must have sinned to bring on the suffering.[13] One author describes this view: 'People who found themselves in a miserable condition must surely have possessed some character flaw . . . individuals who rose high in social standing . . . were naturally thought to have superior moral character.'[14]

Literary context in the book of Proverbs

Three problems have been discussed concerning the interpretation of proverbs: the lack of literary context, the secular versus religious

[13] For a discussion of the health and wealth gospel, its origins, developments, key players and theology see Jones and Woodbridge 2011; for a briefer discussion from an OT scholar see Kaiser 1988.
[14] Crenshaw 1989: 31.

meaning of proverbs, and making the proverbs absolute statements. These problems can be addressed by discussing different contexts that are important for understanding the proverbs.

The literary context in view is the proverb's immediate textual context. Although it seems like the individual sayings grouped together in a chapter have no relationship to each other, there is a growing recognition that there is more literary context in Proverbs than many have thought. Van Leeuwen argues on the basis of structure, poetics and semantics that the poet constructs a coherent, overarching view of reality in Proverbs 25 – 27.[15] Waltke's substantial two-volume commentary applies this method consistently throughout the commentary. If an interpreter understands the poetics used to give compositions coherence and unity, he can discern unstated and often implicit connections between the verses.[16] Poetics include keywords, structure, theme and phonetic connections. For example, Proverbs 16:1–9 is unified by the keyword 'Yahweh' and is framed by the idea that the heart of a man may make plans but Yahweh determines the outcome (vv. 1, 9). The theme of this unit is that Yahweh's sovereign rule encompasses human accountability: Yahweh's sovereign rule through human participation is the focus in verses 1–3, and Yahweh's sovereign justice in response to human morality is the focus of verses 5–7. The middle verse (v. 4) looks backward with clause A asserting that Yahweh brings everything to its appropriate destiny, and looks forward with clause B asserting that Yahweh matches the wicked with calamity.[17]

Longman takes an opposing position concerning the relationship of the proverbs to each other. He interprets the proverbs as individual sayings that have no connection with each other. The proverbs are randomly organized, a reflection of their history of composition and the messiness of life.[18] He interprets each proverb as an individual saying that has no relationship with proverbs that come before or after it. Perhaps the truth lies somewhere between these two positions, depending on the passage. Bartholomew and O'Dowd argue, on the one hand, that the random arrangement of the proverbs parallels

---

[15] Van Leeuwen 1988: 37–39. He even states, 'Indeed, there is some evidence that individual units were either adapted or created ad hoc to fill a role in the larger proverbial composition.'

[16] Waltke 2004: 47–48.

[17] Waltke 2005: 8–9. Waltke includes a brief introduction to each passage, where he explains the structure and poetics of that passage.

[18] Longman 2006: 40–41.

the reality of life because life is not always very orderly. Once the proverbs were written down and collected, however, it was inevitable that literary connections would develop between them whether intended by the editor or not.[19] The challenge is whether there is enough connection between the individual proverbs that a sermon could be preached from a section like Proverbs 16:1–9 or from a chapter like Proverbs 26, where proverbs are grouped by subject matter. Verses 1–12 deal with the fool, verses 13–16 describe the sluggard and verses 17–28 deal with people who stir up trouble. There may be more literary connections between the proverbs than is apparent at first sight and it is appropriate to look for such connections, but they should not be forced.

The context of Proverbs 1 – 9

The individual sayings called 'proverbs' begin in chapter 10. Proverbs 1 – 9 is composed of longer discourses called 'instructions' (see chapter 2). These chapters explain the religious foundation of life (the fear of Yahweh) and set forth the benefits of wisdom so the young person can choose the way of wisdom over the way of foolishness. Many recognize that chapters 1–9 are an interpretative canon for understanding the individual sayings that begin in chapter 10.[20] Others call Proverbs 1 – 9 a hermeneutical prism or guide through which to read the rest of the book.[21] These chapters establish the religious foundation from which the proverbs should be understood and interpreted. This means that none of the proverbs should be understood as secular in nature but should be interpreted from the religious perspective of life laid out in Proverbs 1 – 9.

The canonical context

Proverbs occurs with other books in a collection called the Old Testament. It shares a basic outlook on life with other OT books so that it is not surprising if there are references to ideas in other books in the OT. For example, clear connections exist between Proverbs, a wisdom book, and Deuteronomy, a covenant book that contains law. The connections can be summarized as an emphasis on parental

---

[19] Bartholomew and O'Dowd 2011: 92–93.
[20] Childs 1979: 553.
[21] Longman 2006: 61; Zimmerli 1976a: 186–187.

instruction (Deut. 6:7; Prov. 6:20), the use of standard terms used of
the law (Prov. 6:20), a similar emphasis on binding the commandments
to your person so you can take them with you wherever you go (Deut.
6:7–9; Prov. 6:21–22), and a similar outlook concerning the deed–
consequence relationship, where obedience will bring blessings, and
disobedience will bring negative consequences. Deuteronomy has a
corporate emphasis and Proverbs an individual emphasis. The
previous chapter also showed the close relationship between the law,
wisdom and parental instruction.

Yet there is a clear difference between the way the law is obtained
and the way wisdom is obtained. The law is directly revealed by God
but wisdom comes about by observation, reflection and drawing
conclusions about life (Prov. 24:30–34). These observations, however,
are not made by an autonomous individual who is interacting with
nature as an independent entity, but are made by those who are firmly
grounded in the fear of Yahweh. The object of the observations,
creation itself, was created by God with an order that can be
understood by those who observe creation. Observation is thus based
on the foundation of the law as the sages interact with the world from
a religious base. In other words, the sages stood on the foundation of
special revelation as they interacted with God's general revelation in
creation.[22] These two revelations are juxtaposed in Psalm 19. They
are not opposed to each other but are complementary.[23] So even
though wisdom operates more on the basis of observation, these
observations are not divorced from the law of God or the religious
foundation of the fear of Yahweh.[24]

Life context

The importance of life context, or the various situations in life that
a person may face, is expressed in Proverbs 26:4–5. These two verses
seem to state a contradiction. Proverbs 26:4 states that one should

[22] Longman (2017: 112) concludes that the source of wisdom is God, so that wisdom
can be called revelatory.
[23] Craigie 1983: 179–184. He shows that there are numerous points of contact
between the two halves of this psalm.
[24] Waltke (2004: 80–83) is negative toward the idea that there is an order in creation
that can be discovered through the observation of creation, partly because he thinks
it leads to a natural theology. But if the authors of Proverbs viewed the creation through
the lens of faith based on special revelation (Waltke 2004: 82), then such a pitfall can
be avoided. For a more positive view of the order in creation that is knowable and
useful for educational purposes see Estes 1997: 26–30.

not answer a fool according to his folly and Proverbs 26:5 states that one should answer a fool according to his folly. So how does one decide whether to answer a fool or not? The second line helps a person to know which would be appropriate. Proverbs 26:4b specifies 'lest you be like him yourself' and Proverbs 26:5b states 'lest he be wise in his own eyes'. The second line gives a wise person some direction as to whether a fool should be answered. In some situations it is futile to answer a fool because a fool will not listen and the discussion will deteriorate into using his methods. It is possible to look like a fool yourself (26:4b). In other situations a fool must be answered because his words are dangerous and his arguments must be challenged. An answer in these situations may be fruitful to a fool or to others who are part of the conversation.[25] Wisdom will help a person understand the situation to know whether to answer or not. A proverb is not a universal statement that applies to every situation but is a specific statement that applies to certain situations.[26]

Proverbs that use the name Yahweh are not necessarily situation specific but are more universally true because God is not limited by human limitations. For example, it is universally true that Yahweh

> has made everything for its purpose,
> even the wicked for the day of trouble.
> (Prov. 16:4)

And yet not all proverbs that use the name of God are universally true. Proverbs 16:3 states:

> Commit your work to the LORD,
> and your plans will be established.

This proverb assumes that a person's plans and the purposes of Yahweh coincide with each other, but what if a person's plans are not in line with God's purposes? Proverbs that use the Lord's name but are dependent on human response may not be universally true. Wisdom is needed to understand a proverb and apply it to the many situations of life.

Not everyone understands Proverbs 26:4–5 as being situation specific. Fox acknowledges that these two proverbs originally existed

---

[25] Kitchen 2006: 586; Murphy 1998: 199; Ross 2008: 6.212; Van Leeuwen 2015: 3.913.
[26] Longman 2006: 464; Lucas 2015: 169.

47

independently and applied to different situations, but when they are placed in a literary context juxtaposed with one another, the second proverb becomes a cautionary limitation to the first proverb. The meaning is that it is dangerous to respond to a fool, but the wise have a duty to speak up.[27] The meaning of the individual proverb in 26:4 is changed, because the wise must now speak up. Waltke argues that proverbs are absolutely true, not situationally true, and so Proverbs 26:4 and 26:5 are both true at the same time. Proverbs 26:4 refers to the fool's style of speaking that is rash, deceptive and heated. A wise person should never use this style of speaking and become like a fool. Proverbs 26:5 pertains to the substance of a fool's talk. The wise person must expose the fool's distortions in order to hinder the impact of foolish thinking. The proverb pair instructs the disciple always to answer a fool in order to destabilize him, but to do so without becoming like him.[28]

As a general rule, proverbs should be understood as situationally specific and not universally true. They express truth but not the whole truth. They are partial utterances that are not able to assert qualifications or exceptions that may be significant. This matches the genre of a proverb as a short, pithy saying and avoids the problems that arise when certain proverbs are made to be universal statements. Proverbs are meant to be applied to life situations. Diligent attention is to be given to the words of the wise (22:17–18). They are to be kept within a person, even 'ready on your lips'. Words of wisdom are to be internalized so a person can use them in different situations of life. To say the right thing at the right time is a blessing (Prov. 15:23). Wisdom helps a person understand difficult life situations in order to respond accordingly. The proverb 'Haste makes waste' means that things done in a hurry will lead to mistakes. It would apply to a person who is impulsive and makes rash decisions in life. They need to be more deliberate. The proverb 'He who hesitates is lost' means that in some situations prompt decisions must be made or the opportunity will be lost. It would apply to a person who has trouble making decisions and needs to be more decisive. A wise person will understand what kind of person is in view in order to apply the right proverb.

The structure of Proverbs supports the principle that proverbs are situation specific and not universal statements. Proverbs 1 – 9 lays the

[27] Fox 2009: 794.
[28] Waltke 2005: 349.

religious foundation of the fear of Yahweh and explains why the way of wisdom should be chosen over the way of folly. The proverbs in chapters 10–15 are almost all antithetical proverbs that show the contrast between the wise and the fool or the righteous and the wicked. This contrast is expressed with the conjunction 'but'. Proverbs 10:11 is a good example:

> The mouth of the righteous is a fountain of life,
> but the mouth of the wicked conceals violence.

The antithetical proverbs of chapters 10–15 reinforce the doctrine of the two ways taught in chapters 1–9. If a person follows the way of wisdom, good things will result, but if a person follows the way of foolishness, negative consequences will follow.

Proverbs 16 – 22 contain very few antithetical proverbs. Instead, they contain a number of proverbs, called 'better-than' proverbs, that show exceptions to the general teaching of the two ways. For example, Proverbs 16:8 (see also 16:19; 17:1; 19:1) states:

> Better is a little with righteousness
> than great revenues with injustice.

This proverb teaches that it is better to be poor and righteous than to gain wealth through injustice. This teaches that wealth is a relative and not an absolute good. Some things are better than wealth. It is possible to be poor and righteous or to be rich and wicked. Good things like wealth can become tainted with evil.[29] If wealth is a relative good, then it cannot be used to judge a person's life or relationship with God. Not all poor people are lazy and there are many rich people who are wicked. There are extenuating circumstances that may determine a person's financial condition, such as injustice (Prov. 13:23), poor decisions (17:18; 20:4) and the mystery of God's sovereignty (16:19; 19:21; 30:20–21).[30] One proverb presents only a

---

[29] Van Leeuwen 1992: 31. For a balanced discussion of wealth and poverty see Wilson 2017: 26–30.

[30] This discussion assumes that God is active in governing the world and in the principle of retribution. An early work on retribution (Koch 1955: 1–42), reprinted in English (1983: 57–87), argued that actions have built-in consequences so that the consequences of the actions come from within the actions themselves. God does not have a role in rewarding or punishing people but facilitates something that human action has already set in motion (see Boström 2016: 135–137 for a response to this view).

partial aspect of life and other proverbs are needed to present the whole picture.

Another way to express the applicability of a proverb is that it is 'dependently true now' but will be 'ultimately true then'. Proverbs are dependently true now in the sense that they do not give the whole picture but present only a slice of life, a partial utterance that does not apply to every situation. They give insights of general validity so that the application of a proverb to the right situation is a matter of wisdom. All things being equal, a person who lives according to the principles in Proverbs will live a life that is freer from trouble and is more financially secure than a person who ignores its teaching and lives like a fool. In general, experience validates the teaching of Proverbs. But there are no guarantees that such a person will be free from trouble or free from financial hardship. Life is messy and each person faces different situations and extenuating circumstances. From a NT perspective one could add persecution for the cause of Christ as an extenuating circumstance. Jesus himself experienced difficult living conditions (Matt. 8:20), injustice (Matt. 26:57–61) and a premature death on a cross.

A proverb will be 'ultimately true then' in the sense that in the new heavens and earth the proverbs that are dependently true now will be universally true. For example, in the new heavens and earth no trouble will befall the righteous and there will be no sorrow (Prov. 12:21; Rev. 21:4). The righteous will be wealthy in the sense that all their needs will be met so that there will be no worries concerning the provision of their needs (Prov. 10:22; Rev. 22:17). The wicked will not have a place in the new heavens and earth but will be experiencing the consequences of their wickedness (Rev. 21:8). This viewpoint fits the NT teaching that the kingdom of God is here now in a partial way but will come in its fullness when Jesus returns. The people of God do not expect to receive the fullness of the blessings of salvation now. Although we have received a glorious down payment of that salvation (Eph. 1:11–14), we still live in a world that suffers under the curse of sin (Rom. 8:20–25) and are engaged in spiritual warfare both within ourselves (Gal. 5:16–18) and with the world in which we live (John 15:18–19; Rev. 12:17).

Some of the principles discussed in this chapter are exemplified in the NT. Jesus uses two proverbs that seem to contradict each other in two different passages of Luke. In Luke 9:50 he states that 'the one who is not against you is for you'. The context is that the disciples saw someone casting out demons in the name of Jesus and tried to stop him because he was not one of the disciples. Jesus' response is against an intolerant, narrow exclusivism.[31] In Luke 11:23 Jesus states that 'Whoever is not with me is against me'. The context here is different. Jesus is responding to the accusation that he casts out demons by the power of the devil, a viewpoint that is clearly in opposition to Jesus. The point is that no one can be neutral in relationship to Jesus.[32] You are either on his side or against him.

There are also situations where Jesus does not answer a fool according to his folly. Jesus did not respond to the false witnesses who testified against him in a mock trial, whose outcome was determined beforehand (Matt. 26:63; Mark 15:5). He did not respond in like manner to his accusers; as 1 Peter 2:23 states, 'When he was reviled, he did not revile in return'. But there are other situations where Jesus did answer his opponents. He responded to the question of the high priest concerning whether he was the Christ (Matt. 26:64; Mark 14:62). It was an opportunity to proclaim that he was the Messiah. Jesus also answered people who were trying to trip him up with their questions. He silenced his critics with his own questions to expose their hypocrisy right before he healed a man on the Sabbath (Mark 3:1–4; Luke 14:1–6). When the Pharisees plotted how to entangle him in his words with a question about whether it was lawful to pay taxes to Caesar or not, he called them hypocrites and answered them in a way that astonished them (Matt. 22:15–22). When the Sadducees asked him a question related to levirate marriage in order to show the foolishness of the idea of resurrection, he responded bluntly with 'You are wrong, because you know neither the Scriptures nor the power of God.' His answer left them astonished at his teaching (Matt. 22:23–33). Paul himself took on the strategy of his opponents in boasting to prove his apostleship. He spoke as a fool (2 Cor. 11:1; 12:11) because he knew that a refusal to use their terms would have confirmed his foolish flock in their opinions. Paul answered a fool according to his folly. Wisdom knows how to respond to the various situations of life and whether or not a fool should be answered.

---

[31] Hendriksen 1978: 521.
[32] Edwards 2015: 292. He comments that in 9:50 the issue 'is the relationship of disciples *among themselves*; in 11:23 the issue is the relationship of disciples *with Jesus*' (emphases original).

Chapter Four

The theology of Proverbs

Theology from proverbial sayings

It is difficult to preach or teach from chapters of Proverbs that are collections of individual proverbial sayings.[1] These chapters are not a unified composition like a psalm or narrative. Some commentaries reflect this difficulty by taking a topical approach rather than giving an exposition of each proverb.[2] One way to approach this material is to group the proverbs according to subject matter and preach topical sermons, with the individual proverbs serving as the main points of the sermon (or teaching lesson). This method produces a variety of topics that cover many areas of life. Discussing theology in the book of Proverbs has the same challenge. There are foundational ideas laid out in Proverbs 1 – 9, but the theology of the book is also expressed in the individual sayings that begin in Proverbs 10.[3]

The sovereignty of God

God is presented in Proverbs as the sovereign Creator who is in control of the world that he has created. He 'founded the earth' and 'established the heavens' (Prov. 3:19), a merism that covers the entire cosmos. The world that God created is stable and permanent and he continues to sustain it with life-giving waters that refresh the earth (Prov. 3:20). The use of the covenant name Yahweh is important because it makes clear that the God of the covenant is also the God

[1] Wilson (2017: 45–47) lays out helpful principles for preaching Proverbs and gives a variety of ways to handle the individual proverbs beginning in Prov. 10.
[2] Commentaries that take a thematic or topical approach beginning in Prov. 10 include Atkinson 1996, Hubbard 1989, Ross 2008 and Farmer 1991. Major commentaries usually give an exposition of each proverb beginning in Prov. 10. Some commentaries give both an exposition of each proverb and a topical index that groups proverbs by topics (Kitchen 2006) or offers topical studies (Longman 2006).
[3] Some theological topics are covered in earlier chapters. The view of life and the benefits of wisdom, including Lady Wisdom, are examined in chapter 2, and the topic of divine retribution (the deed–consequence relationship) is covered in chapter 3 in the discussion of the hermeneutics of proverbs.

of creation. The name for God used in Genesis 1 (Elohim) emphasizes the majestic sovereignty of the Creator God in his power and glory. This is the same God who prepares a special place for Adam and Eve so he can have fellowship with them (Gen. 2:8–25). The name for God in Genesis 2 is Yahweh Elohim (LORD God). God is the transcendent, glorious God of creation (Elohim) but is also the God (Yahweh) who seeks fellowship with the one he made in his image. Both sides of God are apparent in the book of Proverbs.

God is sovereign over every aspect of creation because he has ordained all things. Proverbs 16:33 states:

> The lot is cast into the lap,
> but its every decision is from the LORD.

God even controls the outcome of the lot, an event from the human perspective that seems to be driven by chance. But there are no chance events in God's universe, as he controls all things, even the future.[4] God even directs those who are the most powerful on earth. Proverbs 21:1 states:

> The king's heart is a stream of water in the hand
> of the LORD;
> he turns it wherever he will.

A historical example of this is God's power over Pharaoh to bring him to a point where he lets the Israelites go from Egypt through the hardening of Pharaoh's heart.[5] God is also sovereign over the affairs of people. Proverbs 19:21 states:

> Many are the plans in the mind of a man,
> but it is the purpose of the LORD that will stand.

Human beings can make plans but God's purposes will prevail (Prov. 16:9). Human strategy may be important but it will not always lead to success. In fact, if a person's steps are from Yahweh it will be difficult at times to understand the direction of one's life (Prov. 20:24). Sometimes the path of life can be confusing because a person is not

---

[4] Lucas 2015: 125. There is no need to limit this verse to God's settling of matters properly referred to him (Kidner 1964: 122).
[5] Currid 1997: 96–103.

able to see how the purposes of the Lord are being carried out. The proper response is to trust that Yahweh will make the paths of life straight (Prov. 3:5–6). The implication is that God is able to use bad circumstances or the evil intent of people for good as he did in Joseph's life.

God's sovereignty over every aspect of life should bring comfort to God's people. God is not only transcendent, but is also very involved in the events of this world. For one thing, he knows what is going on in this world. He knows everything because his eyes are in every place (Prov. 15:3). He keeps watch over the evil and the good. He even knows what is in the heart of people (Prov. 15:11); he knows what they are thinking and planning. Even Sheol, the realm of the dead, lies open before Yahweh. God is not surprised by anything the wicked are trying to accomplish. If he knows what the wicked are scheming, he also knows the plight and condition of the afflicted. If people mock the poor, they are actually insulting God his Maker (17:5). Serious consequences will come to people who rob the poor or take advantage of the afflicted. God himself pleads their cause and will rob the lives of those who rob the poor (22:22–23). On the other hand, if people are generous to the poor they are actually lending to Yahweh, who will repay them for their generosity (19:17). In the book of Proverbs God is not a distant deity who is unconcerned with the events of life on earth.[6] He is a God of justice who is concerned about how the disadvantaged are treated. God's sovereignty over all things is not a problem in the book because the emphasis is on the blessings that come to the wise and righteous. Trouble is in the world (Prov. 13:23; 28:3), but trouble and wickedness are presented within the confinement of God's purposes so that eventually things will work out well for God's people. Struggle related to suffering will become prominent in the book of Job and the difficulty of understanding the events of life will take centre stage in Ecclesiastes.

Creation order

Common grace and human knowledge

God used wisdom as an instrument to create the world (Prov. 3:19–20) and to establish its boundaries (Prov. 8:25–29). Wisdom is built into

---

[6] Wilson 2017: 23–24. He describes God's relationship to the world as God's kingly rule in everyday life.

creation and is part of the way creation works (see the discussion of Prov. 8 in chapter 2). Creation contains an order that can be explored by human beings. Proverbs 20:12 says:

> The hearing ear and the seeing eye,
> the LORD has made them both.

God has made the faculties of people to work in the world he has created. By the use of sight and hearing people are able to analyse and understand, to a certain extent, the way creation works. This knowledge can be very beneficial to people in making life more comfortable and allowing them to be more productive. Interacting with God's general revelation in creation is part of the way people exercise dominion in creation (Gen. 1:26–28). Adam carried out this role when he named the animals in Genesis 2. In the OT kings are in a position to explore, analyse, organize and thus understand creation. Proverbs 25:2 states:

> It is the glory of God to conceal things,
> but the glory of kings to search things out.

Waltke notes that the use of Elohim for God in verse 2 and the use of heavens and earth in verse 3 suggest that what God conceals in creation includes his wisdom in his acts of creation.[7] Kings are in a position to investigate God's creation in order to understand how it works and to assist others in understanding by naming and explaining the works of creation. Both Adam (Gen. 2:19) and Solomon (1 Kgs 4:33) investigated God's creation to understand it better.

The wisdom by which Yahweh made creation is available to every person. The building of the cosmos with wisdom is compared to the building of a house with wisdom and filling it with riches (Prov. 24:3–4). People are able to have a fuller understanding of the way the world works if they submit to God by fearing Yahweh (Prov. 1:7). The entrance of sin into the world led to a rebellion of people against God's ways (Gen. 6:5–7; 11:1–9) and a hard-hearted blindness toward God. And yet even unbelievers, in a limited way, can understand how creation works.[8] Human civilization develops in the ungodly line in

---

[7] Waltke 2005: 311. Waltke unnecessarily limits this searching by the king to the affairs of state because he is negative toward the concept of an order in creation.

[8] For the relationship of wisdom to natural law see VanDrunen 2014: 367–416. He is very optimistic in his view of what wisdom can accomplish in relationship to natural

Genesis 4 through the family of Cain. They are driven from the presence of Yahweh and separated from the godly community, but develop husbandry, music and metal works (Gen. 4:20–22).

The fact that unbelievers can understand the way creation works and even use that knowledge for the benefit of humanity is called 'common grace'. Such grace does not have a redemptive focus, but refers to God's favour granted to all people. Murray defines common grace as 'every favor, of whatever kind or degree, falling short of salvation, which this undeserving and sin-cursed world enjoys at the hand of God'.[9] God's common grace manifests itself in various ways. God restrains sin so that evil is not as widespread as it could possibly be.[10] God allows history and human life to continue by not immediately exercising judgment against sin. God grants temporal blessings to everyone, such as sunshine and rain, by virtue of his universal love and goodness (Matt. 5:45). Unbelievers are able to know truth, not in an ethical sense of being obedient to God, but in a limited sense of understanding how the world works.[11]

Common grace is particularly important in wisdom literature because most of the topics addressed are common concerns of everyday life. Whether you are an Israelite or an Egyptian you are concerned about how to raise children, as well as being concerned about broader family issues, business practices, financial matters, and so on. There are striking parallels between Israel's wisdom literature and the wisdom literature of the ANE. One explanation of this similarity is that when believers or unbelievers interact with the concerns of life, they many times come to similar conclusions concerning secondary issues. For example, it is good when children are disciplined, when certain financial principles are followed or when fairness becomes a part of business practices. These would be called common-grace insights. Such similarities should not be surprising.[12]

One interesting example of the similarity between Israelite wisdom literature and Egyptian wisdom literature is the possible relationship between Proverbs 22:17 – 24:22 and the Egyptian *The Instruction of*

law; he states that 'Proverbs grounds the moral life in the natural order created by God through wisdom' (375).
[9] Murray 1997: 2.96. He has an excellent discussion of common grace.
[10] Ibid. 2.104, 106. He shows that the unregenerate are recipients of divine favour and that in a relative sense good is attributed to the unregenerate.
[11] Frame 2013: 247.
[12] Common grace does not mean the antithesis between a believer's and an unbeliever's thinking is destroyed. There is an antithesis on the level of one's basic commitment to the ultimate issues of life related to the worship of God.

Amenemope (1186–1069 BC). Some scholars see similarity in structure and content between this Egyptian instruction and Proverbs 22:17 – 24:22. This connection is strengthened by understanding Proverbs 22:20 to be referring to 'thirty sayings' that are supposed to relate to the thirty sayings of the Egyptian instruction. This possible association leads many to argue for some kind of relationship between the two. Some have argued that Proverbs is dependent on the Egyptian instruction, even going so far as to suggest emendations to Proverbs.[13] Another view is that someone adopted and adapted these sayings by putting them into the religious context of Israel with the use of the name Yahweh (22:19).[14] Others argue that there is no direct connection between these two works, but they may go back to a common source.[15]

So what is the best way to understand the connection between these two wisdom works? The evidence is not absolutely convincing that there is a clear relationship between *The Instruction of Amenemope* and Proverbs 22:17 – 24:22. The translation of 22:20 as 'thirty sayings' is based on an emendation of the text. What is written in the Hebrew text (the Ketiv) is *šilšôm*. This word means 'formerly' and would fit with the 'today' of Proverbs 22:19: 'I have made them known to you today, even to you. Have I not written to you formerly of counsel and knowledge?'[16] Scholars have problems with this translation. In poetry the full phrase *'etmôl šilšôm* is used to express the idea 'formerly', or the abbreviated form *'etmôl* is used, but not *šilšôm* (Ps. 90:4; Isa. 30:33; Mic. 2:8).[17] Some point out that this rendering draws an unnatural contrast between the instruction given to trust in Yahweh (v. 19) and the instruction formerly given concerning the ability to answer correctly (v. 20).[18] No translation is without difficulties.

---

[13] Ruffle 1977: 31. He gives the history of the relationship between *The Instruction of Amenemope* and Proverbs 22:17 – 24:22 and lays out the various views of the relationship between the two.

[14] Waltke 2004: 24. He argues that Solomon is the one who adapted the sayings. He also has the best argument for 'thirty sayings' in 22:20 (2005: 219, n. 113) and lays out Prov. 22:17 – 24:22 according to thirty sayings.

[15] Ruffle 1977: 30; Currid (1997: 215) states that if Proverbs was influenced by the Egyptian instruction, it was indirect.

[16] This is my translation of v. 20. The scribes of the Hebrew text want you to read *šālîšîm* in v. 20 (called the Qere). This would give the meaning 'excellent things' (NASB, KJV, NKJV), but it requires a lexical jump from 'officer' (*šālîš*) to excellent or noble things (Waltke 2005: 219, n. 113).

[17] Kitchen (2008: 561–562) argues that the use of *šilšôm* by itself is not an isolated phenomenon in the broader ANE but has precedents going back a millennium in the Babylonian word *shalshumi*.

[18] Waltke 2005: 219, n. 113.

Scholars also point to strong parallels between Proverbs and *The Instruction of Amenemope*, particularly with Proverbs 22:17–18,[19] to bolster the case for some kind of relationship between the two. The parallels cited between Proverbs 22:17 – 24:22 and this Egyptian instruction are very general and scattered throughout the Proverbs material. In Proverbs 22:17–18 the parallels are as follows: give your ears // incline your ears, things that are said // my words, give your heart // set your heart, beneficial // pleasant, make them rest // if you keep them, and in the casket of your belly // in your belly. Other parallels include robbing the lowly, associating with a hothead, riches flying away like a bird, and not moving a boundary stone. These parallels are not unique to these two works. Even the parallel of 'belly' is not unique to Proverbs 22:18 but is used in a similar way to express what is within a person (Job 32:18; Prov. 18:8; 20:27, 30). Plus the verses that are 'parallel' to each other are scattered throughout the Egyptian instruction, and the Proverbs passage does not follow the same order as the Egyptian instruction.[20] Longman thinks the best conclusion is that 'there is not a specific relationship between Proverbs and Amenemope; rather, both texts are part of an international tradition of wisdom that shares many similarities'.[21] The similarities between these two works show that unbelievers interacting with God's creation will at times come to good conclusions in areas of secondary importance. There remain, however, major differences between believers and unbelievers in areas of primary or ultimate import-ance that touch matters of religious commitment and world-view presuppositions.

Order, disorder and the use of Proverbs

God's wisdom is built into creation so that there is an order in creation. People interact with God's creation and seek to understand how it works. People exercise dominion as they seek to understand, preserve

---

[19] Ibid. 221; Fox 2009: 713. Fox not only gives his own translation of Proverbs 22:17 – 24:22 but also highlights in bold those areas that parallel the Egyptian instruction.

[20] Ruffle 1977: 63; Kitchen 2008: 562. Kitchen makes the strongest argument against any relationship between these two texts. Ruffle is willing to acknowledge the possibility of an Egyptian scribe working at Solomon's court producing this text based on memories of a text he had heard and maybe used in his scribal training.

[21] Longman 2006: 54. He also notes that there are similarities between Proverbs and other wisdom literature of the ANE, such as the Aramaic Ahiqar (see also Kitchen 2008: 563–564). In a later work, Longman (2017: 259) uses stronger language when he states that proverbs were 'inspired' by Amenemope and 'adapted and contextual-ized' it.

and use it for the benefit of fellow human beings. One result of this quest for knowledge is the expression of this knowledge in proverbial form. Proverbs are a result of people trying to understand the world in which they live and to express that understanding in ways that will help other people live lives that demonstrate God's wisdom. For the most part, proverbs in the book of Proverbs express confidence in the dependability of the world God has created. They reinforce family, society and the religious values associated with God and the fear of Yahweh.[22]

Creation, however, is not perfect. Disorder in creation is a result of God's curse against sin (Gen. 3:14–19) and the entrance of death into the world. Such disorder can lead to a crisis that causes people to wrestle with the goodness of God and the world he has created. In a crisis the positive teaching of Proverbs seems far removed from the experience of suffering. This struggle many times revolves around the deed–consequence relationship and that the positive blessings taught in Proverbs are not being enjoyed by the person in crisis.[23] Job was a righteous man who suffered greatly. His friends operated with a distorted view of the deed–consequence relationship and so they concluded that Job sinned to cause his suffering. Qohelet in Ecclesiastes wrestles with the breakdown of the deed–consequence relationship and the fact that the righteous experience in life what the wicked deserve, and vice versa. Each book wrestles with a different aspect of disorder in the world. The problems of the world overwhelm the order in creation. Even the wise and righteous can struggle when life is difficult. Disorder in creation raises many questions about life but it does not destroy the ability of people to understand the basic order in creation.[24]

Non-Israelites, general revelation and special revelation

Proverbs 30 – 31 provides an interesting conclusion to the book of Proverbs by giving some clarity to the relationship between general revelation and special revelation from the perspective of non-Israelites. Each chapter begins with an 'oracle' and then deals with experiences in life. Each chapter contains the words of a foreign figure either spoken by or to a son. Each chapter urges temperance by the use of a prohibition followed by negative outcomes (30:6–10; 31:3–4). Also,

[22] Estes 1997: 41–62.
[23] The problem is not the teaching of Proverbs, because it does not teach a mechanical view of the deed–consequence relationship (see chapter 3).
[24] Longman 2017: 140–146.

how people should respond to God frames the two chapters (30:1–9; 31:30). The last section of the book is a positive image of a virtuous woman who is an embodiment of Lady Wisdom and is a contrast to the adulterous woman. The fear of Yahweh frames the book (Prov. 1:7; 31:30). The proverbs in Proverbs 30 – 31 are meant to be read together as a conclusion to the book.[25]

The final two chapters of Proverbs are from non-Israelites. The title of Proverbs 30 is 'The words of Agur son of Jakeh. The oracle.' The title to Proverbs 31 is 'The words of King Lemuel. An oracle that his mother taught him.' It is clear that Agur is a non-Israelite because he did not grow up learning the wisdom of Israel or with the knowledge of the Holy One (30:3). There are also no clues within the text to the identity of King Lemuel: the best conclusion is that both are non-Israelites.

How did teaching from non-Israelites make its way into the book of Proverbs? There are several possible answers to this question. Both chapters deal with issues related to creation order and general revelation (Prov. 24:30–34) but do so within the confines of special revelation. The term *maśśā'* occurs in each title. Although a few take it to refer to the geographical region of Massah to the east of Israel and Judah in the Arabian desert,[26] there is good reason to understand it in the sense of 'oracle'. In Proverbs 30:1 the word *maśśā'* is followed by a term common in the prophets (*ně'um*) used in the phrase 'Thus says the LORD'. Also, the content of Proverbs 30:5–6 concerns the truth of the word of God. If *maśśā'* means 'oracle' in 30:1, it makes sense that it would also mean 'oracle' in 31:1. The teaching offered in each chapter should not be separated from special revelation, although some of it deals with reflections on general revelation.

The numerical sayings (vv. 10–33) of Proverbs 30 interact with creation order (general revelation). They treat life in this world under God's established order. Some see a close connection between the proverbs of this section and formulate themes to explain this relationship. Waltke understands the theme of these verses to be the disruption of the social order.[27] Steinmann argues that these verses deal primarily with God's established order in family and government.[28] These themes are found in this section, but not all the sayings relate to these

25 Koptak 2003: 653–654.
26 Kitchen 1977: 100; Delitzsch 1978b: 6.262.
27 Waltke 2005: 481.
28 Steinmann 2009: 481.

specific topics (particularly vv. 24–28). On the other side, Longman treats these verses as if there is very little relationship between them.[29]

There is a general structure to this section with single-line sayings in verses 10 and 17 followed by longer sayings that are lists. Most of these are numerical sayings that categorize the way life generally works. Items could easily be added to these lists. The first section deals with the character of people. Verse 10 discusses slander and verses 11–14 list different 'generations' (*dôrôt*) that exhibit bad character. This is followed by numerical sayings that deal with greed. The focus is on people who exhibit bad character traits and the results that follow from such traits. The bad character traits include slander, cursing parents, self-righteousness, arrogance, mistreatment of the poor, and greed.

The single-line saying in verse 17 deals with defiant, rebellious children and the horrible outcomes such children encounter. Verse 17 is followed by a brief section, verses 18–20, that features the word 'way' (*derek*). This word is used in Proverbs 1 – 9 to describe the general path of life: either the path of wisdom or the path of foolishness. The ways described in verses 18–19 describe specific ways of how something operates. These ways are wonderful and not easily understood, such as the way an eagle soars in the sky, the way a snake glides across a smooth rock, the way a ship navigates the sea, and the way of a man with a maiden. The last item is likely emphasized and describes the mysterious, wonderful way a love relationship develops between a man and a woman.[30] The way of verse 20 is the way of an adulteress. There is nothing wonderful or mysterious about this way, because it presents the sexual relationship as just the satisfaction of physical desires that is no different from sitting down to eat a meal. The way of the adulterous woman is the way of foolishness, a path that one should avoid. The numerical sayings that follow in verses 21–31 describe the different ways of things in different circumstances without using the word 'way'. There are situations that lead to social disorder because a person is not equipped to handle the responsibilities that come with a position of honour. A slave who becomes king may mishandle authority, leading to anarchy. A fool filled with food does not know how to handle prosperity (e.g. Nabal in 1 Sam. 25). An unloved woman who obtains a husband may act like the quarrelsome woman in Proverbs who cannot rule her tongue (Prov.

[29] Longman 2006: 526–533.
[30] Wilson 2017: 310.

21:9; 25:24), much less a home. A maidservant who displaces her mistress may become haughty, looking with disdain on the rest of the household (as with Hagar in Gen. 16:4). The stability of the community is at stake because people are elevated to a status for which they are not prepared or in which they can do a lot of damage. In contrast to social upheaval there are those who excel in their stride because of confidence. These include the lion, the rooster, the he-goat and the king with his army. Each confidently faces the challenges of life.[31]

Between the situations that lead to social disorder (vv. 21–23) and the situations that describe those who excel because of confidence (vv. 29–31) are situations where a creature from the animal world overcomes limitations to achieve success (vv. 24–28). The limitation of the ant is that it is not strong, yet it shows an ability to survive by storing up food. It provides for the future to compensate for its lack of strength. The limitation of the coney, or rock badger, is that it is not powerful, yet it shows an ability to survive by making its home in cliffs. In this way it provides for its security. The limitation of the locust is that it has no leader, yet it shows an ability to advance in ranks. The limitation of the lizard is that it is caught easily, yet it lives in king's palaces. It reaches the highest place in society. Each of these animals overcomes its limitations and obstacles in life through the wisdom of foresight, discipline and industry. The small, weak and seemingly insignificant can accomplish great things in life. Wisdom is greater than stature or talent. People should not allow the limitations in life to keep them from succeeding. Everyone faces obstacles, but wisdom overcomes those obstacles to achieve success in life.

The numerical sayings interact with God's creation and draw conclusions about how life works. They stress mastery over life by organizing things and enumerating them. They help people understand the way creation works in order to draw conclusions concerning human life. Many times the last item in the list is emphasized (30:18–19, 29–31).

The general revelation of creation order is important for understanding how the world works. And yet it is not sufficient in itself to give a full understanding of God, creation and human life. The words of Agur in 30:1–9, which are usually broken down into a confession (vv. 1–6) and a prayer (vv. 7–9), make this clear. They begin with terms

---

[31] Longman 2006: 533. He notes that each is dangerous in its own way and so needs to be feared.

associated with prophetic literature ('oracle' and 'declares'). There is debate about the clause at the end of verse 1: 'The man declares to Ithiel, to Ithiel and Ucal' (NASB). If this translation is accepted, the terms Ithiel and Ucal refer to obscure personal names.[32] Another option is to divide the consonantal text of the Hebrew differently and to add different vowels to come up with the translation (ESV)

> I am weary, O God;
> I am weary, O God, and worn out.

There is general agreement that 'I am weary, O God' is the right translation, but there is some debate over the last verb, *'ukāl*. The two main options are 'prevail'[33] and 'worn out'.[34] The verb 'prevail' would emphasize that even though Agur is weary in his quest for wisdom and knowledge, he can prevail through God's revelation in his word.[35] The verb 'worn out' would fit better the immediate context of the next few verses, which describe the limitation of human knowledge and the weariness that results in trying to find wisdom apart from God's revelation.

Agur confesses that he has not had access to God's wisdom or the knowledge of the Holy One and is therefore ignorant of God's wisdom. This lack of knowledge has left him 'stupid' and lacking basic human understanding. Apart from the religious base of wisdom that comes only from God, people are left to their own devices and can behave like animals. The word for 'stupid' has the connotation of brutish, like an animal, and may carry that idea here.[36] Limited human knowledge can accomplish much, but the use of that knowledge can be brutish. On the other hand, to know God is to be truly human.[37]

The limits of human knowledge are brought out in a series of questions emphasizing the gulf between God and humanity. Agur recognizes that the dwelling of the Holy One is in heaven and asks who among human beings has ascended into heaven and come down.

---

[32] Kitchen 2006: 678. He prefers this option.

[33] Waltke 2005: 455, 469. He takes the verb as a defective pual participle of *'kl* (see also Murphy 1998: 225–226).

[34] Longman 2006: 520 and ESV. Longman slightly repoints the verb from *'ukāl* to *'ekel*, from the root *klh* (see also Steinmann 2009: 591). Fox (2009: 850, 854) also understands the last verb to be *klh* and translates it as 'have wasted away'.

[35] Waltke 2005: 467–468.

[36] Fox 2009: 854.

[37] Waltke 2005: 469.

God's powerful activity is expressed in the next several questions related to creation to affirm the great gulf that separates people from the divine realm and the characteristics of deity. The answer to these questions is that only God can do such things because only God can bridge this gulf.[38] He asks for the name of the one who has done all these things, and asks for his son's name. If God is the only one who can overcome the gulf that exists with human beings to reveal his knowledge, it makes sense that Israel is the son because Israel is the recipient of the revelation of God and is called the firstborn son (Exod. 4:22). The Davidic king was also called 'son' (Ps. 2:7), and a few kings, such as David and Solomon, received special revelation.[39] Of course, there is another Son, sent by God the Father, who has come down from heaven. He also has the power to direct and provide for creation. He is also the fullness of the revelation of the Father and is the final word spoken to God's people. These ideas are stated in Hebrews 1:1–3 about Christ the Son, who was appointed the heir of all things, through whom God created the world, and who upholds the universe by his power.

Agur's confession of his lack of wisdom and knowledge of the Holy One shows he is a non-Israelite and came to the knowledge of God later in life. He especially knows the value of the word of God[40] and the importance of preserving it (Prov. 30:5–6). The value of the word of God is that it 'proves true' because it has been tested or refined. Something that goes through the testing process is found to be solid or trustworthy. Agur has found God's word to be true and trustworthy for his life. But even beyond that, the God who has given his word to humanity is a shield for those who take refuge in him. God protects those who submit themselves to his word. God's revelation is so important that it should not be tampered with or changed by adding to it (see also Deut. 4:2; 5:22; 12:32). The word of God does not need human wisdom to complete or supplement it. Anyone who claims this authority will be rebuked by God and exposed as a liar.

Agur recognizes that a person can go only so far in understanding God's ways based on general revelation and creation order. Although

---

[38] Waltke 2005: 472, 475. He notes that by asking the name of the one who can do these things, he defines the epistemological crisis in relational rather than intellectual categories. This agrees with Prov. 1:7.

[39] The view that the 'son' could refer to anyone who learns wisdom, including the son addressed in the instructions in Prov. 1 – 9 (Koptak 2003: 657), is too broad if the focus is on the reception of special revelation.

[40] The word 'God' is *ĕlôah*, a name found in some of the oldest poetry of the Bible (Deut. 32:15) and used frequently in the book of Job (Kitchen 2006: 681).

many good things can result from people understanding God's creation, it still leaves people ethically limited because they do not have the special revelation of God in his word. God's word is the sufficient foundation for life and all the challenges inherent to it. It guides people on how to use the knowledge obtained from creation and keeps people within certain boundaries of what to think and how to live.

Agur follows his statement on the sufficiency of the word of God with a prayer that he will not deny God (30:7–9). Falsehood and lying are a denial of the God who is the source of truth and who has revealed that truth in his word. This refers back to verse 6, that those who add to God's words are liars. He also requests that God will provide what he needs in life. The danger of being rich is that he will be satisfied with the abundant provision that wealth brings and forget Yahweh. The danger of poverty is that he will steal what he needs and bring dishonour on the name of God. There is nothing virtuous in poverty. Although having wealth is not wrong (think of Abraham and the many proverbs that speak of wealth as wisdom's fruit [3:16; 8:18; 22:4]), it comes with the spiritual danger of trusting in what wealth can provide and not in God. This is a prayer that the circumstances of life do not cause a person to become misguided and act in a way that dishonours God. Balance and moderation are important aspects of wisdom. This prayer reminds one of the statements in the Lord's Prayer

> Give us this day our daily bread . . .
> And lead us not into temptation,
>   but deliver us from evil.
>   (Matt. 6:11, 13)

The fact that a prayer follows an emphasis on the word of God fits the pattern of Scripture that associates prayer with the prophets who are the recipients of special revelation. Abraham is called a prophet and is told to pray for the household of Abimelech (Gen. 20:7). Prayer is also prominent in the ministry of Moses. Pharaoh asked Moses to pray for him during the plagues (Exod. 8:8–15; 9:27–35; 10:16–20). He prayed for the people after the golden calf incident (Exod. 32:11–14) and interceded for Miriam when she was struck with leprosy (Num. 12:13). At Saul's coronation Samuel stressed the importance of prayer: 'far be it from me that I should sin against the LORD by ceasing to pray for you' (1 Sam. 12:23). It is somewhat surprising when God tells Jeremiah not to pray for the people because of their iniquities and the coming judgment (7:16; 11:14; 14:11–12). As the final Word and the last great prophet, Jesus also had a prayer life (Luke 3:21–22; 5:16; 6:12–13; 9:18, 28–29; 22:44; Heb. 5:7).[41] The apostles did not wait on tables, not because it was beneath them but because it would take away from their ministry of the word of God and prayer (Acts 6:4). It is significant that the association of the word of God and prayer is also found in wisdom literature. It is not as prominent as in other parts of Scripture, but shows that a proper attitude to God's word goes hand in hand with the proper response of submission to God through prayer. This too is part of the fear of Yahweh.

'Life' in Proverbs: one horizon or two?

'Life' is a major theme in proverbs, but is life in Proverbs to be confined only to the horizon of this life or does it also include the horizon of the one to come? Proverbs emphasizes what happens to a person in this life. The rewards that come from living according to God's wisdom are experienced here and now. Proverbs 11:31 states:

> If the righteous is repaid on earth,
> how much more the wicked and the sinner!

This proverb may mean that the righteous will receive blessings in this life and the wicked will experience the negative consequences of their wicked actions.[42] Another view is that if the righteous are repaid for their less heinous offences, how much more will those who are wicked be paid for their wickedness?[43] Either way the focus is on what happens in this life.[44] Proverbs 13:21 states:

> Disaster pursues sinners,
> but the righteous are rewarded with good.

---

[41] For more on Jesus' prayer life as he fulfilled the role of the prophet see Belcher 2016b: 49–51.

[42] Mentioned by Longman 2006: 266.

[43] The phrase 'how much more' supports taking the two clauses the same way (Kitchen 2006: 258).

[44] Waltke's view that the wicked will be punished after death (2004: 514) goes against the reasoning that the wicked will undergo the same kind of repayment as the righteous (Fox 2009: 546).

This proverb teaches that a life in pursuit of sin will end up being pursued by sin, but those who live a righteous life will receive good. The focus of Proverbs 13:22 is also on this life. The fact that a good man will leave an inheritance to his children's children refers to the blessing future generations will enjoy. The wealth of the sinner will not be left for his descendants but will be enjoyed by the righteous.[45] There are also proverbs that state that the wicked will experience sudden disaster (6:15; 28:18; 29:1), which includes premature death.

Certain proverbs also promise the blessing of long life, which is a benefit of wisdom (Prov. 3:16). The fear of Yahweh prolongs life but the years of the wicked will be cut short (Prov. 10:27). Righteousness delivers from death (Prov. 10:2). Death in the OT is always an enemy, but there is both a good death and a bad death.[46] A good death is one like Abraham's. He lived a long life (175 years) and 'died in a good old age, an old man and full of years' (Gen. 25:8). A bad death is a premature death, a violent death or a death where there is no surviving heir.[47] Long life is clearly associated with wisdom. Those who follow wisdom generally avoid the people and circumstances that can lead to disaster, including premature death.[48]

Although there is no doubt that the book of Proverbs focuses on the events of this life, there is debate about whether Proverbs includes a view of life after death. Some proverbs seem to teach life after death, but many scholars deny such teaching and interpret these proverbs as focusing only on this life. Proverbs 10:25 states:

> When the tempest passes, the wicked is no more,
> but the righteous is established for ever.

Generally speaking, this proverb teaches that the wicked do not weather trouble well but the righteous have roots that help them survive catastrophes.[49] But should this proverb be limited to surviving trouble in this life? Fox takes 'for ever' to refer to a lifetime (Deut. 15:17; 1 Sam. 1:22) and not to life after death.[50] Proverbs 15:24 states:

---

[45] Waltke argues that retribution in Prov. 13:22 is not bound to this temporal order.
[46] Alexander 1986: 41–42.
[47] Ibid. 42.
[48] Chapter 3 shows that such blessings associated with wisdom should not be seen as guarantees.
[49] Longman 2006: 241.
[50] Fox 2009: 526. He notes that 'the righteous remain alive while others are eliminated'.

The path of life leads upward for the prudent,
that he may turn away from Sheol beneath.

The direction of a person's life is important. The life of the prudent is on the rise, heading upward. This direction of life avoids the downward path to Sheol, the realm of the dead, by helping the person turn away from death. Murphy understands this proverb to teach that a person is able to avoid a premature or unhappy death; not that there is life after death.[51] Proverbs 24:14 notes that wisdom gives the righteous a future and a hope that will not be cut off. Is this a future and a hope only for this life? Fox understands the future to refer to long life in this world or to a person's descendants who continue to live in this world after an ancestor's death.[52] Proverbs 24:15–17 cautions someone not to do violence against the righteous,

for the righteous falls seven times and rises again,
but the wicked stumble in times of calamity.

Lucas believes this teaches that the righteous will endure the difficulties of this life.[53] And finally, Proverbs 14:32 states:

The wicked is overthrown through his evildoing,
but the righteous finds refuge in his death.

Lucas comments that the hint of an afterlife is unclear in this proverb; rather, it means that the righteous seeks refuge in Yahweh when facing death.[54] Both Murphy and Fox emend the text to change the last clause from 'refuge in his death' to a reference to the integrity or innocence of the righteous, partly because they do not think a belief in the afterlife is attested in the Bible before Daniel 12.[55]

There are also a couple of metaphors for 'life' in the book of Proverbs. One is the 'fountain of life', a phrase that refers to something as the source of life. The fountain of life is associated with 'good sense' (Prov. 16:22) and 'the mouth of the righteous' (Prov. 10:11). These are described as the source of life in contrast to 'the mouth of the wicked' and 'the instruction of fools'. The focus is clearly on the

---

[51] Murphy 1998: 114.
[52] Fox 2009: 749.
[53] Lucas 2015: 160.
[54] Ibid. 116.
[55] Murphy 1998: 102; Fox 2009: 586.

impact of these things in this life. Both the 'fear of the LORD' (Prov. 14:27) and the teaching of the wise (Prov. 13:14) are also associated with the fountain of life and turn one away from the snares of death. Is the reference to death in these verses referring only to avoiding a premature death?

The 'tree of life' is also used several times in Proverbs in relationship to wisdom (Prov. 3:18), the fruit of the righteous (Prov. 11:30), a desire fulfilled (Prov. 13:12) and a gentle tongue (Prov. 15:4). Life is associated with the fruitfulness and vitality of a healthy tree and refers to the good life offered by wisdom,[56] the happiness associated with the life in the teaching of wisdom,[57] a figure of vitality and healing,[58] and a symbol of a long and fruitful life.[59] Should the symbol of the tree of life be limited to blessings received in this world?

Answers to these questions depend on a variety of factors. A clear statement of the resurrection occurs in Daniel 12:2, but many would place Daniel in the second instead of the sixth century.[60] Fox acknowledges that the tree of life in Genesis, but not in Proverbs, refers to immortality. But even if views of resurrection are later in Israel's history, there are reasons to affirm some kind of existence of life after death in the OT.[61] The main reason for this affirmation is the character of Yahweh and his relationship to life and death. He is the origin of all life: 'with you is the fountain of life' (Ps. 36:9). Life is not a power that proceeds from itself or is grounded in itself. If God is the origin of life, then it cannot be limited to this life but must transcend this life because God transcends it. Life is more than the fullness of earthly vitality because life in the presence of God is the highest good. The steadfast love of God is better than life itself (Ps. 63:3). The life that comes from God is greater than anything on this earth and will not be hindered by death. In fact, death itself is under the power of Yahweh (Ps. 139:8). If Yahweh is more powerful than death and if the righteous are in a relationship with Yahweh, then it makes

---

[56] Lucas 2015: 64.
[57] Murphy 1998: 22.
[58] Fox 2000: 159.
[59] Kitchen 2006: 85.
[60] Many take the visions in Dan. 7 – 12 as coming from the second century BC (Goldingay 1989: 328–329; Newsom 2014: 10–11); see Baldwin 1978: 35–46 and Hamilton 2014: 30–40 for arguments that support a sixth-century date.
[61] For arguments that there is a view of life after death before the exile see Greenspoon 1981; Alexander 1986; and Levenson 2006.

sense that the life that they have in Yahweh is greater than the power of death.[62]

Life beyond death is affirmed elsewhere in the OT. Psalm 16 is a psalm of confidence, where the troubles of life are subordinated to confidence in God to overcome them. There is security for the psalmist when God is at his right hand (Ps. 16:8–9). This security extends to the 'flesh' because the life of the psalmist will not be abandoned to Sheol. The language in this psalm pushes toward an unbroken relationship with Yahweh beyond this life,[63] especially with verse 11 following verse 10.[64] The fullness of joy in the presence of God should not be limited to this life but extends to a life enjoyed with God after death.[65] Only then can the fullness of joy and pleasures for evermore be experienced. This means 'the path of life' (v. 11) refers to more than life on this earth. The psalmist's security includes the assurance of not being abandoned to death. A similar view is expressed in Psalm 49, a wisdom psalm that reflects on the prosperity of the wicked. Wealth cannot deliver from death (vv. 7, 17). Instead, fools are destined to be ruled over by death (v. 14), but the upright will be ransomed from the power of death and be received by God (v. 15). The final statement of verse 15 alludes to the translations of Enoch (Gen. 5:24) and Elijah (2 Kgs 2:1, 9), who were taken into the presence of God apart from death.[66] Over against the foolish who have death as their shepherd and whose bodies will be consumed in Sheol, the psalmist has the hope of being ransomed from death to experience the presence of God.[67] Death does not have the final word for those who trust in God.[68]

The example of Enoch brings into focus the picture of life at the beginning of Genesis.[69] Life apart from the experience of death is

[62] Greenspoon 1981: 319. He suggests that the OT belief in a bodily resurrection developed out of themes associated with Yahweh as the Divine Warrior who has power over death and can release those under its control.

[63] Mays 1994: 89.

[64] Some understand the original meaning of Ps. 16 to limit deliverance to this life (Craigie 1983: 158; Goldingay 2006: 233; Kraus 1993: 240).

[65] VanGemeren 2008: 5.192.

[66] Grogan 2008: 104. The allusion is in the verb 'to take'. VanGemeren (2008: 5.425) argues that Ps. 49:15 refers to the resurrection.

[67] For the view that Sheol is the realm of the dead primarily reserved for the wicked see Alexander 1986: 41–46; Johnston 2002: 81; Levenson 2006: 73.

[68] Alexander 1987: 6–11.

[69] There are a variety of views of the provenance of Gen. 3, from Moses to the fourth century BC. This question depends a lot on one's presuppositions. According to the biblical account, the Israelites spent almost 400 years in Egypt and the Egyptians were known for their robust view of life after death.

the original state of Adam and Eve. Even after the entrance of death because of their disobedience, the hope of life that conquers death is held out as a goal. The one who brought death will be defeated (Gen. 3:15) and the tree of life is associated with living for ever (Gen. 3:22). Although sin triumphs in Genesis 4 in the death of Abel and sin reigns in the genealogy of Genesis 5 in the phrase 'and he died', hope is expressed that death will not have the final word. They are looking for the one who will bring relief from the curse of sin and death (Gen. 5:29) and there is hope in life beyond death in the 'taking' of Enoch (Gen. 5:24).[70]

Life in the book of Proverbs should not be limited to life in this world because the fullness of life associated with Yahweh cannot be limited to life in this world. The association of the tree of life with the blessings of wisdom (Prov. 3:18) has implications for this life (Prov. 13:12; 15:4) but also for life beyond death.[71] The 'fountain of life', when associated with the fear of Yahweh, turns away the snares of death (Prov. 14:27). If Yahweh is the source of life and the fear of Yahweh is a fountain of life that turns one away from the snares of death, then a relationship with Yahweh will include the abundant life that extends beyond death. When Proverbs 10:25 states that the wicked cannot survive the tempest but that the righteous is established for ever, the hope is expressed that not even the greatest misfortune can shake the righteous. Waltke notes that the fate of the righteous and the wicked is escalated to an eternal dimension.[72] When Proverbs 15:24 states that the path of life leads upward for the prudent to avoid Sheol, this must refer to more than an untimely death; otherwise, the path of life will be swallowed up by death.[73] Proverbs 24:14 states that wisdom gives the righteous a hope for the future and 24:16 states that the wicked should not do violence to the righteous because the righteous falls seven times and rises again. Without denying that these verses refer to this life, if seven symbolizes completeness so

---

[70] For arguments that the phrases 'to be gathered to one's people' (Gen. 25:8, 17; 35:29; 49:33; Num. 27:13; 31:2; Deut. 32:50) and 'to be gathered to one's fathers' (Judg. 2:10; 2 Kgs 22:20; 2 Chr. 34:28) refer to life after death see Alexander 1986: 45 and Levenson 2006: 73.

[71] Waltke notes that the tree of life as a representation of eternal life is part of the ANE culture of Israel's day (2004: 259).

[72] Ibid. 475.

[73] Waltke calls this an unthinkable thought in Proverbs (ibid. 634). Longman notes that the opposite of Sheol must be heaven as the dwelling place of God (2006: 321), although he is not convinced that this verse expresses an eschatological sense.

that the righteous will always get up,[74] it makes sense that not even death can keep the righteous down.[75] And finally, Proverbs 14:32 asserts:

> The wicked is overthrown through his evildoing
> but the righteous finds refuge in his death.[76]

The death mentioned at the end of this verse must refer back to the righteous because the 'evildoing' earlier in the verse refers back to the 'wicked'. The last phrase marks the circumstance in which righteous people prove themselves to be worshippers of Yahweh: they trust Yahweh in their death.[77]

Eternal life after death in a resurrection is clearly taught in Daniel 12 and in the NT. The tree of life appears in the new heavens and earth referring to eternal life (Rev. 22:2). Even if resurrection is not clearly taught early in Israel's history, life with Yahweh beyond death is present in many texts of the OT. If Yahweh is the source of life and offers abundant life to those who follow him, it follows that the greatest enemy that human beings face, death itself, would not stand in the way of a continuing relationship with Yahweh after death for those who trust in him. Yahweh is more powerful than death so that there is real hope for abundant life beyond death for those who trust in him.

---

[74] Longman 2006: 439.

[75] Waltke 2005: 283.

[76] Although Murphy (1998: 102) and Fox (2009: 585–586) follow an emendation of the text that reads 'in his innocence' instead of 'in his death', Waltke (2004: 383, n. 53) argues against the emendation because Proverbs consistently encourages faith in Yahweh; not faith in one's own piety.

[77] Waltke 2004: 608. He translates the last phrase 'in his dying' because the process of death is in view, not the state of death (383, n. 53). Kitchen (2006: 320) also understands this verse as referring to the final condition of the righteous and the wicked.

Chapter Five

Theological issues in Job 1 – 3

A brief introduction to the book

Several introductory questions concerning the book of Job are important for its interpretation. The structure of Job raises questions concerning its coherence. The following outline identifies the main parts of the book:

1. Prologue (1 – 2)
2. Job's lament (3)
3. The cycle of speeches (4 – 27)
4. The wisdom poem (28)
5. Job's last speech (29 – 31)
6. Elihu's speeches (32 – 37)
7. God's speeches and Job's responses (38 – 42:6)
8. Epilogue (42:7–17)

The prologue and epilogue are prose and the rest of the book is poetry. Some have argued that the original form of the book consisted of the prologue and epilogue, and the other parts were added later.[1] And yet the prologue and epilogue do not contain much of a story and are not really intelligible without the speeches.[2] There are also problems with some of the speeches. The wisdom poem of chapter 28 and the Elihu speeches seem out of place. The first two cycles of speeches are complete, but the third is incomplete. Is it appropriate to try to complete the third cycle or is an incomplete third cycle significant for understanding the book? The best approach is to accept the book in its current form as a basis for understanding its message. The prose prologue gives the context in which the dialogues take place.

---

[1] Fohrer 1968: 325.
[2] Wilson 2015: 13. The following scholars approach the book of Job as a whole: Andersen, Habel, Hartley, Longman, Newsom, Smick, G. Wilson.

The poetic dialogues lend credibility and a human face to an otherwise one-dimensional story. God's speeches confront Job with assertions he has made about God's justice. The epilogue reflects the dialogue between Job and the friends and brings the story to a close.

There are also questions related to the origin of Job. Two boundary points set its parameters. The book itself reflects the patriarchal period in the description of Job's wealth (1:3), the length of his life, and the account of his death (42:16). These factors parallel Abraham's life in his wealth (Gen. 13:2; 14:14), length of life (Gen. 25:7) and manner of death (Gen. 25:8). Job also acts as a priest for his family (1:5). The other boundary point is Ezekiel 14:14, where Job is mentioned as a righteous person, along with Noah and Daniel, who would not be able to stop the judgment of God if Job lived in Judah. Ezekiel was a prophet living in Babylon before the destruction of Jerusalem in 587. Some form of the book of Job must have been known by then.

There are a variety of suggestions concerning the date of the book. Some date it close to the time of the patriarchal period, claiming Moses as the author.[3] Others date the book in the era of Solomon because of the proliferation of wisdom literature during this time (1 Kgs 4:31–34).[4] Hartley places the book in the eighth century because of parallels he sees between Job and Isaiah.[5] Others date the final form during the period of exile to encourage Israelites to hold on to their faith amid suffering.[6] A date during the exile, however, is difficult if a comparison is made between the suffering of Job and the suffering of Israel because Israel suffers for her sin but Job is innocent in his suffering.[7] A date during the era of Solomon fits with the flowering of wisdom literature during this period.[8] Parallels between Job and the other books of the Bible could support a date during the period of the monarchy. Job 28 is similar to Proverbs 8, and Job 7:17 may be a negative allusion to Psalm 8.[9] Some leave the

[3] Archer 1974: 458.
[4] Young 1952: 309; Delitzsch 1978a: 4.20–21.
[5] Hartley 1988: 19–20.
[6] Wilson 2007: 2.
[7] Hartley 1988: 19.
[8] Delitzsch (1978a: 4.20) notes that the era of Solomon was a peaceful era that allowed the development of wisdom literature as represented in 1 Kgs 4:31–34 (see also Young 1952: 309).
[9] Kynes (2012) presents the best argument that Job refers to several psalms in the debate with his friends. Van Leeuwen (2001: 205–215) argues against Job's use of Ps. 8. Wisdom traditions are both ancient and international, so the question of borrowing is not necessarily decisive.

date open because a particular date does not necessarily have an impact on its interpretation.[10] The message of Job is not tied to a particular time period.
The genre of the book of Job is not an easy question. Genre discussions are based on comparisons between literatures, but there is nothing in the ANE that handles suffering quite like the book of Job.[11] Genre suggestions come from elements within the book. The term 'lawsuit' is used because of the legal elements in the book that relate to the innocence or guilt of Job.[12] Job certainly wants a hearing in order to present his case before God, but the legal aspects of the book do not explain its totality. The many laments in Job have led some to the conclusion that Job is a dramatization of a lament, a story with lament elements.[13] Certain parts of the book, like Elihu's speeches, do not fit well with this genre identification.[14] Dell discusses parody as a genre related to Job's speeches because they have the purpose of critiquing in a sarcastic tone traditional positions held by the friends.[15] Parody is more a rhetorical device used by an author and is hardly all-encompassing as a genre.[16] Job is in many ways 'unique in its structure . . . in the coherence of its sustained treatment of the theme of human misery . . . and in its intellectual integrity with which it faces the "unintelligible burden" of human existence'.[17] Job is best understood as a debate about how to respond to suffering that leads to the question concerning where wisdom is to be found.[18]

---

[10] Longman 2012: 27; Habel 1985: 42.

[11] For discussions of genre comparisons that deal with the suffering of the righteous and the issue of theodicy (the defence of God's justice in the face of evil) see Lucas 2013: 132–134 and Belcher 2016a: 359–360.

[12] Seow (2013: 59–60) discusses this genre. He also discusses a number of other genres and concludes that there is no precise parallel to Job. Habel (1985: 54–56) discusses Job as having a narrative plot that uses the legal metaphor as a major literary device that integrates the narrative and the theological motifs of the book. The legal metaphor is key to the book for Habel.

[13] Westermann 1977: 8–13.

[14] Wilson 2015: 245. Westermann understands the Elihu speeches as an addition and must trim aspects of the book to fit his argument.

[15] Dell 2017: 34. She recognizes that parody is not really a genre classification and that it feeds on other genres in order to exist. Some examples would be the way Job uses laments and the way Job 7 uses Ps. 8.

[16] Seow 2013: 83.

[17] Andersen 1974: 32. The above quote is just a few lines from his full statement on the uniqueness of Job (see also Hartley 1988: 38; Wilson 2015: 7; Gordis 1965: 4, 7). Longman (2017: 158) also comments that there is nothing like the book of Job in ANE literature.

[18] Longman (2012: 31) calls Job a wisdom debate.

Theological questions raised in Job 1 – 2

Important information is given to the reader in chapters 1–2 that is essential for understanding the book. This information is not available to Job and his friends as they debate his suffering, but is essential for understanding the message of the book, along with key questions raised in the prologue.

The character of Job is important. He is described as 'blameless' (1:1), a word that signifies wholeness and is used to describe sacrificial animals that are without blemish. When used of a person, it does not describe someone who is sinless but someone who is not a hypocrite. The term 'upright' (1:1) emphasizes faithful adherence to what is right, including a just treatment of others. Job is a person of integrity who fears God and turns away from evil. The fear of God emphasizes an awe and reverence for God. It is common in the wisdom literature of the OT and will be a key theme in a later chapter (Job 28). Job is a man who is righteous and wise.[19] He demonstrates his righteousness by showing concern for the spiritual welfare of his children and by functioning as a priest for them. He offers burnt offerings in case they have sinned by cursing God in their hearts (1:5).

Job is also a non-Israelite from the land of Uz who worships Yahweh. The land of Uz has associations with the area of Edom (Lam. 4:21). Even though Job was a non-Israelite, he worshipped the God of Israel and used the name Yahweh, the covenant name of God.[20] The name Shaddai occurs more in the book of Job than in the rest of the OT and is the name associated with the patriarchs (Gen. 17:1; 28:3; 35:11; 43:14; 48:3; 49:25; Exod. 6:3).[21] The wealth and stature of Job are expressed in the statement that he is 'the greatest of all the people of the east' (1:3). Job is a very wealthy man blessed with many children (1:2). Job's life and character are foundational for the events that follow.

God is presented in the prologue as the sovereign God who is king over the world. He sits in council with the heavenly hosts of angels, who present themselves before him to give an account of their activities. They submit to his authority. When Satan appears, God

---

[19] Ibid. 79. Longman points out that the terms used to describe Job's character are commonly used of the wise in Proverbs.

[20] The name Yahweh occurs in Job 1:6–9, 12, 21; 2:1–4, 6–7; 12:9; 38:1; 40:1, 3, 6; 42:1, 7, 9–12.

[21] The title Shaddai occurs forty-eight times in the OT. Thirty-one of these occurrences (65%) appear in the book of Job.

initiates the discussion concerning the character of Job. Satan always operates within the limits set by God (1:12; 2:6), even though he is clearly an adversary. The noun *śāṭān* with the definite article[22] can refer to an accuser or an adversary (Num. 22:22; 1 Sam. 29:4; Ps. 109:6), a meaning that fits very well in Job 1 – 2 because this figure brings accusations against Job. Some are hesitant to identify this being with Satan because not much is said in the OT about him. However, many passages talk about beings or spirits working against God's purposes (Gen. 3:1; 1 Sam. 16:14), a role that fits the heavenly being in Job (see also Zech. 3). The NT also mentions Satan, identified as the devil, who seeks to make trouble for God's people (Rev. 12:15–17).

The dialogue between God and Satan raises key theological issues that will be important for the rest of the book. God asks Satan if he has considered Job, 'that there is none like him on the earth, a blameless and upright man who fears God and turns away from evil' (1:8). Satan's response is that the only reason that Job fears God is because God has protected him and has blessed him with great blessings. If God takes away his protection and blessings, then Job will curse[23] God to his face (1:9–11). Satan's response raises the question of the relationship between piety and prosperity. Job is pious only because he is prosperous. This challenges Job's religious commitment to God as nothing more than self-interest. It also challenges the character of God. Is God worthy of worship only because of the blessings that he gives people? Is God worthy of worship because of who he is apart from a person's situation or condition of life? In Satan's first attack Job loses most of his family and wealth (1:13–22), but does not curse God. Satan responds with the accusation that God has not really hurt Job because he still has his life. The key phrase is 'All that a man has he will give for his life'

---

[22] There is debate about the use of the definite article with the noun *śāṭān*. Some argue that the article makes the term a title rather than a personal name (Hartley 1988: 71) and that it should be translated as 'the adversary' or 'the accuser'. However, there is a grammatical category where the noun plus the article becomes equivalent to a proper name (Waltke and O'Connor 1990: 249; they use *haśśāṭān* as one of the examples of this grammatical category).

[23] Several times in Job the word translated 'curse' is the Hebrew word for 'bless' (*bārak*). Scholars debate the reason for this practice. Perhaps the author does not want to use the word 'curse' so close to the word 'God' (Longman 2012: 81). There are other passages, however, where the words 'curse God' appear (Lev. 24:15). This could be a stylistic preference of the author or part of the artistry of the story (Newsom 2015: 3.39–40). Could the author be making a point about the ambiguity between blessing and one's condition in life?

(2:4–5). If Job's health is taken away, then he will curse God. Job is struck with loathsome sores from his feet to his head (2:7–8). Now the challenge will be whether a relationship with God is more valuable than life itself.

Some have problems with the way God is presented in the prologue.[24] He comes across as uncaring, not very concerned about Job but only concerned about whether he can win this argument with Satan. What kind of God would put someone through such suffering just to prove a point? Is this a God who is fickle and unstable, who can be manipulated by Satan ('you incited me against him without cause', 2:3)? Does God really care about Job, or does he just want to win a wager against Satan? God, however, is not really making a bet with Satan. In a wager a person does not really know the outcome.[25] God knows the outcome because he has ordained the outcome. But does this make it any easier to worship this God?

Although Job will struggle with how he perceives God is treating him, he does not abandon God as the ultimate hope of his deliverance. The sovereignty of God is a great mystery but is also a tremendous comfort. If God is not in charge of the events of this universe, and the events of our lives, who or what is? Any other option, such as Satan or chance, leaves us with no hope of deliverance. The sovereignty of God gives us hope because, even in suffering, God is able to bring unimaginable good out of it. We struggle with this because we are limited in our human understanding. Many times all that we can see are the bad things that result from suffering. We do not see how God can use it for good. We do not see the invisible and innumerable consequences that our suffering can have on ourselves, on others and for God's glory.

The connection between piety and prosperity will be at the heart of the debate between Job and his friends, but it will manifest itself in the relationship between righteousness, suffering and sin. If Job is really pious, as he claims, then he has nothing to worry about because his suffering will not last long (Job 4:6). The friends operate with a mechanical view of the deed–consequence relationship, so that if Job is suffering he must have sinned to cause it. This issue will dominate the discussion.

---

[24] Clines 2004: 233–241; Dell 2010: 174–176.

[25] Carson (1990: 177) uses the term 'wager' to capture the scene in the first chapter and to connect the suffering of Job to the larger cosmic struggle between God and Satan, where the outcome is certain but the struggle is horrible. He recognizes that the use of the term could make God appear capricious or participating in a game, which he rejects.

The book of Job tackles suffering head on but not in the way that is expected. The natural human response to suffering is to ask, 'Why did this happen to me?' The book of Job does not answer the 'why' of suffering. God never tells Job about the events of chapters 1–2. The focus of the book is how someone should respond to suffering. The point of Satan's challenge is that Job will respond a certain way to God if God allows Job to suffer. Job responds in several ways to his suffering, his wife responds and his friends respond. Are some responses better than others? How should people react to suffering? This is a wisdom issue because wisdom helps people evaluate life situations in order to respond appropriately. As the debate deteriorates, the question of the source of wisdom becomes more important. It becomes apparent that the friends fail to provide wisdom and that wisdom can be found only in God. Thus it is appropriate to see Job as a wisdom debate on how to respond to suffering.

There are several initial responses to Job's suffering in Job 1 – 3. Job's first response clearly shows that his faith is not self-interest and that he does not worship God only for the good things he gives him. After he loses everything, except his health and wife, he responds with actions that express grief and worship (1:20). He demonstrates pious submission to Yahweh in his actions and words. People come into the world with nothing and will leave the world with nothing, so anything that they receive in this world is a gift of God. There is no entitlement mentality in Job. God sovereignly gives and takes away, so no matter what people are experiencing in life the name of Yahweh is to be blessed. Job did not sin or charge God with wrong (1:22).

After Job loses his physical health, his wife responds with the words 'Do you still hold fast your integrity? Curse God and die' (2:9). Some react negatively to her response because her words 'Curse God and die' reflect the words of Satan.[26] If Job had cursed God, then Satan would have been correct in his assessment of Job. However, the first words she utters about Job's integrity are a reflection of the words of God (2:3). She raises the crux of the issue that will be debated in the rest of the book in a pointed way.[27] One must remember that she too has lost her wealth, her position and her children. When people lose their security, it is easy to respond out of panic because life is no longer sure and the future is uncertain. She also expresses pity toward

---

[26] Konkel 2006: 6.42. He notes that the early church fathers were generally negative toward Job's wife, calling her assistant of Satan (Augustine) and claiming that one of the trials of Job is that his wife did not die (Chrysostom).
[27] Wilson 2007: 31.

Job.[28] She offers a solution to end his suffering. She responds out of desperation,[29] and says some things that she would not normally say. Job answers his wife by recognizing her frail position and the desperation of her words, while at the same time calling her to a better perspective.[30] He first states, 'You speak as one of the foolish women would speak' (2:10). He does not call her foolish but recognizes that her words express a foolish view. He then raises the question whether we should expect to receive only good from God and not adversity.[31] This agrees with his first response: God does not owe anyone anything; he sovereignly gives and takes away. Once more it is stated that Job did not sin with his lips (2:10). Job passes the test and demonstrates that piety does not necessarily guarantee prosperity. In fact, Job's response cuts the cord between piety and prosperity because he recognizes that God does not owe him anything in this life. A pious life is no guarantee of wealth and great material blessing. If everything we receive in this life is God's gift because we come into this world with nothing, then there is no necessary connection between living a righteous life and prosperity. This view will be challenged in the debate that follows.

The first response of Job's three friends is to show him sympathy and comfort (2:11–13). They mourn with him by weeping aloud, tearing their robes and putting dust on their heads. They sit with Job at the ash heap, and they sit with him for seven days. The remarkable thing is that no one said a word to him during this time because they saw that his suffering was great. The friends should be commended for their presence with Job, their identification with him and their sympathetic silence toward him in his suffering. It is a great temptation to offer shallow platitudes of hope, or even to speak principles of truth, before a person is ready to hear them. A silent, sympathetic presence is many times the best initial response to suffering.

[28] Konkel 2006: 6.42. The response of Job's wife can be characterized as panicked pity.

[29] Smick 2010: 4.720.

[30] If Job's friends in the ensuing dialogue had treated him the same way, much of the book of Job would not have been written!

[31] The word 'adversity' is the Hebrew word *ra'*, which can mean 'evil' or 'calamity'. This Hebrew word combines into one word what English expresses in two words. One meaning refers to what is morally evil, which is the meaning when Job is described as a man who turns away from evil (1:1; 2:3). This word can also be used to accentuate the grievousness of something that is intrinsically harmful to one's physical well-being, even though no moral judgment has been made (Baker 1997: 3.1154). In Job 2:7 this word is used to describe the sores that afflict Job as 'loathsome'. The best nuance in Job 2:10 is 'calamity' or 'adversity'.

Job's curse-lament in Job 3

Job 3 begins the first cycle of speeches and launches the dialogue between Job and his three friends. Their sympathetic silence gave him the confidence to unburden his heart to them about his suffering. This chapter is being covered here because it is a further response of Job to his suffering that seems very different from his response in chapters 1–2. Many things change in Job 3. The prose narrative of chapters 1–2 ends and the poetic speeches begin. The divine perspective is gone and the reader is left with a limited, human perspective. Job's attitude toward his suffering also changes. A major theme of Job 1 – 2 is whether he will curse God and die (mentioned in 1:11; 2:5, 9), but he does not sin or charge God with wrong (1:22; 2:10). Thus the reader is shocked when chapter 3 begins, 'After this Job opened his mouth and cursed'. The Job of chapter 3 seems hardly the same person as the Job of chapters 1–2. How can this be explained? Does Job curse God?

Job 3 can be divided into two parts, with verses 1–10 being the curse of Job and verses 11–26 being the lament of Job. They both argue the same point: Job wishes he were never born. He curses the day of his birth in verses 1–10. Job pleads that the day of his birth will be obliterated so that the events on that day never occurred. He desires for darkness to overtake that day so that it never existed (vv. 4–6, 9). Job calls on skilled sorcerers to rouse the powers of evil to curse the day of his birth (v. 8). Leviathan is a mythological sea monster who represents the forces of chaos associated with the evil of this world.[32] If such forces were unleashed against the night of his birth, that night would be barren with no joy and no hope for light. The culminating reason for Job's curse is that if he were never born, he would not be experiencing trouble in his life (v. 10). Job does not curse God; rather, he curses a day in the past that cannot be changed, which is a parody of a curse.

The lament of Job continues his desire that he had never been born (vv. 11–26). It is similar to the lament psalms but also very different from them.[33] The lament psalms ask a lot of questions but the

---

[32] Fyall 2002: 142–143.

[33] The intent of Job's words is hard to discern. Wilson (2016: 62–65) sees the laments in Job as similar to the laments of the psalms and understands Job as expressing a robust faith in God. Longman (2017: 45) highlights the differences between the laments in the psalms and Job's lament of ch. 3 and argues that Job is closer to the grumbling Israelites in the wilderness than to the words of the psalmists. Both Wilson (2016: 63) and Longman (2017: 273) agree that it is appropriate for a believer to seek God by using lament.

psalmist also pleads with God to deliver him. He expresses confidence that God has heard his prayer or that he will answer his plea. Job's lament is different. He does not call on God to deliver him.[34] The 'why' questions in Job's lament continue the curse of 3:1–10 and focus on why Job did not die at birth (vv. 11–12, 16, 20, 23). If Job had died at birth, he would be at rest. Instead, his way is hidden because he has lost all purpose in life. He feels trapped in his suffering. Satan uses a word in Job 1:10 to express that God has protected Job, but instead of feeling protected by God Job feels God has hedged him in so he cannot escape (3:23). Job's longing is not for deliverance but for death (3:21). He ends the lament with a self-centred focus on his suffering evidenced by an accumulation of the pronouns 'my' and 'I' (3:24–26). He has no rest, he is full of trouble and he wishes he had never been born.

What are we to make of Job's words? How are we to explain the move from the God-centred outlook in Job 1 – 2 to the self-centred perspective in Job 3? How are we to explain the move from Job's patient submission to God in Job 1 – 2, where he blesses the name of Yahweh after he has lost everything, to a position of protest over his suffering, including how God is treating him, in Job 3? The answer is not that there are two Jobs or that the real character is introduced in Job 3.[35] Rather, both responses are legitimate because there is more than one way to respond to innocent suffering.[36] The simple explanation is that suffering can have an impact on the way people view their life and relationship with God. The patient, submissive Job of chapters 1–2 highlights the intellectual dilemma faced by the people of God: God is sovereign over the events of this life and yet suffering can overtake a person who fears God. The protesting Job of chapter 3 shows that believers may wrestle with this dilemma by venting their anguish and anger.[37] Job now views his life negatively, consumed by darkness and fear. His life is full of spiritual, emotional and psychological turmoil. An insight is given into the psychological nature of his suffering when he states:

[34] Hartley 1994: 89–91.
[35] Dell 2017: 41. She argues that the real character of Job comes to life in Job 3. See also Brenner 1989: 37–52, who argues that the pious Job of the prologue is superficial, an ironic exaggeration of conventional piety that is later rejected when found in the speeches of the friends. But the Job of the prologue denies the connection between piety and blessing, a view that does not correspond to the argument of the friends.
[36] Clines 1989: 66.
[37] Konkel 2006: 6.48.

> the thing that I fear comes upon me,
> and what I dread befalls me.
>
> (v. 25)

It is natural for people to fear what the future may bring and Job has become consumed with angst concerning his situation. This statement, however, does not mean that Job believes he is getting what he really deserves. Such a view would subvert the purpose of the book. These words show that Job has thought about these matters enough to know that he cannot consider himself exempt from the possibility of disastrous loss.[38] If God is sovereign, it is natural for people to wrestle with his role in their suffering. The response of Rabbi Harold Kushner to his son's illness and death is a well-known example. He wondered how God can be both all-powerful and good if he allows such bad things like his son's death to happen. He felt like he had to choose between a God who is all-powerful but not good, and a God who is good but not all-powerful. He came to the conclusion that God is a good God but that he is limited in what he can accomplish. If God is both all-powerful and good, then his son would not have become sick and died.[39] Job will also wrestle with the character of God but will not change his basic conception of God. In the dialogue with the friends Job will struggle with the response of God to his suffering; but as the debate progresses, Job will realize that he has no hope in anyone other than God. Even as Job perseveres in his protesting, his argument is primarily an argument with God because God is the only one who will be able to respond to his suffering in a satisfying way.

Job may come across as impatient with God in the curse-lament of chapter 3. In fact, the friends are going to see him as impatient because he will argue that God has mistreated him, that God will not respond to his request for a hearing and that he is frustrated with the counsel of the friends. Job even asks the rhetorical question in 21:4 'Why should I not be impatient?' The book of James refers to the character of Job in a section where believers are exhorted to be patient until the coming of the Lord (Jas 5:7–11). But was Job truly patient? Has James misunderstood the character of Job? Although Job is mentioned in the context of farmers and prophets who are patient in waiting upon

---

[38] Carson 1990: 159. He also states that because Job has thought about this issue, he is prepared for it (as best as one can prepare for such a devastating loss). This may explain why his initial response is so noble.

[39] Kushner 1981.

the Lord, Job is introduced with a word that emphasizes 'endurance' and 'fortitude' (*hypomenō*). Those who remain steadfast are blessed, says James, even as Job was steadfast. James has not misunderstood the character of Job.[40] Looking at Job's overall life, he did persevere until God spoke to him and vindicated him before his friends.

The distinctions between Job 1 – 2 and Job 3 show that there are two different situations in the book, and it is helpful to distinguish between them. Job is not suffering because of sin he committed and did not sin or charge God with wrong in his early responses to his suffering (1:22; 2:10). As the dialogue with the friends progresses, however, Job will say some things that challenge God's justice in the way he governs the world. Job will say some things about God that are wrong (see Job 9 and God's statement in 40:8). Thus it is helpful to distinguish two situations in the book of Job. One situation deals with whether Job has sinned to cause his suffering. This is the main point of the debate with the friends. God even affirms in Job 1 – 2 that Job has not sinned to cause his suffering. This can be designated as Situation A. The other situation is how Job responds in his suffering. He does not always respond in the debate with the friends in a way that honours God. This situation can be called Situation B. Distinguishing these two situations will explain why Job must repent of things he says about God (Situation B) and how God can say that Job has spoken of him what is right but the friends have not (Situation A). Job is correct concerning the main point of his debate with the friends and the reader knows this from the statements in Job 1 – 2.

Job is a wisdom debate about how to respond to suffering. Job's initial response is patient submission. Job's wife responds with panicked pity. The friends' initial response is silent sympathy. Job's response in chapter 3 can be called persevering protest. The friends will then respond by accusing Job of sin as the reason for his suffering. How one responds to suffering or a person who is suffering is important. Suffering can bring confusion, turmoil and darkness into people's lives. It is natural for questions to arise and for people to struggle with God's role in suffering. It may take time for people to process their suffering in order to come to some kind of resolution. Wisdom is needed to help people respond to suffering. Ultimately, such wisdom comes from God and the reader of the book of Job

[40] Longman (2012: 281) argues that James is not using the Job of the OT but the Job of the LXX or the *Testament of Job* as his example.

should grow in wisdom, thereby helping people react to suffering.[41] Christians have more clarity in the light of the suffering of Christ and the victory of his resurrection, but this does not always make suffering easier to explain or endure. Yet followers of Christ have even more reason to persevere in suffering than Job because we see his victory over suffering, sin and death.

---

[41] Wisdom helps people discern how to respond to different situations of life. Thus it seems strange to argue that Job's friends in the debate do not provide instruction in how to give counsel or comfort (Walton and Longman 2015: 70). If they are wrong in their counsel, then people should avoid their counsel (see Bartholomew and O'Dowd 2011: 153–154 for why the book of Job is important pastorally).

Chapter Six

Divine retribution, suffering and God's justice: Job 4 – 26

Job 1 – 3 establishes several things. Job is a righteous man whose suffering is not caused by any sin he has committed. One of the main questions of the book is the connection between piety and prosperity. Do people worship God only because of the blessings that he gives or is God worthy to be worshipped apart from those blessings? Satan challenged Job's faith as mere self-interest and also challenged the character of God as not worthy of worship apart from his blessings. God allowed Satan to take away the blessings of Job's life and his health. How Job and others respond to his suffering is important. Job's initial response is to affirm the sovereignty of God in granting both good and adversity and that everything we receive in this life is a gift from God. Job passed the test even when his wife encouraged him to curse God and die.

Job's friends visit as he sits on the ash heap. They mourn with him, staying silent for seven days. Job shares with them the struggles of his suffering in his curse-lament (Job 3). His perspective changes from a God-centred pious submission to a self-centred protesting stance. The ensuing dialogue with the friends raises the issues of suffering, divine retribution and God's justice. Of course, Job and his friends are not aware of the discussion between God and Satan in chapters 1–2 and the pronouncement of Job's righteousness before his affliction. The dialogue continues the wisdom debate of how someone should respond to suffering and raises the question of where the wisdom needed to answer this debate is found.

The three friends agree on the main point of their debate with Job although they approach him in different ways. They agree that he must be suffering because of sin he has committed. This is the doctrine of divine retribution that draws a connection between deeds and consequences so that what people experience in life, whether blessing or adversity, is related to how they live. The book of Proverbs also expresses the deed–consequence relationship, but Proverbs has a nuanced view that does not draw a mechanical relationship between the deeds of people's lives and what these people experience in life (see chapter 3). A rigid view of divine retribution could easily develop, however, so that if someone is experiencing adversity he must have sinned to cause the adversity. The friends operate with a mechanical view of divine retribution that argues that Job is suffering because he has sinned.[1]

Eliphaz: a counsellor who misses the mark

Eliphaz speaks first (Job 4 – 5).[2] He is the most prominent and eloquent statesman, for in each cycle his speeches are longer than those of the other two friends. He is also the most articulate in terms of rhetoric and is likely the oldest of the friends. He approaches Job cautiously at first but feels compelled to speak because of Job's reaction to his suffering. Job's words in the past have been a source of instruction and strength to those who were weak and in danger of stumbling (4:3–4), but now Job finds himself in a position of weakness and it seems he is about to stumble. Twice Eliphaz asks whether Job is impatient. Job has lost his calm confidence and is rattled by the events of his life. He has failed to live up to the standards he has raised for others.[3] Job's confidence should be in his fear of God, and his hope should be in the integrity of his actions (4:6).[4] In other words, if Job has been upright and if he responds in the right way his suffering should be temporary.

The basic principle of the argument is stated in verse 8: those who sow trouble also reap trouble. Eliphaz may be responding to Job's words that if he had never been born, then he would not be experiencing trouble (3:10).[5] The word 'remember' in verse 7 reminds Job of the truth they will both affirm.[6] Two rhetorical questions in

---

[1] Clines (1982: 199–214) has a fascinating article on the arguments of Job's three friends, where he shows both coherence and distinctiveness in their views. They agree on the fact that Job is suffering for his sin, but argue their case in different ways. He also contends that the basic position of each of the friends remains the same throughout the speeches. I will argue that the positions of the friends change in a negative way toward Job as the debate progresses and then collapses.

[2] For a fuller exposition of the speeches of the friends see Belcher 2017b: 41–172.

[3] Hartley 1988: 106.

[4] Clines 1982: 210. He notes that Eliphaz argues from the piety of Job to offer consolation to Job.

[5] The word 'trouble' (*'āmāl*) is used in both passages.

[6] Clines 1989: 124.

verse 7 introduce the principle.[7] Has the innocent ever perished?[8] Where has the upright ever been cut off? These questions do not deny that the righteous suffer, but when they do suffer it will not lead to death. The righteous will not experience a premature death.[9] The innocent and the upright do not perish, because they avoid the negative consequences of those who sow trouble. Job is not dead yet, so is able to have confidence in his piety (v. 6). In Eliphaz's view Job is suffering because of sin he has sown, but Job's sin must not have been bad enough to cause death. This explains why Eliphaz appeals to Job's piety as the basis of his confidence. Job's suffering is a temporary setback that can be alleviated by his right response.[10] Divine retribution works because there is a connection between piety and prosperity.

Eliphaz's first speech, especially 5:18–27, emphasizes Job's suffering as a means for restoration. God disciplines people as a faithful father. He may wound and shatter, but the ultimate purpose is to heal (v. 18). Restoration brings one into a position where the blessing of God can be poured out again. The numerical saying of verse 19 shows that even though there may be many difficulties in life (six troubles), the final blow of death will not be struck ('in seven no evil shall touch you').[11] In the light of these blessings Eliphaz encourages Job not to despise the discipline of God. His suffering is for his good and will lead to blessing.

Eliphaz paints a picture of a fool who is destroyed by the strong emotions of anger and jealousy (5:2–7).[12] Even though the fool seems to be secure, he is always in danger of losing what is dear to him. His children and harvest can easily be lost. Eliphaz paints this picture with the hope that it will act as a warning to Job.[13] He does not directly call Job a fool nor does he say that Job has lost his children and his crops because he is a fool. The implication, however, seems clear that Job should consider whether this picture of a fool fits his own situation. Maybe he has done something foolish to cause his suffering. Eliphaz's counsel is that Job should seek God and commit

---

[7] Wilson (2016: 67) cites Hopkins and Koppel (2010: 21), who argue that rhetorical questions encourage defensiveness and are not good to use in pastoral situations.

[8] This question may also be a response to Job's statement 'Let the day perish on which I was born' (3:3). Both statements use the verb *'ābad* for 'perish'.

[9] Clines 1989: 124.

[10] Wilson 2015: 223.

[11] Hartley 1988: 126.

[12] Ibid. 117.

[13] Longman 2012: 123.

his way to God, who does great and marvellous things (5:8–16). Instead of cursing the day of his birth and wishing he were never born, Job should seek help from the God who brings about great reversals.

Eliphaz can be characterized as a counsellor who misses the mark. He asserts many general things that are true.[14] People do reap what they sow. Human beings are not always right or pure before God. People should seek God. God does discipline his people. The question is whether these are good explanations for Job's suffering. Job 1 – 2 has established the blameless character of Job and that his suffering is ultimately from the hand of God. The problem with Eliphaz is not his theology, but the application of that theology to Job's situation. He misuses proverbs by misapplying them. Although he does not attack Job directly, he makes enough allusions to Job's situation to make his point. Twice children are mentioned. The first time is in the description of the fool whose children are far from safety (5:4). The second time is in the restoration of children as a result of God's discipline (5:25). It would be hard for Job not to make the connection that he has done something foolish to cause his suffering.

Eliphaz is much less cautious toward Job in his second and third speeches because of the way Job has responded in the debate.[15] In the second speech (Job 15) Eliphaz expresses the same basic argument (15:20, 34–35) and confronts Job directly by telling him that his own mouth condemns him (15:6). He offers a poem on the fate of the wicked (15:20) to show that the wicked do not prosper except for the briefest moment. He does not hold out hope for Job as he did in his first speech. In the third speech (Job 22) he gets specific by trying to pinpoint Job's wickedness. He mentions again Job's fear of God, like the first speech (4:6), not as a basis for Job's hope but as a statement of scepticism concerning Job's fear of God (22:4). Job's suffering is evidence that his evil is abundant and a list of possible sins is presented that Job must have committed (22:6–11),

---

[14] The fact that Paul can quote Eliphaz (Job 5:13) in 1 Cor. 3:19 to establish the point of the foolishness of the wisdom of the world in God's sight shows that the friends say many things that are true in general that may be used for their instructional value (Robertson 2017: 137). For a discussion of this quote in 1 Cor. 3:19 see Ciampa and Rosner 2007: 704.

[15] Walton and Longman (2015: 67) argue that each cycle of speeches has its own emphasis. In the first cycle the friends offer advice to Job, in the second they turn their attention to the wicked and in the third they accuse Job directly. The friends move from offering advice to humiliating Job with insults and insinuations.

such as exacting pledges for nothing, stripping the naked of clothing, withholding water from the weary and bread from the hungry, and mistreating widows and the fatherless. His solution is that repentance will lead to restoration (22:23).[16] Eliphaz does not understand Job's situation or how God relates to it. He is asking Job to repent of sin he has not committed. Thus he has no real solution to Job's suffering.[17] He does not realize that at the end of the book he will be the one who is guilty and must repent through Job's mediation (Job 42:7). Job does not need to repent of any sin that has caused his suffering, but Eliphaz will need to repent of speaking falsely concerning God.

Bildad: the defender of God's justice

Bildad, the second friend to speak, posits that all of God's ways are just (Job 8). Although Bildad is more direct with Job than Eliphaz, he couches his speech with possibilities through the use of the word 'if'. He calls the words of Job a great wind and asks whether God perverts justice (8:2–3). His answer is that God punishes the wicked and blesses the righteous and that this principle is evident in the events of the world. For example, he tells Job:

> If your children have sinned against him,
> he has delivered them into the hand of
> their transgression.
>
> (8:4)

He clearly draws the connection between the death of Job's children and sin. Although the wicked may flourish for a short time, they are soon destroyed (8:11–19). Job's hope is that God will not reject a blameless man (8:20), so that if Job is pure and upright, as he claims, then he will be restored by God (8:6–7, 20–22). Bildad is wrestling with how to explain his understanding of divine retribution in the light of the experience of Job's life. If Job is truly blameless, then he should not be suffering. His suffering must mean that he has sinned.

---

[16] Clines 1982: 212. He has a more positive view of Eliphaz's third speech because he believes the arguments of the friends remain the same as the debate progresses. Eliphaz is still trying to offer consolation to Job based on his piety. Thus he understands Eliphaz's call to repentance of specific sins to be referring only to things that Job has failed to do (sins of omission).

[17] Andersen 1974: 206–207.

There is no category in Bildad's thinking for a person who is blameless and suffering.

Bildad's position hardens in his second and third speeches. His basic argument in the second speech (Job 18) is that the lamp of the wicked is snuffed out (18:5). No hope is offered to Job in this speech. He offers a description of the wicked and their destruction (18:6–14). Eliphaz already presented such a picture in 15:17–35. He focused on the mental worries of the wicked, and Bildad focuses on their outward troubles, but the connection to Job's situation seems clear.[18] Bildad mentions several things that can apply directly to Job, including the loss of the skin of the wicked (v. 13), the loss of his place in society (v. 14) and the loss of vitality (v. 16). The clear implication is that Job is caught in the trap of his own wickedness. There is no mention of Job's blamelessness or any hope connected to being upright; only the picture of the suffering of the wicked and their demise.[19] Bildad's third speech is very short (Job 25:1–6). He compares the greatness of God with the insignificance of human beings. He attacks Job's claims of innocence and leaves no room for mercy. If the splendour of the moon and the stars is overshadowed by God's brightness, then how much more insignificant are human beings in the light of God's greatness. In fact, human beings are so insignificant that they are compared with maggots and worms. These terms symbolize a wretched existence, carrying with them the smell of death. The frail condition of human beings makes them susceptible to death, where the body will be consumed by worms.[20]

Zophar: the interpreter of God's ways

Zophar's first speech (Job 11) is the most antagonistic of the first speeches among the friends (vv. 11–12). He perceives Job as an idle mocker of God who continues to assert his purity. He wants God to speak to Job to show him the secrets of his wisdom. This would put Job in his place by showing him that his punishment is less than his guilt deserves (vv. 5–6). Job must have sinned in greater ways than he can imagine. Any hope held out for him because of his piety is gone

---

[18] Ibid. 187, 190.

[19] Clines (1982: 211) argues that Bildad's first speech offers a warning to Job based on the contrast between the fates of Job and his children. This becomes the hermeneutical clue for the second speech of Bildad so that his description of the wicked is only a possibility that can still be avoided.

[20] Hartley 1988: 357.

because he must be a condemned sinner. It is impossible to discover the limits of God's understanding for it is higher than heaven and deeper than Sheol. It is impossible to escape God's gaze for he knows worthless men and will deal with iniquity when he sees it. The implication is that he has seen Job's iniquity and is dealing with it through his suffering (vv. 7–11). Zophar's solution for Job is to repent so that he can be restored (vv. 13–19). The speech of Zophar ends with a statement concerning the wicked (v. 20). Those who do not repent will have a horrible end. They will suffer physically, they will experience hopelessness and they will long for death as their only escape. Zophar pictures the wicked in ways that Job himself has suffered in order to encourage him to repent of his wickedness. He seeks to interpret the ways of God for Job's life. He offers Job little comfort except for the elaborate picture of the peaceful security of repentant sinners.

Zophar has a second speech (Job 20) but does not have a third speech. In his second speech he does not advance the argument, because he is convinced that Job is suffering because of his sin. He paints a picture of the destruction of the wicked in order to show Job what will happen to him if he does not repent of his sin. He demonstrates that there is no hope for wicked people because everything in their life will turn out for their ruin (vv. 4–11). The wicked will experience the consequences of their wicked actions (vv. 12–23) and their lives will end in total disaster (vv. 24–29). Zophar's description of the destruction of the wicked is important because the way he frames it is meant to highlight Job's place among the wicked. When he describes God as a warrior pursuing his enemy, he is alluding to Job's earlier statement that he feels like one who is being chased down by God (Job 16:13–14). Job should count himself among the wicked.[21] Zophar does not call Job to repentance and does not have a speech in the third cycle of speeches. This is his final word to Job and he does not leave him with any hope, because he believes his fate is certain.

---

[21] Clines (1982: 210–211) understands Zophar's basic position, based on his first speech, as denouncing Job as a sinner because of his suffering. The second speech of Zophar is a description of the future he sees in store for Job if he does not repent of his sin, not the reality of his present situation. Clines does not see any development in Zophar's speech. It is better to see the debate between Job and the friends deteriorating and the friends becoming more hardened in their accusations against Job.

A summary of the theology of the friends

Divine retribution

The friends believe that Job is suffering because he has committed sin. Early in the debate they cautiously hold out hope that if Job's claim of being upright is true, then his suffering will only be temporary. Eliphaz specifically states that Job's integrity is his hope (4:6) and Bildad agrees that if Job is pure and upright God will restore him (8:6). Even though Job is suffering because of sin, his upright character will compensate and bring about his restoration. The suffering in a person's life is related to the amount of sin he or she has committed.[22] As the debate progresses, the friends become convinced that Job is not righteous and so his hope is not in his blamelessness but in repentance for his sin.[23] They operate with a mechanical view of divine retribution that sees all suffering as a result of sin. Zophar even argues that Job's suffering is much less than his guilt deserves (11:6). The only hope for Job is to repent of his sin so that he can be restored by God. Eliphaz even comes up with a list of sins that Job should use to examine his life (22:5–11). Both Bildad and Zophar paint a picture of the wicked and their destruction hoping that Job will see the true end that is coming to his wicked life unless he repents (18:5–21; 20:6–29).

The friends' theology of divine retribution is flawed because of its mechanical connection between suffering and sin and because they have no category in their thinking for an innocent sufferer. Zophar himself affirms that God does not reject a blameless man (Job 8:20). He cannot conceive how Job can be blameless and experience suffering. The problem is not that the OT does not have examples of

[22] Wilson (2015: 220) defines retribution as 'Whatever a person deserves, that should be their punishment, no more or no less.'
[23] For a more positive analysis of the view of the friends see Newsom 2003: 90–129. She argues that what separates Job and the friends is not so much the fact of Job's innocence or guilt, but that they operate with different moral imaginations. The friends operate with a different narrative from Job. When they tell Job that he must seek God, they are encouraging the spiritual practice of prayer that has a capacity to reorder the disordered and to help Job find a way beyond the turmoil of his life. In her discussion of prayer there is little said about repentance and in some places it is downplayed as only part of the pious engagement in preparation for prayer (see particularly the explanation of Zophar's words in Job 11). But, to the contrary, if Job's suffering has been brought on by his sin, then repentance is the key response that Job must make to restore his relationship with God. And if Job's sin is not the cause of his suffering, then the exhortation to seek God in repentance is not the solution to Job's problem.

unjust suffering (Gen. 4) or that it does not have a better view of divine retribution (see the discussion in Proverbs), but that it is easy for the deed–consequence relationship to harden into a mechanical view so that there is no place for a righteous sufferer.

The friends' view of God

The friends make many statements about God that are true. Eliphaz argues that God stands behind the principle that those who sow trouble will reap it. The wicked suffer the consequences of their actions but may also find themselves the direct object of God's wrath (4:7–9). God is like a father who disciplines his children so that those who are disciplined by God are blessed. God can use suffering to restore and heal people (5:17–18). God is also a God of justice and governs the world with justice. The friends defend God against some of Job's assertions that question God's justice. But what does it mean for God to govern with justice? Bildad applies their principle of justice to Job's situation when he argues that if his children have sinned, then God delivered them into the hand of their transgression (8:4). There are two groups of people and God acts toward each group according to whether they are blameless or wicked (8:20–22). Zophar argues that God knows worthless men and deals with their iniquity (11:7–11). The implication is that God has seen Job's iniquity and is dealing with it through his suffering.

In the second and third cycles of speeches the views of the friends concerning God's justice harden. In Eliphaz's second speech God sees to it that sinners get paid in full without any recognition that God may exercise mercy or love toward sinners (15:12–35). In Zophar's second and last speech he does not even offer Job any hope (20). In Eliphaz's third speech he presents God as transcendent and self-sufficient to the extent that he is not concerned with people and their claims to being blameless (22:13–30). Each of the friends paints a portrait of the wicked, who are destroyed by God. In Bildad's short final speech he has no mercy to offer Job but only the insignificance of human beings before God (Job 25). In the final analysis, the friends can only offer Job a false repentance or death.

A mechanical view of divine retribution leads to a narrow view of God and his justice. The God who disciplines people for their good has become a distant, uncaring God who punishes people in a mechanical way. The reader understands that this view of God goes against the way God reacted in Job 1 – 2 where he is very concerned about Job and is willing to invest in him as an example of someone who exercises true piety apart from prosperity. If Job abandons his piety in the crucible of suffering, then Satan will be right that Job's faith is self-interest and God is worthy of being worshipped only for the blessings he gives people. God has something to gain from Job's response.[24] The logical conclusion of a mechanical view of divine retribution is that God becomes depersonalized, unable to interact with people in real life situations.[25] In the final analysis the friends' view of God is distorted because their view of God's justice is distorted.

Job defends his innocence

Job's speeches do not develop in a linear fashion from start to finish. He goes back and forth between despair and hope, defending himself against his friends and seeking a conference with God. There are times when Job despairs of his situation because he has lost hope, but there are other times when flashes of hope shine through his suffering. Despair and hope can be strongly expressed in the same speech (Job 16 – 17; 19) If there is progression in any area of Job's thinking, it is that his expressions of hope for vindication increase until his final claim of innocence in Job 31.

In Job's first response to Eliphaz (Job 6 – 7) he defends his curse-lament of chapter 3 by demonstrating the reality of his suffering (6:1–7). His words have been rash because his suffering has been horrifying. His grief is unbearable because his vexation is heavier than the sand of the sea. As long as an animal has food, it does not make any noise. Andersen notes, 'Job also has a right to bray like a hungry wild ass and to bellow like a starving bull.'[26] The friends, represented by Eliphaz, have dishonoured Job by not showing him compassion. They are like an empty stream that gives hope of water but then disappoints with a dry bed (6:14–20). They have forsaken the fear of the Almighty by not showing kindness and have demonstrated a lack of 'loyalty' (ḥesed) to Job (6:14). He pleads his innocence with the statement 'I have not denied the words of the Holy One' (6:10). He also pleads with the friends to speak upright words and to treat him fairly because his vindication is at stake (6:25–30).

Many times Job proclaims his innocence and expresses his desire to have a consultation with God so he can prove it. In chapter 9 Job

[24] Belcher 2017b: 149–150.
[25] Clines 2006: 551, 553.
[26] Andersen 1974: 128.

considers whether he can resolve his suffering by presenting his case to God. Will a debate with God uncover God's hostility toward him? This chapter is filled with legal language and Job speaks of God in the third person.[27] To present a case before God is not possible because it is impossible to answer the questions God will ask (9:3). God is full of wisdom and mighty in strength (9:4–10), but is also hidden (9:11). It is impossible to give an answer to God even if Job is in the right (9:14–15). Job perceives that God is behind his suffering (9:16–18), but no one can contend against such a powerful God and summon him to court. Job feels he has no escape and the conviction of his moral purity does not help his sense of meaninglessness. When the hope of a trial fades, he expresses the need for an arbiter to bring him together with God (9:33) and takes up a lament addressed to God that lays out the terrible nature of his affliction (10).

In Job's response to Zophar (Job 12 – 14) he offers two complaints against the friends (12:1–12; 13:1–12), and after his second complaint resolves to try to argue his case before God regardless of the consequences (13:18 – 14:22). He is willing to risk his life in challenging God to hear his complaint. Job has prepared his case and is ready to meet with God because he knows he is in the right (13:18–22). If God will only remove his hand from Job so he can be free from his dread of God, then the lines of communication will open up and there can be a resolution to his suffering. Otherwise, Job has little hope, trapped in a situation that he cannot escape, wasting away like a garment that is moth-eaten. He does not know how to bring his case before God or to find the court in which God resides (Job 23:1–7). If he can only have a hearing with God, he can be acquitted. He takes an oath that he will not speak falsehood or utter deceit as a way to reject the view of the friends and to affirm his integrity (Job 27:1–6). His final oath of innocence is his last speech (Job 31).

Job wrestles with despair

Abandoned by family and acquaintances

Job's despair arises from his suffering but is also a result of being abandoned by everyone (including God). So he seeks someone who will understand his situation and be a witness for him. He is

---

[27] Hartley 1988: 165. When Job contemplates litigation, he generally speaks about God; and when Job laments, he speaks directly to God (Wilson 2015: 242).

frustrated with the way family and acquaintances are treating him (Job 19:13–20). Job's brothers have grown distant from him. Job's trusted friends are estranged from him. His relatives have abandoned him. The guests in Job's house, to whom he has shown hospitality, and his servants act like they do not know him. Job is even estranged from close family members. There is little intimacy with his wife because of his putrid breath; his illness causes him to be a stench to his close family. Even young children despise him and talk against him. Job's body has also failed him. He experiences no consolation from anyone and no one supports him. It is the world against Job.

Abandoned by his three friends

Job's relationship to his three friends deteriorates and the counsel they give to him is a problem. He rejects their mechanical view of divine retribution and continues to assert his innocence throughout his speeches. In his first response to Eliphaz (Job 6 – 7) he expresses that he feels betrayed by his friends because they have not shown him 'kindness' (*ḥesed*), the word for 'loyalty' or 'faithfulness'. Rather, they are acting treacherously against Job like those who cast lots over the fatherless. They should give him latitude by showing compassion instead of uttering words that miss the mark (6:14–30).

Job offers several reasons for rejecting the view that he is suffering because of sin. He appeals to his own experience. A just and blameless man is now a laughingstock, but the reality is that the robbers are at ease and those who provoke God are secure (12:4–6). These examples are common because the view of the friends does not match the reality of life. He explores the power of God at work against the mighty of the earth (Job 12:13–25). God exercises his sovereignty with both wisdom and might so that no one can hinder his actions in the world. If he tears down, no one can build up. If he imprisons, no one can set free. His wisdom overpowers both the deceived and the deceiver. He exercises authority over kings, judges, priests and the nations. The world is more complicated than the view of the friends. The combination of wisdom and power creates a sense of mystery to the events of the world and implies that the reason for Job's suffering resides with God. Thus their arguments are morally deficient (13:4–5) and he accuses them of speaking falsely on behalf of God (13:6–12). They are worthless physicians and should be terrified of God because their maxims are proverbs of ashes.

Job takes on the friends' view of retribution (Job 21) in responding to Zophar's description of the destruction of the wicked (Job 20). He asks:

> Why do the wicked live,
>   reach old age, and grow mighty in power?
>
> (21:7)

This question introduces verses 7–16, where he describes the peaceful prosperity of the wicked and their children.[28] Job gives a list of the prosperity of the wicked: their children are established, they live peacefully in their own homes, they do not know the fear of sudden disaster, their animals do not miscarry and they live out their days in peace even as they reject God. The wicked live without experiencing the judgment of God, which makes it hard to discern God's ways in the world (vv. 22–26). The friends' view that there is quick retribution for the wicked is false. One person dies at ease, secure with an abundance of health and possessions (vv. 23–24), but another dies after living a hardened, bitter life of poverty without experiencing blessing and prosperity. There is no connection between how one lives life, how one relates to God and what the quality of that life is. The friends' view of retribution cannot explain the reality of life. Their words offer him no comfort because they are nothing but falsehood (21:34).

Job gives evidence of the wickedness of the wicked to support the view that many suffer because God does not judge them (Job 24). The discrepancy between experience and the theology of the friends is not only revealed through Job's suffering (Job 23) but also through widespread injustice carried out by the wicked (24:1–17). The simplistic view of the friends fails to explain experiences in life and Job's situation. Job again explores the mysterious ways of God in the world in response to Bildad's short speech (Job 25). God is in control of every aspect of the universe (Job 26). The works of God are mysterious because we know very little about his purposes (26:14). No one can understand the way God exercises his power in the world because God's ways are greater than the human mind can comprehend. Our knowledge of God is like a whisper in the vast display of the

---

[28] Habel 1985: 325. He comments, 'Thus Job's disputation on the wicked is a calculated refutation employing both major themes and key emotive language used by the friends in their portrait of the wicked.'

thunder of his power. The view of the friends fails to recognize the mystery of God's works in the world, including the mystery of Job's own suffering.

Job's growing confidence

Job goes back and forth between despair and confidence but confidence grows as the debate continues. Job's despair arises from his treatment by family and friends, but particularly because of his treatment by God. At times Job expresses that God is his enemy. Job also recognizes that God is the only real source of his hope and several assertions of confidence relate to his hope of being vindicated by God. This section will focus on Job's perception of God and his statements of hope.

Job has problems with the way God is treating him. As a rationale for his rash words he presents God as a hunter who pursues his prey, causing Job to be filled with the terror of God (Job 6:4). This is in contrast to Eliphaz's depiction of God as a father disciplining his children (Job 5:17). Job speaks directly to God in chapter 7 as he laments his hard lot in life (vv. 1–10) and complains that God is harassing him (vv. 10–17). He asks God to leave him alone for just a few moments, as long as it takes to swallow spit (Job 7:19), so he will have relief. In a possible allusion to Psalm 8, Job asks:

> What is man, that you make so much of him . . .
> visit him every morning . . .
>
> (7:17–18)

Instead of expressing wonder at the exalted place God has given human beings within the vastness of creation, Job expresses concern over God's overbearing gaze upon him. Job sets forth the hypothetical situation 'If I sin' to argue that his sin is not grievous enough for the suffering he is experiencing.[29] God can pardon his iniquity and restore the relationship.

In Job's response to Bildad (Job 9 – 10) he despairs of ever being able to present a case for his innocence to God. Job believes he is being mistreated by God (9:16–18) and that even if he can speak to God it will be a useless exercise (vv. 19–21). In seeking to assert his own blamelessness, he calls into question God's justice. It does not

---

[29] Longman 2012: 148.

matter if a person is blameless or wicked because God destroys both the blameless and the wicked (v. 22). When the innocent die young, God is mocking them (v. 23). Wickedness rules the world because God allows judges to exploit the weak and the poor. Job drives home the point with the question 'if it is not he, who then is it?' (9:24). He believes there is a great barrier between him and God, so expresses the need for an arbiter who can bring them together. He envisions someone who can lay his hand on both of them in order to allow Job to speak to God without fear (vv. 32–35). This one will remove the rod of God from him so he can speak to God without being terrified. Job in the lament of chapter 10 speaks freely from the bitterness of his soul. He is trapped by God in his affliction with no way of escape. In a more positive statement he understands that God has granted him life, steadfast love, and care that have preserved his spirit. God has a purpose but Job does not know what that purpose is or whether it will turn out to be good (10:13–18). Job's suffering makes him appear guilty whether or not he has sinned. In the end God hunts Job like a lion, increases his vexation against Job and brings fresh troops against him. Job ends his lament with thoughts of death that echo the curse-lament of chapter 3 (10:18–22).

Job expresses both futility concerning his situation and remarkable assertions of confidence in God (Job 12 – 14). After Job's complaint about the worthless arguments of the friends (13:1–12), he resolves to continue to pursue a hearing with God (13:13–22). He is even willing to risk instant death in challenging God to hear his complaint.[30] Job even says, 'Though he slay me, I will hope in him' (13:15). This is a strong affirmation of faith. There is debate, however, concerning the translation of this verse.[31] The RSV translates it as an affirmation of resignation, 'Behold, he will slay me; I have no hope'. Hartley translates it as an affirmation of uncertainty, 'If he were to slay me, I would have no hope.'[32] Habel understands it as an affirmation of perseverance, 'Yes, though he slay me, I will not wait.'[33] The context of verses 14–16 favours a positive statement of confidence. Job asserts that he will continue to argue his case before God because he is convinced that it will turn out for his salvation (vv. 15a–16). He is confident of this outcome because the godless are not able to come before God, and he is convinced of his own innocence. Thus the

---

[30] Hartley 1988: 222.
[31] For the translation difficulties and options see Belcher 2017b: 85–86.
[32] Hartley 1988: 221.
[33] Habel 1985: 224.

affirmation of faith or the affirmation of perseverance fits the context of these verses.[34] The former asserts Job's ultimate hope in God and the latter affirms he will not wait to speak because he knows it will end in his salvation. Job is ready to meet God (13:18–22).

After asserting confidence in his vindication, he quickly falls back into despair because God hides his face and treats him like an enemy (13:24). Job feels trapped with no way to escape. He is wasting away like a moth-eaten garment (13:28). A lament concerning the general condition of human life as short and full of suffering follows (14:1–22). He compares the life of man with that of a tree and concludes that there is more hope for a tree than there is for a man (14:7–12). When a tree is cut down, there is hope that it will sprout again, but such hope does not exist for human beings who stay dead until the heavens are no more. There is a glimmer of hope for his renewal (v. 14), but Job ends this lament by focusing on the terrors of death (vv. 18–22). Suffering erodes hope until it is gone.

The conflicting emotions of a sufferer are also expressed in chapters 16–17. Job has flashes of insight about his suffering that bring encouragement before he descends into the abyss again. He sees no help coming from the friends and little help coming from God. He views God as the enemy because he believes God is behind his suffering (16:7–17). Job is exhausted because there is no relief to his suffering. God pursues Job as his prey and wages war against him (vv. 9, 14). God has treated him this way even though he has not done anything wrong (vv. 14–17). Job expresses a desire that his testimony will not go unnoticed. He also affirms that he has a witness in heaven, called 'my witness' (v. 19), who will testify on his behalf. There is debate concerning the identity of this witness.[35] One view is that the heavenly witness does not really exist,[36] but this does not take into account the growing confidence of Job that he will eventually be heard by God. Another view is that the heavenly witness is one of the angels, even Satan himself.[37] But the angels do not play a role in the book beyond chapters 1–2 and it is hard to conceive that Satan would testify on Job's behalf. Another view is that Job's restless cry is personified

---

[34] The affirmation of faith is based on what is read in the text (called the Qere) and the affirmation of perseverance is based on what is written in the text (called the Ketiv).

[35] See Belcher 2017b: 104–106 for a fuller discussion of this question.

[36] This view is discussed by Habel (1985: 276) and Wilson (2015: 98).

[37] Habel (1985: 275) argues for a figure from the heavenly court and Oblath (1999: 189–201) argues for Satan.

as his witness in heaven,[38] but in the context of the book the witness seems to be a person (9:33; 16:19; 19:23–27).[39] The final view is that God is the heavenly witness. The difficulty with this view is that God would be a witness against himself. But this view fits with Job's vacillation between confidence in God and despair with the way God is treating him. Job at times sees God as his enemy, but there are also increasing instances where Job responds with confidence that he will be vindicated by God. Perhaps Job is not pitting God against God but is affirming confidence in God regardless of the way God is treating him.[40] In true form Job utters another lament that is full of despair because of the way he is being treated by people and by God (17:1–6). Job is resigned to the fact that his life is broken, his plans and desires are dashed and his best days are behind him. Job's hope seems to fade again as the future holds only the certainty of death (17:7–16).

Job expresses frustration with how he is being treated by everyone, including God (Job 19:7–12, 21–22). No one has stood with him, and yet he is convinced that he will be vindicated by a kinsman-redeemer (19:21–27). This is the most famous passage in the book but there are many questions and translation decisions that have an impact on its meaning.[41] Job is certain that his kinsman-redeemer lives, but who is this kinsman-redeemer? A 'kinsman-redeemer' (*gō'ēl*) is many times a close relative who comes to a person's defence when he or she is in trouble (Lev. 25:25, 47–49; Num. 35:19). But God is also a kinsman-redeemer (Isa. 43:14; 48:17; Prov. 23:11–12). Some question whether God can be Job's kinsman-redeemer because Job's dispute is with God. Thus it seems more likely that Job's cry of innocence will go on speaking for him after death and will act as his kinsman-redeemer.[42] Yet it is unusual for the term 'kinsman-redeemer' to be used in this way. Job has been abandoned by his friends and family so it is unlikely he has any of them in mind as his redeemer. The use of the adjective 'living' in 19:25 stands in bold relief against Job's fear of dying and reminds one that God is the 'living God' (Deut. 5:26; Josh. 3:10; Jer. 10:10). Job can see God as his redeemer because

[38] Seow 2013: 739.
[39] Jones 2007: 141. He argues that the Hebrew word for 'cry' in v. 18 is feminine and the one who is to argue Job's case as witness in v. 21 is masculine, which makes the identification of the two difficult.
[40] Hartley 1988: 264.
[41] See Belcher 2017b: 122–128 for a fuller discussion of the issues and the options.
[42] Clines 1989: 455–459.

he has conflicting views of God at war in his mind depending on his emotional state at any given moment.[43]

Job knows that his redeemer lives but how and when he will act and what the results will be are debated. The important question is whether Job expects to see God in this life or after his death. The three translation decisions that have an impact on the meaning of this passage are the meaning of the Hebrew word *'āpār* ('dust' or 'earth'), the reference of the word *'aḥărôn* (at the last), and the translation of the phrase *mibbĕśārî* ('in my flesh' or 'apart from my flesh'). The traditional understanding is that Job's redeemer will stand on the 'earth' 'at the last day' after his skin has been destroyed and he will see God in his resurrected body ('in his flesh'). Job's vindication will come after his death at the time of the resurrection. Some argue that the idea of resurrection develops later in Israel's history and so is not an option for understanding this text.[44] Yet 'dust' can mean 'grave' and the idea of resurrection is taught in Isaiah 26:19.[45]

Another view is that Job's vindication will come after his death but before his resurrection. A written testimony (19:23–24) will not be needed if Job is going to be vindicated before his death.[46] The word 'dust' can refer to the grave and the phrase 'at the last' suggests an interval of time and expresses something eschatological, after Job's skin has been destroyed in his death. The phrase 'in his flesh' can be translated 'apart from his flesh' referring to the state of Job after death.[47] Vindication after death, however, seems rather anti-climactic for the great struggle Job is having with his friends. If Job's vindication comes after his death, then who will witness it? If Job dies, the friends will appear to win the argument.

Although Job says many things in the despair of his suffering, his basic desire is to have a hearing before God so he can be vindicated (Job 13:16). Job wishes for death at times because it will end his suffering, but also knows that death will bring his days to an end without hope (Job 7:6). Job is not confident that he will have an opportunity to meet with God, so looks for a way to defend his integrity if he dies (Job 19:23–24). His great desire is to be declared

---

[43] Hartley 1988: 295.

[44] Walton 2012: 219.

[45] Many would argue that Isa. 26:19 is from a later period than Isaiah, but such an argument is circular if Isa. 26 must be late because it has an idea that scholars consider late.

[46] Andersen 1974: 194; see also Habel 1985: 307 and Smick 2010: 4.787.

[47] The preposition *min* can mark something as missing or lacking (Arnold and Choi 2003: 118).

innocent by God before he dies and he expresses this hope in Job 19.[48] Job's redeemer will stand in the 'future' (*'aḥărôn*) at the very place where Job is suffering ('dust' or 'ash heap') and even though his skin is being destroyed by his illness, he will see God 'in the flesh'. It is significant that this is what happens later in the book as Job is vindicated by God while still alive and suffering (Job 42:7).[49]

In the remaining speeches the darkness and despair are still there but Job's statements of assurance are evident. Job does not even respond to Eliphaz's accusations of possible wicked deeds of which he should repent (Job 23 – 24). He speaks directly to God and expresses confidence even though God is hidden (23:8–12). He knows that God sees his suffering and expresses the assurance that his suffering will turn out for his good: 'when he has tried me, I shall come out as gold' (v. 10). Job expresses confidence even while asserting that he is terrified of God (23:13–17). God's plans cannot fail, so he will complete what he has appointed for Job's life. The freedom of God leaves room for the mystery of his ways, but it also leaves Job terrified of God. The darkness of the situation presses in on him but he is not silenced by the darkness. His speeches will end with confident assertions of innocence (Job 31).

---

[48] Commentators who argue that Job is hoping for vindication before his death include Hartley, Longman, Whybray, Jones, Konkel and G. Wilson.

[49] Does the view that Job is vindicated before his death mean that the traditional view of resurrection is wrong? Not if Job 19 is understood in the light of the whole canon. Our hope of vindication parallels Job's hope of vindication, but our hope is even greater because of the certainty of our resurrection in Christ. Thus Job 19:25–27 can be understood in a fuller way as referring to resurrection hope.

Chapter Seven

Where is wisdom to be found? (Job 27 – 42)

The collapse of the debate

There are not three complete cycles of speeches between Job and the friends. Table 1 shows the cycles of speeches.

Table 1: The cycles of speeches

First cycle	Second cycle	Third cycle
Eliphaz (4 – 5)	Eliphaz (15)	Eliphaz (22)
Job (6 – 7)	Job (16 – 17)	Job (23 – 24)
Bildad (8)	Bildad (18)	Bildad (25)
Job (9 – 10)	Job (19)	Job (26 – 27)
Zophar (11)	Zophar (20)	
Job (12 – 14)	Job (21)	

Bildad's third speech is very short and Zophar does not have a third speech. Some of the words attributed to Job sound like the argument of the friends (Job 27:13–23). Attempts to complete the third cycle have been made by rearranging the text.[1] Some take parts of chapters 26–27 and add them to Bildad's speech or try to give Zophar a third speech. A better approach is to accept the incomplete third cycle as evidence that the debate has collapsed. The friends have not been able to help Job in his suffering. They have not been a source of wisdom for Job.

As the debate progresses each side becomes entrenched in its own position. The debate deteriorates to hurling insults back and forth. Bildad calls Job's words 'a great wind' (8:2). Zophar characterizes

---

[1] For the various attempts to complete the third cycle and problems with those attempts see Belcher 2017b: 168.

Job's speech as babble and mocking (11:2–3). Job sarcastically comments that the friends

> are the people,
> and wisdom will die with you.
> (12:2)

Eliphaz calls Job's talk unprofitable and words that do no good (15:2). Job calls them miserable comforters (16:2). Bildad complains that Job sees them as cattle and stupid in his sight (18:3). Zophar is also agitated because he has been insulted by Job's condemnation of the friends (20:3). Bildad's third speech is short and Zophar has no third speech. Frustration has increased and an impasse has been reached concerning God's justice and Job's integrity. To try to complete the third cycle of speeches takes away from what the incomplete third cycle is teaching. Wisdom is not to be found among the friends. The issue that Job has been wrestling with has not been resolved. Wisdom must come from another source.

Job's final words

Although scholars debate the identity of the speaker in some of the final speeches, headings seem to make it clear who is speaking. After Bildad's short third speech, Job 26 has a heading attributing it to Job ('Then Job answered and said'). Job 27 has a heading ('Job again took up his discourse, and said') that includes Job 28, which does not have a heading. Job 29 has a heading ('And Job again took up his discourse, and said') that includes Job 29 – 31. Although some have trouble with the calm speech of Job 28 being a speech by Job, if it is not Job's speech then it is the only chapter not included under a heading. The fact that Job 29 – 31 is under one heading provides evidence for taking Job 27 – 28 as under the heading of chapter 27. If one accepts these headings, then Job 26 is Job's response to Bildad, Job 27 – 28 is Job's reflections on his dialogues with his friends, and Job 29 – 31 is Job's final speech that ends with strong assertions of his innocence.

A warning to the friends (Job 27)

After Job complains about the useless counsel of Bildad (Job 26), he gives his last response to the friends before making his final appeal. The problem with Job 27 is that verses 13–23 sound like an argument of the friends when they describe the destruction of the wicked. Even the children of the wicked are mentioned as destined for the sword. The wicked pile up money for the righteous to receive and the security of the wicked is not lasting. Terrors overtake the wicked and quickly they are gone. Job has struggled with similar descriptions of the wicked in the speeches of the friends. How can these words be Job's?

At the beginning of chapter 27 Job asserts his innocence by taking an oath in the name of the God who has made his soul bitter. Job appeals to the God who is the very source of his trouble (27:2–3). The oath asserts that he will never utter falsehood but will continue to affirm his integrity (27:4–6). Then he utters a curse against his enemy (27:7–12). Job and the friends cannot both be right, and if the friends are wrong, then they have treated him unfairly and have acted toward him as an enemy. They have sinned against him and have misrepresented God. They are the enemy who should be treated as the wicked. Job turns to the friends in verse 11 to teach them concerning the way God works in the world ('the hand of God'). The fate of the wicked is then expounded in verses 13–23. These verses can be explained in a number of ways as the words of Job. He could be quoting the meaningless words of the friends, especially if verse 12 refers to 'meaningless talk'.[2] Others may argue that Job does not disagree with the general argument of the friends about the fate of the wicked, but that he objects to their identification of him with the wicked because of his suffering.[3] A more likely explanation is that Job is instructing the friends by turning their argument against them, warning that this could happen to them.[4] This view fits well with the emphasis in verse 11 that Job is going to instruct them, and it makes sense if the friends are seen as the enemy (v. 7) who will receive the portion of the wicked (v. 13). The friends have misrepresented God and have wronged Job with their counsel so that their possible identification with the wicked is an appropriate warning to them.

The quest for wisdom (Job 28)

Scholars have a hard time accepting Job 28 as the words of Job because the peaceful tenor of Job 28 is different from the heated

---

[2] Alden 1993: 265.
[3] Andersen 1974: 219–220. It is true that Job does not deny divine retribution in general but has trouble with the mechanical view of it argued by the friends. The question is whether this is the best explanation of Job 27.
[4] Talbert 2007: 149–150.

discussions of the speeches.[5] It is calm in tone and orthodox in content with the use of the fear of the Lord. And yet a case can be made for understanding Job 28 as the words of Job.[6] There is no evidence that Job has rejected the fear of the Lord. People who are suffering may explore many different avenues of thought that are related to their particular emotional state at the time. Job has fluctuations of mood and thought as he debates the friends. Once the debate is over, there is time to reflect on what has transpired.[7] Job comes to see that wisdom can be found only in God, and he affirms the fear of the Lord as the proper response to God.

Job shows the ingenuity of people to mine the earth for precious metals (28:1–11). People can accomplish wonderful things through their ability to ascertain how the world works and use that information to their advantage. Although humans exhibit tremendous skill in mining the earth, human ingenuity is not able to discover wisdom (Job 28:12–19). Verse 12 asks, 'But where shall wisdom be found?' This question is answered in verses 13–19, where two problems are emphasized. The first is that wisdom is not a commodity that can be discovered by people using their natural abilities. The second is that people do not understand the true value of wisdom. People do not seek wisdom because they do not understand that it is more valuable than silver or gold.

The source of wisdom is the focus of verses 20–28, introduced with the question 'From where, then, does wisdom come?' The answer is that wisdom is hidden from people, animals and even the realm of the dead. In other words, wisdom is not accessible anywhere in the world. People do not understand the value of wisdom, they do not know where wisdom is to be found and they are unable to discover it by human ingenuity. The conclusion Job comes to is that only God knows the way to wisdom because God knows everything and God sees everything (Job 28:23–28). He has created the world and established wisdom as a part of his creation, and then reveals wisdom to human beings when he says, 'Behold, the fear of the Lord, that is wisdom' (v. 28).[8]

---

[5] Smick 2010: 4.823; Andersen 1974: 224. Not everyone who denies that ch. 28 is from Job believes the chapter is a later addition.

[6] Longman 2012: 327. Lo (2003: 209–210) analyses the role of contradictory sayings spoken by Job as a basis for arguing that ch. 28 is the words of Job. However, Lo also concludes that Job does not affirm the ideas in Job 28.

[7] Both Robertson (2017: 164) and Longman (2017: 52) describe Job 28 as a soliloquy, a speech where a person reflects on his thoughts or feelings.

[8] For problems scholars have with 28:28 see Lo 2003: 11–14.

Job 28 raises two issues that are linked together. The first issue is that the inaccessibility of wisdom in Job 28 seems to contradict the accessibility of wisdom in God's creation in Proverbs. According to Job 28, wisdom cannot be found by people who are seeking it (28:13). Wisdom is inaccessible, hidden where people cannot find it, only known by God (28:13–23). The second issue is whether the fear of the Lord is the solution to Job's problem. Job does not have to learn the fear of the Lord because he already fears him before the tragic events of Job 1 – 2. The placement of the fear of the Lord in Job 28 and not in the speeches of Yahweh or the epilogue raises questions concerning whether it is the answer to Job's suffering. One view is that the statement that the fear of the Lord is wisdom in 28:28, is an excessive claim that wisdom is exhausted by this phrase based on a fossilized misunderstanding of Proverbs. The idea that the fear of the Lord exhaustively encompasses wisdom needs to be corrected because wisdom cannot be reduced to this phrase. The fear of the Lord is thus not the solution to Job's struggle of faith.[9] In fact, to offer it as the solution is to discount the protest and complaint of Job in the earlier chapters.[10]

The view that Job 28:28 is an excessive claim based on a fossilized misunderstanding of Proverbs has several problems. First, although this expression occurs in a speech by Job, it is spoken by God himself. God is the one who says 'the fear of the Lord, that is wisdom'. Second, this view of 28:28 would make Job agree with the friends in their misunderstanding of the deed–consequence relationship, but Job has argued against the friends' view. A better view is that wisdom and the fear of the Lord are closely associated because there is no wisdom without the fear of the Lord. Job is not denying the foundational role of the fear of the Lord for wisdom. Job can affirm this principle intellectually even as his emotional turmoil continues in Job 29 – 31.

The book of Job is a wisdom debate but it is a debate about a topic that is inaccessible to people through normal channels of information. Job's dialogue with the friends concerns the cause of his suffering, a question that cannot be answered on the human level because only God knows the answer to this question. Even Proverbs recognizes the mystery of God's ways in the world and that there are certain things

[9] Wilson 2015: 260–266.
[10] Habel (1985: 292–293) argues that the use of the traditional fear of the Lord means a return to a posture of unquestioning submission that the friends have advocated and Job has rejected. For more discussion of this see Belcher 2017b: 187–188.

beyond human knowledge (Prov. 20:24; 27:1). Every human answer to Job's suffering fails, and when God responds he does not give an answer to this question. God is concerned, however, with how Job will respond. Although the fear of the Lord is not used in Job's responses, his repentance is in line with how someone who fears the Lord would respond. This is the right response to suffering and the debate centres on the fact that one who fears the Lord can indeed suffer. Just because someone is righteous, or wise, or fears the Lord does not mean he or she is automatically exempted from the troubles of life. When the friends tell Job to trust in his piety as a way to end the suffering, it is the wrong solution. There is mystery to God's ways in the world that cannot be encapsulated by a narrow view of the deed–consequence relationship. Job 28 is a needed corrective to the friends' view and shows that wisdom has not yet been discovered in the debate. Job turns away from the friends to petition God directly.[11] If wisdom concerning Job's suffering cannot be discovered on the human level and can be found only with God, then it is imperative for God to speak. Job 28 fosters a desire to hear from God.

Job's last speech (Job 29 – 31)

These chapters are framed by statements that these are the words of Job (29:1 and 31:40). They are Job's public testimony that functions as his final attempt to prove his innocence and to force God to answer him. In chapter 29 Job gives an account of his glorious past before his suffering to show how much he has suffered and to demonstrate his own integrity. He had a wonderful relationship with God and enjoyed the blessings of life (vv. 1–6). Job also had a prominent place in the community. He was known for his wisdom in legal matters and for his beneficence to the poor. His reputation was so great that others deferred to him out of respect. This description of Job matches the picture in Job 1 – 2. His righteous life will become the basis of his oath of innocence in chapter 31.

Job turns from a description of his glorious past to give an account of his present humiliation (Job 30). He is mocked by fools who are much younger than him and whose fathers he would not even trust with the dogs of his flock. He is mocked by fools who have no moral standing in the community. He is a laughingstock and is taunted by their songs. Not only is Job mocked by fools (30:1–15) but he is also mired in his suffering by God (30:16–23). He feels hemmed in by his

---

[11] Hartley 1988: 384.

suffering as if he is in a straightjacket. God is the cause of his suffering, casting him into the muddy clay, not answering him when he calls for help, using his powers to persecute him, and treating him like an enemy. Despair overtakes Job as he vents his frustration with the way God treats him. He ends this chapter with a lament (30:24–31) that he has been overcome by darkness and abandoned by everyone.

Job dramatically expresses that he is innocent of all charges brought against him by asserting several oaths (Job 31). He declares his innocence by calling down curses on himself if he has committed any of the forms of wicked behaviour he lists. There is disagreement among scholars about how many oaths of disavowal Job expresses.[12] Here is a possible list:

1. Lust (vv. 1–4)
2. Falsehood (vv. 5–6)
3. Covetousness (vv. 7–8)
4. Adultery (vv. 9–12)
5. Mistreatment of one's servants (vv. 13–15)
6. Mistreatment of the poor (vv. 16–23)
7. Trust in wealth (vv. 24–25)
8. Idolatry (vv. 26–28)
9. Rejoicing at a foe's misfortune (vv. 29–30)
10. Failure to extend hospitality to a sojourner (vv. 31–32)
11. Concealment of a sin without confession (vv. 33–34)
12. Abuse of the land (vv. 38–40)[13]

An example of the oath he utters and the curse he calls down on himself can be seen in verses 7–8:

> if my step has turned aside from the way
>   and my heart has gone after my eyes,
>   and if any spot has stuck to my hands,
> then let me sow, and another eat,
>   and let what grows for me be rooted out.

Such oaths are a legal challenge offered in a court of law that demands a response from the other party in the case.[14] Job desires that God

---

[12] See Clines 2006: 1013 for a list of the different proposals.
[13] For an explanation of this list and an exposition of the text see Belcher 2017b: 210–222.
[14] Wilson 2007: 334.

will respond to his oath by declaring him innocent of the charges. Job is a model of how a person who fears God lives. He proclaims his innocence both in his outward actions and in his inward attitudes. If God remains silent and the curses uttered by Job do not fall on him, then his innocence will be established.[15] There is expectant hope, however, that God will respond to Job's oaths of innocence.

Elihu: friend or foe?

The expectation that God will answer Job is put on hold by the speeches of Elihu. He is a difficult person to understand, partly because his character is ambiguous and the meaning and role of his speeches are difficult to understand.[16] Some think he is brash and opinionated and adds nothing new to the debate.[17] Others argue that he is sincere, even prophet-like, and contributes positively to the debate.[18] Others take a mixed view of Elihu, recognizing that his approach to Job is different, as are some of his arguments. And yet, in the final analysis, it is hard not to conclude that he agrees with the friends' view of divine retribution. Both positive and negative aspects of Elihu will be examined.

Positive aspects of Elihu

Elihu is introduced in Job 32. He did not enter the debate earlier because he is younger than the other participants. Although he deferred to those who were older, he concludes that the breath of the Almighty, not age, is what brings wisdom. Elihu is angry at both Job and the friends. He is angry at Job because he justified himself rather than God (32:2) and is angry at the friends because they were not able to answer Job. They declared Job wrong without any evidence. The silence of the friends makes it look like Job has won the debate.[19] This also leaves God open to the charge of injustice. Part of the reason Elihu enters the debate is to defend the honour of God against these charges.

Elihu also promises a different approach to Job from that of the friends. He identifies with Job so that Job has no reason to fear him (33:6–7). He tones down the rhetoric of the debate by acknowledging

---

[15] Habel 1985: 431.
[16] For a summary of the different views of Elihu see Belcher 2017b: 226–229.
[17] Habel 1985: 443–447; Rodd 1990: 63.
[18] Ash 2014: 326–328; Green 1999: 118–136.
[19] Hartley 1988: 428.

that his involvement is not personal. He promises to use different arguments from the friends (32:14) and offers a different approach. He will begin many of his speeches by quoting the words of Job before giving an answer (33:8–11; 34:5–6; 35:2–3) as a way to promote understanding. He will try to answer the specific words of Job.

Elihu views suffering as God's discipline to turn people from the error of their way.[20] Misfortune may overtake people to awaken them to a wrongful attitude or an unconscious error to keep them from a wrong course of action. Thus suffering may be more an expression of God's mercy than his wrath.[21] Suffering has a divine purpose whereby God seeks the sufferer's purification.[22] Some argue that Elihu confines his words to what Job has said in his speeches and does not deal with the main argument between Job and the friends concerning whether Job sinned to cause his suffering.[23] In this view Elihu does not really address the main argument of the debate but focuses on how Job has responded to his suffering. Thus his view of divine retribution may not necessarily be the same mechanical view of the friends. Elihu defends the thesis in Job 34 that God rules the world with justice. Then in his last speech he emphasizes the sovereignty and majesty of God (Job 36:1 – 37:24). He shifts from a defence of God's justice to a description of God's power and wisdom in controlling the elements of creation (36:26 – 37:24). This speech anticipates the speeches of God, who will demonstrate his power over creation. The rhetorical question Elihu uses to stress Job's limited knowledge (37:15–20) also anticipates God's speeches, which will use rhetorical questions to expose Job's limited knowledge.[24]

There are several positive functions to Elihu's speeches. If God had answered Job right away, it would have appeared that God was at his beck and call.[25] Elihu provides space between Job's assertions of innocence that call his accuser to present his case (Job 29 – 31) and God's response. Elihu also reminds the readers of Job's arguments by summarizing them. This keeps the main issue of Job's innocence and

[20] Eliphaz presents a similar view in his first speech (Job 5:17–18).
[21] Hartley 1988: 427.
[22] Jones 2007: 226.
[23] Talbert 2007: 170. In other words, Elihu limits himself to situation B (how Job responded to his suffering) and does not deal with situation A (the reason for Job's suffering).
[24] McCabe 1997: 79.
[25] Ibid. 77–78.

God's justice before the reader.[26] The fact that Elihu is given a genealogy (32:2) and several chapters of speeches (Job 32 – 37) leads some to conclude that his arguments must be important and that they add something significant to the debate. Why would so much space be given to someone who only repeats what the friends have said? Plus God does not answer Elihu when he responds to Job, leaving the impression that Elihu does not need to be addressed because his words were helpful.[27]

Negative aspects of Elihu

Whether or not Elihu is brash and opinionated, he does say some things that seem peculiar. Elihu asserts that his words are not false and 'one who is perfect in knowledge is with you' (Job 36:4). He clearly seems to be referring to himself. Those who take a positive view of Elihu believe that he claims a fuller knowledge of God's ways than Job or the friends,[28] or that he claims to be an accurate communicator of divine truth,[29] or that he speaks as a prophet with the voice of one perfect in knowledge because he speaks God's words (33:23).[30] Of course, those who take a negative view of Elihu see these words as arrogant, condescending, presumptuous and even blasphemous.[31] If one gives Elihu the benefit of the doubt, it seems strange that he would use terminology that he later uses of God (37:16) to refer to himself. It raises questions about his role in the debate and the speeches he gives.

Perhaps the major question in the speeches of Elihu is whether he agrees with the friends that Job is suffering because of sin he has committed. Elihu may emphasize other things about suffering and he may not make retribution the central focus of his speeches, as the friends do, but in the final analysis his view is no different from that of the friends. It is hard to limit what Elihu says about Job to his response to suffering. In Job 33:8–11 Elihu quotes Job's words in chapter 13, where he responds to Zophar over the issue of whether Job's sin has caused his suffering.[32] Elihu's accusation that Job asserts he is clean is the same accusation that Zophar levelled against Job

---

[26] Ibid. 73–75.
[27] Talbert 2007: 168–169; Jones 2007: 227.
[28] Jones 2007: 253.
[29] Talbert 2007: 187.
[30] Ash 2014: 361.
[31] Wilson 2015: 173; Whybray 1998: 151; Andersen 1974: 284.
[32] In Job 33:9–11 Elihu seems to be referring back to Job 13:23, 27.

(11:4). It is difficult to avoid the conclusion that the starting point for the discussion is the same as that of the friends. There is no evidence that Elihu is trying to limit the discussion to Job's response to his suffering. At best, he is ambiguous about the matter and so does not offer wisdom because wisdom should bring clarity to the situation. In Job 34 Elihu argues for the justice of God on the basis that God repays a man according to his work (v. 11). This means that God has repaid Job for his sin and everyone can see the results of God's actions.[33] Elihu condemns not just what Job has said, but what he has done, and offers Job a possible confession related to his deeds: 'if I have done iniquity, I will do it no more' (v. 32). If both Job's deeds and words come under condemnation, then the statement of Elihu that Job 'adds rebellion to his sin' (v. 37) refers to both the sin that caused his suffering and his words as a response to his suffering. He specifically states that Job is experiencing the suffering that falls on the wicked (36:17). This agrees with the view of the friends. He also agrees with the friends that Job must repent of his sin, but does not manufacture a list of sins from which Job must repent.

Some argue that Elihu must be understood in a positive way, providing a partial answer to Job's dilemma, because so much space is given to his speeches.[34] But this argument could also be used to argue for a positive view of the friends who take up nine chapters in the book, versus Elihu who has six chapters. Wisdom literature is concerned about the right answer, but is also concerned about how one gets to the right answer. The application of wisdom to life is not always easy and there are difficulties in trying to comprehend different situations. Wisdom is not always able to give a quick answer, because life is complex. Thus the amount of space given Elihu in the book of Job is irrelevant to whether his teaching should be understood as offering wisdom to Job.

One issue where Elihu is wrong is whether God will answer Job's complaint. Elihu presents himself as the arbiter of Job's legal case with God (Job 33:5), but if that is the case, then God will not need to answer Job. Yet the role of Elihu as mediator will fail to bring about the desired outcome for Job. Elihu does not realize this failure so gives Job several reasons why God will not answer him. First, Job needs to

---

[33] Wilson 2007: 391; Habel 1985: 485.
[34] Green 1999: 124; Talbert 2007: 191. Whybray (1998: 23) argues that the fact that Elihu is the only human speaker who speaks at great length with no interruptions suggests that he makes a substantial contribution to the debate. A more important question is how Elihu lines up with God's evaluation when God finally speaks.

consider whether God has already answered him and he has not perceived it (33:14–18). He speaks to people in dreams or visions of the night while they are sleeping. He may also speak to people through the pain of illness to rebuke them (33:19–22). Second, Elihu argues that God has no compelling need to commence litigation with people (34:23). He does not need to convene a court to find evidence, because he already knows it. Thus he is able to shatter the mighty without an investigation (34:24–27). Third, Elihu argues that God does not respond to an empty cry (35:9–13). People call to God for help when they experience hardship because he has the power to deliver them. The problem is that people look to him only when they are in trouble. Elihu sees Job's cry to God as empty (35:14–16), the implication being that God will not answer Job. In fact, he ends his speeches with the words 'he does not regard any who are wise in their own conceit' (37:24). But Elihu is wrong because God does answer Job (38:1).

When God finally speaks, he does not even mention Elihu or his arguments. This does not mean that God agrees with everything Elihu has said. God may not respond to Elihu because his view of divine retribution is no different from the view of the friends. The very fact that God responds to Job when Elihu has repeatedly said that God would not respond marginalizes his role.[35] God ignores Elihu and his silence pronounces a negative verdict on Elihu's position.[36] Elihu is another example of the failure of human wisdom to provide an answer. Wisdom resides only with God (Job 28) and the reader longs to hear from him. The fact that God speaks is a welcome surprise giving hope that the issue can be resolved.

God's speeches and Job's response

Elihu dashed Job's hope that God would answer him, so it is a surprise when the next chapter begins 'Then the LORD answered Job out of the whirlwind and said' (38:1). The surprise is not just that God answers Job but also the way God answers Job. He does not directly address Job's complaint, he does not respond to his avowal of innocence in chapter 31 and he does not reprove Job for wrongdoing. Rather, he confronts Job on what he has said about God's justice and his governing of the world.[37]

---

[35] Fyall 1995: 100–101.
[36] Wilson 2007: 368; Habel 1985: 516.
[37] Hartley 1988: 487; Longman 2012: 425.

God's first speech: divine interrogation about God's works (38:1 – 40:2)

The way God addresses Job is important, bombarding him with a list of rhetorical questions that show Job's ignorance and powerlessness in the vastness of God's creation. This form of address will allow Job to accept what God says without it being imposed on him from the outside.[38] God approaches Job in a dramatic way in the whirlwind and uncovers his inability to understand the mysterious, glorious way God works in the world. The goal is that Job will surrender his complaint against God and trust his destiny to the sovereignty of God.[39]

The majesty of God is highlighted when God 'answered Job out of the whirlwind'. Elements of the storm are used to describe theophanies of God (Exod. 19:16–20; Ezek. 1:2–4; Isa. 29:5–6). It represents God's personal presence, demonstrating his control in the middle of chaos.[40] God confronts Job with the question 'Who is this that darkens counsel by words without knowledge?' (38:2). The word 'counsel' (*'ēṣâ*) refers to the plan of Yahweh by which he governs the world.[41] This question highlights that Job has spoken about matters of which he has no knowledge. Then God tells Job to get ready for his questions to see if he can answer them.[42]

God overwhelms Job with a series of questions about the way the world works. He asks Job if he was present when the world was created (38:4–7) and whether he witnessed the limits that God put in place in creation (38:8–14). The wicked are specifically mentioned because God is able to control them (38:13, 15). Job has not seen the gates of death and does not know the origins of light and darkness (38:16–21). God then moves to question Job on his maintenance of the world. He asks Job if he understands how he governs the inanimate world (38:22–38). Does Job know where the storm originates, how God uses the storm to water desolate places of the earth or how the dew forms or how the waters become frost? Can Job control the heavenly constellations (38:28–33)? God is active in places where no

[38] Hartley 1988: 489.
[39] Belcher 2017b: 283–284.
[40] Talbert 2007: 198.
[41] Habel 1985: 536.
[42] God tells Job to 'dress for action' (from a Hebrew phrase that means 'to gird up the loins'), an action that symbolizes using one's strength to meet a difficult task (Hartley 1988: 492).

people live. Job is being shown that the ways of God cannot be understood from the limited viewpoint of human beings. God not only governs the heavenly world, but also governs the animal world. God describes animals that typically live in desolate places and some are a threat to human beings. A beauty and wonder is associated with some of the animals that act in strange or humorous ways. God takes great pleasure in what he has created and no part of the world is outside his control. Both the lion and the raven ultimately depend on God for their food (38:39–41). Job must also learn to live in dependence on God. The mountain goats give birth apart from Job's help (39:1–4). Job has nothing to do with the free spirit of the wild donkey and is not able to force the wild ox to submit to him (39:5–12). Who can explain the strange behaviour of the ostrich that has great ability to outrun a horse but also seems to act in foolish ways (39:13–18). God shows the mysterious wonder of his creation that cannot be comprehended by human understanding. God gives wisdom to some animals and not to others, for he is the source of wisdom.[43] All these examples highlight that Job, or any human being, cannot understand the way God works in creation and how he exercises his sovereign rule.

Job's first response: humbled (40:3–5)

God invites Job to respond with the question 'Shall a fault-finder contend with the Almighty?' (40:1). Job has questioned and found fault with the way God governs the world (10:3) and now responds to God by declaring he does not know how he should answer (40:3–5). He is of small account before the majesty of Almighty God and recognizes his insignificance before the vast panorama of creation.[44] Job is reduced to silence, not because he has been beaten down by God's power but because of the grandeur of God's wisdom and power to govern the world. The first speech of God addresses Job's self-centred focus at the end of the curse-lament of chapter 3. Job has been shown the vastness of creation to move him beyond his narrow view that the world revolves around him and his suffering. It is not that Job's suffering is unimportant, but if Job is not able to understand the way God governs the world, there is no way he can understand the mystery of his own suffering. This theme supports the point of Job 28, that wisdom is found only with God. Job's suffering

---

[43] Longman 2012: 436.
[44] Alter (1985: 87, 92) uses this phrase.

is not beyond the wisdom of God and so Job should trust the wise rule of God even for his own life.

God's second speech: Can you establish justice? (40:6 – 41:34)

God's second speech begins like the first speech, except the emphasis is on God's justice. Does Job really want to condemn God so that he can be right? Job has declared his innocence and has wrestled with the possibility that he is suffering unjustly.[45] Job and his friends are caught on the false dilemma that either Job's suffering is justified because of his sin or that God is unjust in the way he is treating Job. This has led Job to question the character of God (Job 9:20, 24; 27:1–6). God confronts Job with the accusation that he has treated Job unjustly. The questions in verses 8–9 focus on whether Job has the power to control events in the world in order to accomplish his purposes. Power and justice go hand in hand. In order to establish justice, power is needed. Job should be able to demonstrate such power by stopping the wicked from accomplishing their purposes (40:10–14). If Job can do that, then God will acknowledge that he has the power to save himself. Of course, he does not have the power to establish justice on earth in the face of wickedness. He cannot save himself but is dependent on the power and justice of God to do so.

God drives home this point by the examples of Behemoth (40:15–24) and Leviathan (41:1–34). There is debate concerning whether these creatures are literal animals, mythological creatures or a description of literal animals using mythic metaphors. The evidence that these creatures are literal animals is seen in the way their habitat and diet are described (40:15–16, 23), in the description of how someone might try to capture them (40:24; 41:1–8, 25–32) and in the designation they are creatures created by God (41:33) just as God created Job (40:15). Behemoth and Leviathan are also used in the OT without any symbolic meaning (Pss 8:8; 50:10; 73:22; 104:26; Joel 1:20; 2:22; Hab. 2:17).[46] There are problems with identifying these creatures with literal animals. There is no agreement concerning which

---

[45] See the discussion in chapter 6. Wilson (2016: 76) summarizes Job's dilemma as his belief that God is just and that he is not dealing with him justly. God has taken his right to justice (27:2), treating him wrongly as an enemy (6:4; 13:24–28; 16:9–14; 19:6–12), oppressing and unfairly condemning him (7:21; 9:19–20, 25–35; 10:14–17; 14:3–4).

[46] Commentators on Job who take a literal view of the animals are Andersen, Konkel, Alden, Rowley and Talbert; see also Fox 2012: 261–267.

animals are being described. Behemoth has been identified with a hippo or an elephant and Leviathan with a crocodile or some kind of sea creature. Leviathan is also described in ways that go beyond the description of a literal animal with fire coming out of his mouth and smoke from his nostrils (41:18–21).

Others argue that these animals are mythological creatures, symbols of the forces of chaos, used in ANE myths that describe the battles among the gods. Links with the hippopotamus and crocodile come from the use of these figures as symbols of chaos in Egypt where the god Seth assumes the form of the hippopotamus and a crocodile in the battle with Horus.[47] Support for this view is found in the fact that Leviathan is used in Scripture to refer to the chaos dragon of the sea (Isa. 27:1; 51:9; Ps. 74:14).[48] There are problems with the mythological view. The focus of God's second speech is not on the dim mythological past but on the present vast universe as it is governed by God. Also, Behemoth is placed in the same category of creature as Job as part of the natural world (40:15).[49]

Another view is that these creatures are described as literal animals, but the poetic language is symbolic of something beyond the natural, animal world. The description of these animals comes after God challenges Job to establish justice on the earth. The mythological terminology is used to present graphic descriptions of the powers of evil.[50] Fyall develops these concepts further by associating Behemoth with death and Leviathan with the embodiment of evil, even Satan himself. The description of Behemoth's habitat (40:20–22) has a deeper meaning pointing to the underworld. He identifies Behemoth with Mot, the god of death. Leviathan is the climax of supernatural imagery. He is a guise of Satan, who is the sinister power behind death. The Satan/Leviathan figure is unmasked as the climax of the imagery and theology of the book.[51]

Perhaps the best conclusion is that Behemoth is an animal of the natural world and Leviathan is a supernatural creature. Behemoth is a creature created by God just as Job was created by God (40:15). The description of Behemoth is not horrendous and predatory as in the creation myths, but he is described as a herbivore, peacefully lying

---

[47] Habel 1985: 557.
[48] Day 1985: 76–83.
[49] Gordis 1965: 571.
[50] Smick 2010: 697–706. He has an extensive discussion on the use of mythopoeic language to describe mythological concepts by the writers of Scripture.
[51] Fyall 2002: 135, 137, 157, 165.

in the river.[52] The description of his tail as 'stiff as a cedar' does not
fit the description of the tail of an elephant or a hippopotamus. This
could, however, refer to the sexual organ of the animal because
the loins are the seat of procreative powers.[53] The description of the
animal's strength and his habitat as peacefully lying in the river fits
the hippopotamus. The point is that Job is powerless before a living
creature of God who is created like Job. If Job cannot control
Behemoth, a living creature of God, how can he control the proud
(40:12a)?[54] Only God has sufficient wisdom and power to rule the
world. Leviathan, however, is more than just a normal animal. His
eyes shine like a light and sparks of fire leap from his mouth like
flaming torches. His breath is hot enough to kindle coals (41:18–21).
He is a supernatural creature engaged in physical violence in the
natural world. Job has questioned the justice of God. When God
confronts Job with Leviathan, he confronts him with the impossibility
of subduing evil, wickedness or even Satan himself.[55] Job is not able
to establish justice because he is not able to control evil or subdue
the wicked. Divine justice includes the power to rule and the
authority to control the well-being of his subjects. The power of evil
is under the sovereign rule of God and is beyond Job's ability to
control.

Job's second response: repentance (42:1–6)

The meaning of Job's response to God's second speech is debated.[56]
Some see Job protesting against and refusing to submit to God
the divine bully.[57] Of course, this does not fit the picture of God in the
rest of the OT, or in the book of Job. Some understand Job's response
as a hypocritical, 'tongue-in-cheek' response made to calm God in the
whirlwind.[58] But it is peculiar that Job, who is outspoken and honest
about his situation in the speeches, would now become shifty and
evasive.[59] The best way to understand Job's response is that he acknowledges his limitations and repents for calling into question in some of

[52] Gordis 1965: 571.
[53] Konkel 2006: 6.231. There is also the suggestion that Behemoth is a dinosaur (Steel 2001: 42–45).
[54] Talbert 2007: 212.
[55] Fyall 2002: 135, 137; Ash 2014: 421.
[56] For a fuller account of the translation issues and the different views see Belcher 2017b: 309–312.
[57] Curtis 1979: 510.
[58] Robertson 1973: 466.
[59] Fox 2013: 20.

his speeches God's justice.[60] He does not repent for any sin that has caused his suffering but recognizes that his response to his suffering has not always been appropriate. He begins his answer to God by quoting the same question that God asked (42:3), showing that he now views himself from God's perspective, not his own limited viewpoint.[61] He confesses that he spoke beyond his knowledge when he complained that God ruled unjustly. He had heard about God, but now sees him. His deepest longing, to see his redeemer, has come to pass. This transforms his view and he repents in dust and ashes. Job's repentance while still suffering shows that he is willing to fear God and submit to his purposes even if he is never publicly vindicated.[62]

Job does not withdraw his avowal of innocence (Job 31) in his repentance because he was correct on the main point of the debate with his friends, that he was not suffering because of any sin he had committed.[63] He repents of his response to suffering.[64] Those who do not make this distinction must argue that Job withdraws his avowal of innocence,[65] or that Job does not really repent,[66] or that there must be some sin discovered as the cause of his suffering of which he must repent.[67]

The epilogue: the renewal of God's blessing

The epilogue resolves the debate between Job and his friends with the public vindication of Job and gives an account of the renewal of God's blessings in Job's life. Job's vindication is indicated in several ways. First, God is angry at the friends and addresses Eliphaz, the representative of the friends, with the words 'for you have not spoken of me what is right, as my servant Job has' (42:7). This statement seems strange coming right after Job has repented for speaking words without knowledge. How has Job spoken what is right about God

---

[60] Newell 1992: 453–455.
[61] Newsom 2015: 3.261.
[62] Wilson 2007: 468.
[63] God's appearance to Job means that Job's call for litigation is no longer needed. He comes to see the folly of arguing his case with God, so it is appropriate to understand Job as renouncing his legal case (Wilson 2016: 71), especially his view that he is being mistreated by God. Job, however, still affirms his innocence in reference to the cause of his suffering.
[64] Carson 1990: 174. He comments that Job repents of his arrogance in impugning God's justice and of the attitude whereby he demands an answer.
[65] Hartley 1988: 537.
[66] Bartholomew and O'Dowd 2011: 147. They argue that guilt and repentance are not in view but that it is a lesson in human finitude about wisdom in a broken world.
[67] Wilson 2007: 468.

over against the view of the friends? Some argue that Job's words are more honest than those of the friends,[68] but this view downplays the negative statements about God in the speeches and argues against Job's need to repent in his response to God. Others argue that God's statement refers to Job's confession of his sin of speaking arrogant words without knowledge and that the friends need to do the same.[69] This is true to a certain extent but does not get at the heart of the debate between Job and the friends. The best way to understand God's statement in 42:7 is that Job is correct that he is not suffering because of his sin. The friends are wrong on this point and in arguing their case misrepresent God. Second, Job is called 'my servant' four times in two verses (42:7–8). This is a title of honour for one who serves God. Job maintained his honour by not following the counsel of the friends in repenting of sin he had not committed. If Job had confessed to sins he had not committed to satisfy the friends or to get relief from his suffering, he would have lost his integrity.[70] Third, Job prays for his friends while suffering on the ash heap, a demonstration that his suffering is not a mark against his integrity. It is ironic that the one the friends condemned as a sinner is the one they are dependent on for restoration.[71] When Job prays for his friends, God restores the fortunes of Job with great abundance by giving him twice as much as he had before. The doubling of Job's fortune shows God's full acceptance of Job[72] and proves that Yahweh is a life-giving God, not a capricious deity who takes pleasure in suffering. The description of Job's death resembles the death of other servants of God, such as Abraham (Gen. 25:8), Isaac (Gen. 35:29) and David (1 Chr. 29:28), who died after a long and blessed life.

The theological message of the book of Job

Suffering

It is clear that suffering is integral to the story of Job.[73] But the book of Job does not answer the question of why there is suffering. When

---

[68] Andersen 1974: 293; Habel 1985: 383.
[69] Jones 2007: 293; Talbert 2007: 232.
[70] Carson 1990: 167.
[71] Wilson 2007: 472–473.
[72] Hartley 1988: 540.
[73] For a general review of the causes of suffering, responses to suffering, God's relationship to suffering, and the resolution of suffering in Psalms, Lamentations, Proverbs, Job and Ecclesiastes see Belcher 2008: 775–781.

God responds to Job's complaints, he does not give him a list of reasons for his suffering. He does not tell Job about the heavenly council and the discussion with Satan that precipitated his suffering. God focuses on Job's response to his suffering. This is one of the key issues of the book. How people respond to suffering is more important than the reasons behind suffering. All of this leads to a basic question: What are appropriate responses to suffering? There are many responses to suffering presented in the book of Job that fail to offer him real hope. The friends' initial response of sympathetic silence is good. Job's first response of patient submission is also worthy to emulate because he does not charge God with wrong (1:22). His response in Job 3 shows how suffering can take its toll on a committed believer and lead to questioning God's purposes. Such questioning is not necessarily bad, as demonstrated in many of the lament psalms. But Job crosses the line when he questions God's just governing of the world and when he accuses God of treating him as an enemy. Believers may struggle with the tragedies and trials of life. God is able to handle our questions when we do not understand the circumstances of life and wrestle with events that cannot be explained. Questions arise because we do not see the promises of God being fulfilled in our lives. But we must be careful not to impugn the character of God.

If a major theme of Job is how people should respond to suffering, an idea connected to that is how to counsel someone who is suffering. The book of Job asks the question 'Where is wisdom to be found?' It becomes clear that wisdom is not found in any of the participants in the story of Job, including Job's wife, the friends and Elihu. Each of these falls short in helping Job respond appropriately to his suffering. The conclusion that Job comes to is that wisdom is found only in God (28:23) and so God must be the one to respond to his suffering. Job also comes to the conclusion that if wisdom is to be found only in God, then the proper response is to fear the Lord (28:28). Job is described in 1:1 as a man who fears Yahweh and his initial response to his suffering exemplifies such an attitude toward God. After wrestling with his relationship with God and the false arguments of the friends, Job comes back to this response in Job 28. This does not make Job's struggles and questions irrelevant, but shows that the fear of the Lord should not be lost in the struggles of suffering. The fear of the Lord is the foundation from which questions should be addressed to God. Thus people who counsel those who suffer must allow such questions and work with people through the process of mourning and grief without expecting that people will quickly come to a resolution of their suffering. The fear of the Lord, however, should never be out of sight, so that even if not at first, those who suffer will be able to affirm 'blessed be the name of the LORD' (Job 1:21) and 'we know that for those who love God all things work together for good' (Rom. 8:28).

Another factor related to how one should respond to suffering is the question Satan raises about Job's fear of God. He accuses Job of honouring God only because of the blessings that God has given him and that if those blessings are taken away, then Job will curse God. This accusation challenges Job's faith as self-interest and questions whether God is worthy to be worshipped apart from his blessings. God allows Satan to put Job through the test and Job passes the test, not only in Job 1 – 2 but also in the debate with the friends. Although Job questions God's rule of the world and, at times, expresses that God is treating him as an enemy, Job never abandons God but keeps pursuing him to the end. He never gives up on God as his witness and redeemer and confirms this response by his strong assertions of innocence (Job 31). Job passes the test: his faith is not self-interest and God is not worshipped just because he is the source of blessing.

The sovereignty of God

The sovereignty of God is also a major theme in Job. Every step of the way God takes the initiative concerning the character of his servant Job and in each response to Satan God puts limits on what he can do. God resides over the council of the sons of God. Although the friends also affirm God's sovereignty, they have a narrow view of that sovereignty concerning the way he reacts to the wickedness of the world: he always punishes wickedness in such a way that if people are suffering they must have sinned to cause their suffering. Job explores the freedom of God's sovereignty by recognizing that the world does not work according to the narrow definition of divine retribution. There are wicked people who prosper and there are innocent people who suffer. Job explores the mystery of God's sovereignty when he acknowledges that people are not able to explain everything that happens in the world. The mystery of God's sovereignty is affirmed when God leaves Job in the dark about the reason for his suffering and emphasizes his wondrous, mysterious works. These works in creation go beyond the limits of human under-standing and show that God has purposes for parts of the world that have no direct relation to human beings. The vastness of God's creation shows the majesty of his works and the impossibility of comprehending the manifold purposes that God is accomplishing in the world. People know so little of the ways of God, including the way he governs the world in justice. There are many things we do not understand; yet we must bow before his purposes and trust him with our lives.

Divine retribution

The major argument of the friends is a narrow view of divine retribution that looks at suffering as a result of sin that a person has committed. Such a view is a distortion of what is taught in the book of Proverbs (see chapter 3), but it is easy to absolutize the proverbs to come to this conclusion. The book of Job dismantles this mechanical view of divine retribution in a number of ways. The first response of Job to his suffering cuts the connection between piety and prosperity when he acknowledges that we come into this world with nothing and leave with nothing, and that all that we receive in this world is a blessing from God (1:21). Job does not expect an entitlement to blessing because he is a righteous man.

Job pushes back on the narrow view of divine retribution when he explores the possibility of innocent suffering. The friends do not have the category of an innocent sufferer, but God affirms it when he finally speaks. Although he confronts Job for calling into question his just rule of the universe, he condemns the friends' mechanical view of divine retribution because it fails to explain God's activity in the world. It also fails to explain Job's suffering. Thus Job has been correct concerning the main topic of the debate with the friends (42:7). His innocence is demonstrated in chapters 1–2 and confirmed by God in 42:7.

When Job is vindicated before the friends, God restores his fortunes by doubling his blessings. Some struggle with the way the book ends because it seems to affirm the false view of divine retribution held by the friends. But this view does not take into account the fact that Job submits to God after the second speech without any indication that he will be rewarded or that his suffering will end. If the mechanical connection between suffering and sin has been destroyed, so that suffering is not the consequence of sin, then it is also true that blessing is not the result of obedience. It is within God's sovereign power to restore Job. God allows Job to suffer for a higher purpose and once that purpose is fulfilled there is no reason for Job's suffering to continue. The ending of the book of Job shows that suffering is not the final destination of the one who fears the Lord, a teaching that is clearer in the light of the work of Christ.[74]

The message of Job and Jesus

The life and death of Jesus confirms the message of the book of Job and brings clarity to the issues raised in the book. Jesus is confronted with suffering during his earthly ministry and does not answer the problem of suffering by giving reasons for suffering; instead, he emphasizes the importance of the response to suffering. When Jesus is told how Pilate mingled the blood of the Galileans with their sacrifices, he deflects any connection between their suffering and sin by asking the question 'Do you think that these Galileans were worse sinners than all the other Galileans, because they suffered in this way?' (Luke 13:2). His answer is a clear 'No,' with a statement on how they should respond, 'but unless you repent, you will all likewise perish' (Luke 13:3). He answers the same way concerning eighteen people on whom the Tower of Siloam fell. Jesus does not get caught up in the why of these events but focuses on how people should respond. When Jesus and the disciples pass a man blind from birth in John 9, they ask him whether this man sinned or his parents that he was born blind. Jesus' answer is clear that it was not the sin of this man or his parents that caused his blindness. Rather, Jesus pushes them to think of the higher purpose of suffering as a display of the works of God. The healing of this man will glorify Jesus and highlight how different people respond to him.

These two examples clearly show that Jesus does not operate with a mechanical view of divine retribution. The important issue in suffering is not who sinned to cause the suffering, but how someone will respond to suffering. Jesus also reveals the purpose of the suffering of the blind man as a way that the works of God can be revealed.

Jesus demonstrates in his life and death the limitations of a narrow view of divine retribution. Jesus was blameless in the ultimate sense because he had no sin. Even though he was a righteous man he did not have great temporal blessings during his earthly ministry. He was cut off in his prime and died a death that associated him with criminals. He exemplified in his life the tension with which the friends of Job wrestled with how one can suffer and still be righteous before God.

---

[74] Contra Rodd (1990: 127), who cannot see what message the ending of Job has for today.

The fact that Jesus died on a cross caused many to question him, as even the chief priest declared, 'He trusts in God; let God deliver him now, if he desires him. For he said, "I am the Son of God"' (Matt. 27:43). How can Jesus be the Son of God and be suffering on the cross? Of course, the answer is that Jesus is an innocent sufferer and that his suffering is the means through which God will save his people.

Job expresses the need for a mediator to help bring him together with God. Yet how can Job appeal to God as his witness and redeemer if God is also perceived as his enemy? How can God be a witness for Job against himself? Part of the answer is the changing attitudes of Job toward God as he wrestles with his suffering, sometimes in despair over the way God is treating him, and sometimes confident that God will vindicate him. The life and death of Christ also make clear how God can intercede with God for human beings. Jesus is both fully God and fully man and is the one who can bring God and human beings together. The Greek translation of the OT translates 'arbiter' (Job 9:33) with the same word that is used in 1 Timothy 2:5 to refer to Christ as our 'mediator' (*mesitēs*). Christ is able to fulfil this role in a unique way because he is both man and God. He can act as a mediator, a witness, an advocate for his people who suffer, and is the redeemer who will vindicate his people. He has defeated the forces of darkness and sin, represented by Leviathan, and now rules this universe for the benefit of his people (Eph. 1:22–23).[75]

There is a higher purpose to suffering that is not always obvious to people, but those who have faith trust that God is working out his purposes through suffering. Jesus' followers understand the reason for Jesus' suffering and understand the nature of the kingdom that he came to establish. The 'now but not yet' nature of that kingdom means that those who follow Jesus will not receive the fullness of the blessings of salvation until Jesus comes again. Until then, disciples are to respond in a self-denying way by taking up the cross and following Jesus. This response renounces our agenda in order to live for the glory of God's purposes. Following Jesus may include hardship, difficulties, persecution and even death. The believer does not look for the fullness of salvation in this life and so is willing to sacrifice for the sake of Christ. This kingdom perspective understands that suffering is not necessarily a direct result of sin, but is a result of living in a fallen world and many times is a consequence of following Jesus.

---

[75] For Job as a type of Christ in his suffering and in his intercession for the friends see Belcher 2017b: 53–55, 332–333.

Chapter Eight

Key questions concerning the book of Ecclesiastes

Authorship

The majority of modern scholars argue that Solomon did not write the book. Most date the book late because the Hebrew of the book seems to match late Biblical Hebrew prominent after the exile.[1] Some date the book in the Persian period of the fifth century BC because of the sombre tone of the book or because the book is supposed to reflect the economic realities of that period.[2] Others argue that the author was a Palestinian Jew of the third century BC who was heavily influenced by Greek thought.[3]

Only a few scholars, based on statements in the book that seem to point to Solomon as the author (1:1, 12), argue that Solomon is the author of Ecclesiastes. The unusual nature of the Hebrew is explained in a number of ways. Some point to the philosophical content of the book,[4] and others point to the use of a local dialect.[5] Fredericks's analysis of the Hebrew leads to a date in the eighth century BC.[6] Young highlights the diversity of the linguistic situation in pre-exilic Canaan and argues that the Hebrew of Ecclesiastes is a local dialect

---

[1] For an analysis of the Hebrew of Ecclesiastes that concludes it fits late Biblical Hebrew see Seow 1997: 11–21; Schoors 2004; Holmstedt 2013: 283–307; and Cook 2013: 309–342. Delitzsch's statement summarizes the issue well: 'If the book of Koheleth were of old Solomonic origin, then there is no history of the Hebrew language' (1978b: 6.190).

[2] Delitzsch (1978b: 6.212–215) and Hengstenberg (1960: 6–15) cite the sombre mood of the time reflected in the book, and Seow (1997: 21–29) cites the economic realities reflected in the book.

[3] Fox 1999: 6–8; Krüger 2004: 22; Perdue 2007: 168–186. Crenshaw (1987: 50–51) places the book before the Maccabean revolt, which began about 168 BC, when the upper echelons of Jewish society experienced prosperity. Bartholomew (2009: 54–55) argues for the Greek period because the book wrestles with problems of individualism and autonomy that became prominent in the third century BC.

[4] Archer 1974: 478–488.

[5] Isaksson 1987.

[6] Fredericks 1988.

of pre-exilic Canaan.[7] The fluidity of the linguistic situation in the pre-exilic period opens the door for the possibility that Solomon could have written Ecclesiastes.[8]

The author of the book, however, is not identified as Solomon. The term used for the author is Qohelet (*qôhelet*), a feminine participle from the verb *qāhal*, which means 'to assemble'. English translations translate this term with 'Preacher' or 'Teacher' based on the meaning of the Hebrew and the description of the author in 12:9. The best way to handle this term is to leave it untranslated as Qohelet,[9] but is it an artificial name,[10] or a nickname of some sort?[11] Some argue that it is used to distance the author from Solomon. In other words, the author is not Solomon but adopts a Solomonic persona to show that not even Solomon could have fared any better in a search for meaning.[12] Others argue that the self-designation of Qohelet as 'son of David, king of Jerusalem' (1:1) and 'king over Israel in Jerusalem' (1:12) can apply only to Solomon.[13] Although Solomonic authorship can make a difference in the interpretation of the book, it is not integral to the message of the book.[14]

Genre

There are different views concerning the genre of the book. Ecclesiastes is compared to several ANE texts, including the Gilgamesh Epic,[15] Royal Testaments from Egypt,[16] West Semitic Royal

---

[7] Young 1993.

[8] Young does not argue for Solomonic authorship (Young et al. 2008: 2.65), but argues that the language of Ecclesiastes should not be used to date the book. Fredericks seems to favour Solomonic authorship (Fredericks and Estes 2010: 36). Also, the linguistic fluidity of the pre-exilic period does not deny the development of standard Biblical Hebrew in connection with the rise of the monarchy.

[9] Commentaries that follow this approach include Bartholomew, Crenshaw, Fox, Longman, Murphy and Ogden.

[10] Eaton 1983: 23.

[11] Whybray 1989: 2; Longman 1998: 1.

[12] Fox 1999: 159.

[13] Modern scholars who affirm that Solomon wrote Ecclesiastes include Archer, Kaiser, Garrett, Bollhagen and O. P. Robertson.

[14] For a defence of Solomonic authorship that discusses the strengths and weaknesses of the evidence see Belcher 2017a: 21–29.

[15] Brown 2000: 5–7.

[16] Von Rad (1972: 227) applies Royal Testament to the whole book, but Crenshaw (1987: 29) limits it to 1:12 – 2:26. See Shields (2013: 130–135), who thinks connections between Ecclesiastes and ANE royal autobiophies are well established and seeks to show how this would have an impact on the reading of Ecclesiastes.

KEY QUESTIONS CONCERNING THE BOOK OF ECCLESIASTES

Inscriptions[17] and Akkadian fictional autobiographies.[18] The similarities between Ecclesiastes and other ANE literature demonstrate that the book reflects the ANE environment. However, it is hard to point to another work and confidently say that Ecclesiastes fits a particular genre, because of the many differences between Ecclesiastes and the other texts. In the end there is no consensus concerning the genre of Ecclesiastes.[19] There is no clear genre category of the ANE to which the book of Ecclesiastes is analogous.[20]

Structure

The structure of Ecclesiastes is important for understanding the book and the several different interpretations of the book. Ecclesiastes is similar to some of the Akkadian texts in its use of the first-person style of autobiography. A first-person account runs from 1:12 to 12:7. Longman defines autobiography as 'an account of the life (or part thereof) of an individual written by the individual himself'. It must be written in the first person and include reminiscences of the past life of the individual.[21] Isaksson argues that an 'autobiographical thread' composed of perfect verbs in the first-person singular runs through the whole of 1:12 – 12:7.[22] The first-person autobiography is framed by third-person narration. The first eleven verses of the book introduce the author, state the motto of the book, ask a key question and then present words of Qohelet that preview the argument of the book. The end of the book (12:8–14) restates the motto of the book, gives an evaluation of the words of Qohelet and points to the solution of the problems Qohelet addressed. The structure of the book can be called an autobiography cast in a narrative frame, or a framed autobiography.[23] In the light of this, the term Qohelet will refer to the first-person autobiography (1:12 – 12:7), Ecclesiastes will refer to the book as a whole, and the frame narrator will refer to

---

[17] Seow 1995: 284–285.

[18] Longman 1991: 103–116.

[19] Bartholomew 2009: 61.

[20] Koh 2006: 72. This work is one of the best treatments of the genre of Ecclesiastes in the context of the ANE.

[21] Longman 1991: 40–41.

[22] Isaksson 1987: 43, 48. He argues that the perfect forms of the verb may suggest a looser kind of narration that relates points of interest in the life of an author rather than telling a story of connected events.

[23] Longman 1998: 17; Bartholomew 1998: 157.

135

the one who presents the words of Qohelet and evaluates them (1:1–11; 12:8–14).

Approaches to Ecclesiastes

The structure of a first-person autobiography that is framed by third-person narration with a third-person intrusion in 7:27 raises questions concerning the interpretation of the book. Is Qohelet, the author of the first-person autobiography, the same person who added the third-person prologue (1:1–11) and the third-person epilogue (12:7–14)? If he is not the same person, then why would someone want to present the words of Qohelet to a wider audience? Another question is whether the evaluation of the message of Qohelet in the epilogue is positive or negative. In other words, does the epilogue basically agree with the views of Qohelet or not? These questions are determined by a number of factors, but a major question is how the message of the autobiography of Qohelet is understood. Everyone agrees that the epilogue confirms traditional wisdom teaching in 12:13–14, but there are a variety of ways the words of Qohelet are understood.[24]

One of the difficulties in understanding the message of the book is how to handle the positive statements, usually termed the 'calls to enjoyment' (2:24–26; 5:18–20; 9:7–10), and the negative statements of the book (2:15, 17; 3:20–22; 9:1–6). There is even a contradiction expressed in 8:12–14. Qohelet first says in verse 12 that a sinner does great evil and lives long, but then he states the opposite in verses 12b–13: it will not be well with the wicked and his days will not be prolonged. But then Qohelet notes in verse 14 that the righteous are not rewarded for their righteousness and the wicked are not rewarded for their wickedness; rather, the righteous get what the wicked deserve and the wicked get what the righteous deserve. So which is it? Do the wicked live long or not? Does the deed–consequence relationship really work or not? Should the positive statements about the righteous take precedence over the negative statements about the wicked? The answers to these questions determine, to some extent, how one understands the book.[25]

Some argue that Qohelet has abandoned the faith and is no longer a believer. He has deviated from orthodox wisdom and rejects the

---

[24] For approaches to Ecclesiastes in the light of recent trends of biblical theology related to wisdom literature, including postmodernism, see Dell 2017: 81–99.
[25] For a fuller analysis of the different approaches to Ecclesiastes see Belcher 2017a: 37–51.

claim that wisdom can secure one's existence.[26] Many who argue this view see several redactors in the book. The first redactor did not change anything but the second redactor made dogmatic corrections to the words of Qohelet. For example, 8:12b–13 is a dogmatic correction to 8:12a.[27] The problem with this view is that the second redactor did not do a very good job of making corrections because the negative statements still get the last word, as in 8:14.

Many argue that although Qohelet is struggling with various aspects of life, faith wins the day. He is an orthodox wisdom teacher and his message is the same as that of the book of Proverbs. The epilogue to Ecclesiastes affirms the positive message of Qohelet.[28] Ogden argues that the keyword *hebel*, which he understands as stressing the incomprehensibility of life, is not the conclusion or thesis of Qohelet. Rather, Qohelet's main advice comes in the calls to enjoyment, which are theological affirmations of faith in a just and loving God despite signs to the contrary. Faith is aware of the mysteries of life but moves forward to enjoy life. By putting the anomaly (8:14) alongside the tradition (8:12b–13), readers must come to terms with how life operates in the real, but less than ideal, world.[29] Eaton calls Ecclesiastes an essay in apologetics that 'defends the life of faith in a generous God by pointing to the grimness of the alternatives'. The pessimistic view of life is a result of God's being left out of the argument. Instead of beginning with the fear of God as a premise, Qohelet starts from a humanist standpoint to show that such a starting point leads to the meaninglessness of life. But then God is introduced and the pessimism gives way to joy and purpose. The statement of 8:12b–13 is the answer of faith.[30] Waltke does not view Ecclesiastes as an intentional apologetic against secularism but as a debate within the mind of Qohelet between scepticism and faith, with faith winning the argument. It is an agonizing struggle of an honest man. The orthodox statements in the book are the key to understanding the book. Ecclesiastes 8:11–13 is a confession of faith against the contrary evidence. The epilogue confirms this confession, for the narrator understands Qohelet's sayings as upright and reliable.[31]

---

[26] Crenshaw 1987: 28.
[27] Barton 1993: 45–48.
[28] Whybray 1982. He calls Qohelet a preacher of joy.
[29] Ogden 2007: 14–18, 26, 148–149; also see Ogden and Zogbo 1997.
[30] Eaton 1983: 44–45, 122–123.
[31] Waltke and Yu 2007: 951, 954–955.

The main problem with the positive view of the message of Qohelet is that the positive statements of the book are given precedence over the negative statements even when the text indicates otherwise. Although the calls to enjoyment are positive exhortations, it is debatable whether they should be seen as theological affirmations of faith. The premise of Qohelet is not secularism, as in the apologetic view of Eaton, but the failure of wisdom itself to produce what is promised. Commentators regularly give the final word to the positive statements when, in reality, Qohelet gives the final word to the negative statements. For example, in discussing 8:11–15, it is hard to understand 8:12b–13 as winning the day when it is followed by 8:14. Qohelet could have written the text differently, but gives the negative statements the final word, a move that happens throughout the autobiography of Qohelet.

Other approaches to the book stress the negative message of Qohelet as he struggles with the meaning of life. The tensions in the book are evidence of the author's intense struggle to understand life. Bartholomew argues that the juxtaposition of *hebel* and joy (the calls to enjoyment) provides contradictory answers to Qohelet's search for meaning that creates a gap that needs to be filled. For example, the tension in 8:11–14 creates a gap that is filled by 12:13–14. This makes the epilogue necessary for understanding the book. The narrator, who adds the epilogue, reads Qohelet positively and agrees with his basic message.[32] Fox argues that one must allow the contradictions of the book to stand in order to grasp the main argument concerning the problem of the meaning of life. Once the contradictions are recognized the way is paved for a more constructive approach to life. In 8:11–14 Qohelet states both sides without resolving them. He knows the principle of retribution and does not deny it (8:12b–13), but is also aware of situations that violate the principle (8:11, 14). Qohelet allows both to stand and is at one time a man of faith who trusts in God and a man of doubt, who knows the realities that violate his beliefs. The frame narrator in 12:9–14 keeps a distance from Qohelet's views even while echoing certain elements of Qohelet's teaching. The certainty of the statements in 12:13–14 contrasts with the uncertainty of all knowledge expressed by Qohelet. Part of the purpose of the epilogue is to allow a reader to affirm the book even if he rejects the views of Qohelet.[33] Longman understands Qohelet to be a wisdom

---

[32] Bartholomew 1998: 238; 2009: 79–82.
[33] Fox 1999: 3, 51, 55–56, 134; 1977: 103–104.

teacher who struggles with the reality that what he observes in life does not support the normative traditions represented in Proverbs. Pessimism permeates the book because Qohelet takes an 'under the sun' approach, a limited human perspective that does not take into account heavenly realities. In 8:11–14 Qohelet contradicts himself as he wrestles with the meaning of life based on his observations of life. The traditional view of divine retribution is stated in 8:12b–13, but he does not affirm it because he states the opposite in 8:14. Qohelet is a confused wise man who is full of doubt and whose thoughts are filled with tensions and contradictions. The epilogue sets forth a view contrary to Qohelet as he shows the dangers of speculative wisdom and states the normative teaching of the OT.[34]

There are certain exegetical decisions that one must make concerning Ecclesiastes that will determine how one understands the view of Qohelet and the message of the book as a whole. The first-person autobiography (1:12 – 12:7) was written by Qohelet. It is likely that someone presented his work by adding a prologue to the work (1:1–11), using Qohelet's own words, and by adding an epilogue that evaluates the work. Everyone agrees the epilogue affirms the traditional teaching of Proverbs, but the key question is how to understand the words of Qohelet. The best approach is to affirm that Qohelet is a wisdom teacher who is struggling with the teaching of Proverbs in the light of what he observes in the world. He does not give priority to wisdom but seeks to explore both wisdom and foolishness as he searches for the meaning of life. He does not use his knowledge of God to solve the problems with which he struggles. The troubles of life dominate his thinking so that he questions the traditional view of divine retribution. This shows the danger of speculative wisdom and is why the frame-narrator presents the words of Qohelet as a warning to show how easy it is to move away from a solid foundation of wisdom. The following points seek to establish this view exegetically.

The role of the calls to enjoyment

Many understand the calls to enjoyment as theological affirmations of faith that are an answer to Qohelet's struggle to find meaning in life. The elements of the calls to enjoyment are gifts from the hand of God (2:24; 3:13; 5:19) and people are exhorted to enjoy the benefits of eating and drinking that come from labour. An important

---

[34] Longman 1998: 32–39.

distinction puts the calls to enjoyment in proper perspective. The main question of the book concerns the results of labour (1:3): 'What profit is there for a person in all his labour at which he labours under the sun?'[35] This question occurs also at 2:22, 3:9 and 5:11. This is the fundamental problem that Qohelet seeks to answer. The term for 'profit' (*yitrôn*) is a commercial term that refers to a surplus or gain, but it has a wider meaning in Ecclesiastes as it is used in reference to wisdom (2:13). When two things are compared, *yitrôn* refers to an advantage one thing might have over another thing (2:13; 3:19; 5:8; 6:8, 11; 7:11–12; 10:10–11). When it is used by itself, it refers to any net gain that allows one to get ahead in life,[36] or to a desired result produced by effort or labour. The basic answer to the question of 1:3 comes in 2:11, where Qohelet considers all his activities and concludes that there is no profit to labour under the sun. This answer does not change throughout the book. There may be some things that give a relative advantage over other things (2:13–17), but there is no real profit to anything. If something seems to provide a net gain or a desired result, it always falls short of the desired outcome.

Although Qohelet denies that there is any profit to labour (2:11), he acknowledges that there is benefit to labour that people should enjoy (2:10). The pleasure he found in labour is called his 'portion' (*ḥēleq*),[37] a term that occurs with several of the calls to enjoyment (3:22; 5:18–19; 9:6, 9; 11:2). The calls to enjoyment are not the profit that comes from labour, because there is no profit from labour (2:11). They are only the portion that one should enjoy from labour. In other words, there is no lasting benefit from labour so one may as well enjoy the limited benefits of this portion that comes from labour. The calls to enjoyment are not on the level of profit and are not the answer of faith.

The epistemology of Qohelet

This question deals with the methodology behind Qohelet's search for meaning in life or the basis upon which Qohelet draws conclusions about life. In Proverbs interaction with God's creation through observation and reflection play a role in drawing conclusions about life (Prov. 24:30–34). However, observation in Proverbs is not the

---

[35] Unless otherwise noted, all translations in the book of Ecclesiastes are my own.
[36] Fox 1999: 112.
[37] This word is translated 'reward' in 2:10 by the ESV, NASB, NIV, and 'lot' in 3:22 and 5:18 by the ESV and NIV.

source of knowledge, because the wise person does not operate from a neutral standpoint when interacting with God's creation. There is a foundation for knowledge grounded in the fear of Yahweh and divine revelation.[38] Observations, reflections and conclusions conform to what the sages believe concerning God.

Experience takes on a more central role for Qohelet in his search for meaning. The first common singular form of the verb 'to see' (rā'â) is used about nineteen times in Ecclesiastes. Six times it is used with the word 'all' (1:14; 4:1; 4:4; 7:15; 8:9, 17), emphasizing the comprehensive nature of the observations. The whole process of investigation is based on observation. Experience is Qohelet's primary source of knowledge.[39] Although there are statements in the book about God and justice that are not based on experience (3:17; 8:12b–13), these statements do not alter his conclusions. The question 'How do you know?' is to be answered, 'Because I saw it.'[40] Bartholomew concludes that Qohelet's epistemology should be described as autonomous and that his use of wisdom to investigate the world means he will use his powers of reason in the light of his observations to understand the world.[41]

Qohelet does not privilege wisdom in his search. He states several things about his search in 1:13, including the fact that he is totally committed to a personal, disciplined pursuit[42] ('I devoted myself') and that he is going to carry out his search 'by wisdom'. Wisdom here is not the object of the search but is used as an instrument in the search.[43] Qohelet also makes wisdom the object of his search (1:17). He wants to investigate how wisdom works and the consequences that come from wisdom. But he takes his investigation a step further – he not only wants to 'understand wisdom'; he also wants to 'understand maddening folly' (1:17).[44] In other words, he seeks to investigate 'maddening folly' and the consequences that come from it. This phrase occurs in 2:12, 7:25, 9:3 and 10:13 and is also associated with

---

[38] Waltke 2004: 55.

[39] Fox 1999: 76–77.

[40] Ibid. 85.

[41] Bartholomew 2009: 269–277. Bartholomew 2009 and Fox 1999 have the best discussions of Qohelet's epistemology. For a critical review of epistemological studies in Ecclesiastes see O'Dowd 2013: 196–201. He argues that epistemological questions arise out of what it means to be human and that the Pentateuch and Jewish wisdom literature are the most fruitful contexts for examining Qohelet.

[42] Longman 1998: 78.

[43] Seow 1997: 120.

[44] The phrase 'maddening folly' consists of the two words 'madness' and 'folly' that are taken as a hendiadys and translated as one phrase.

wickedness (7:25; 9:3; 10:13). Hubbard concludes that the phrase refers to behaving badly, wildly or irresponsibly.[45]

Qohelet's preliminary conclusions concerning wisdom are negative, whether wisdom is the instrument in the search for meaning (1:13–15) or the object of the search for meaning (1:16–18). The main point is that Qohelet does not privilege the place of wisdom but puts it on the same level as maddening folly in order to investigate both of them. Instead of starting from the standpoint that there are two ways of life where only one way is correct (as in Proverbs), he starts from the standpoint that both ways need to be investigated to see whether either way is beneficial.[46] Qohelet does not operate with the same foundation of wisdom as in the book of Proverbs.

The phrase 'under the sun'

This phrase occurs in the book twenty-nine times. Parallel phrases include 'under heaven' (1:13; 2:3; 3:1) and 'upon the earth' (8:14–16; 11:2). It focuses attention on this world over against the heavenly world, which is God's domain.[47] It is commonly used with words for human activity ('āśâ) and human 'toil' ('āmāl), along with the verb 'to see' (rā'â), indicating the world people experience while they are alive, the observable world of work and human activity. This phrase restricts Qohelet's thinking to this earthly life and the limited horizon of an earthly perspective apart from divine revelation. Qohelet does not allow the theological reflections he makes to correct the conclusions he draws on the basis of his observations. Qohelet could have used a theological reflection about God, or what he knew about God, to solve the problems he was investigating (3:18–22; 9:1–6), but each time he allows his empirical observation to stand without correction. God is never brought in as a solution to the problems that plague Qohelet. These factors support the empirical epistemology of Qohelet.

The role and meaning of hebel

The word hebel is used about thirty-eight times in the book.[48] No other word is used as frequently as this word. It occurs in a superlative

---

45 Hubbard 1991: 64.
46 Qohelet denies the doctrine of the two ways taught in Proverbs in 7:15–18.
47 Fox 1999: 165.
48 Ogden 2007: 21.

sense in the motto of the book that frames the book (1:2; 12:8).[49] It is also the word that Qohelet uses to draw conclusions about the various aspects of life he examines. But what does he mean by the word *hebel*?

The basic meaning of *hebel* is 'breath', as seen in its use in Isaiah 57:13, where it parallels the word 'wind' (*rûaḥ*). Most of the time it is used in a metaphorical sense, either referring to time or to the meaning of the world or activity in the world. On the temporal level it stresses the idea that something is fleeting. Fredericks argues for this view because the emphasis on death reinforces the brevity of life.[50] Others understand *hebel* related to meaning that can have several nuances. Some understand *hebel* to mean 'incomprehensible', a meaning that stresses either that life is hard to understand because humans are unable to grasp fully the meaning of God's ways, or that life is not able to be understood by humans. The former approach translates *hebel* as 'enigma'[51] and the latter as 'vanity' (in the sense of 'futility' or 'without purpose') or 'meaningless'.[52] The view that *hebel* connotes 'futility' or 'meaningless' has the support of some ancient versions (the LXX and the Vg) and many English translations (KJV, NKJV, NASB, NIV, NRSV, ESV). Both Christiansen and Longman examine the use of *hebel* outside Ecclesiastes, where it occurs about thirty-two times. Both of them conclude that although *hebel* can mean 'fleeting', it almost always designates something that is false, futile or empty or is used in parallel with those concepts.[53]

The best way to understand *hebel* in Ecclesiastes is in the sense of 'futility', which can be expressed by the word 'senseless'.[54] The scenarios in life that Qohelet examines do not make sense and do not accomplish what is expected. Its superlative use in 1:2 and 12:8, and its constant use throughout the book, shows that *hebel* is the main theme of the autobiography of Qohelet (contra Ogden). Its use with 'all' or 'everything' implies that there is a meaning common to the

---

[49] The superlative indicates something complete, absolute and unqualified (Whybray 1989: 34–35).

[50] Fredericks 1993: 30; Fredericks and Estes 2010: 50–54.

[51] Ogden 2007: 17.

[52] Longman 1998: 62–64. Fox (1999: 36–42) argues that *hebel* refers to what is contrary to reason and prefers the translation 'absurd'.

[53] Christiansen 1998: 79–80. Longman (1998: 62–64) notes that even in passages where *hebel* may mean 'fleeting' (Pss 144:4; 39:4–5, 11; Job 7:16; Prov. 31:30), the connotation of 'meaningless' is not out of the question.

[54] Fox 1999: 31–32. He suggests the meaning of 'senseless' after acknowledging some of the drawbacks to the word 'absurd'.

various occurrences of the term so that, for the most part, it should be translated by the same word throughout the book.[55]

Apart from the linguistic use of *hebel*, there are other reasons for understanding *hebel* as expressing the idea of futility.[56] It fits the empirical epistemology of Qohelet that undermines confidence in knowledge. It fits the view of the calls to enjoyment as being all that one can hope for in a world where there is no profit, or lasting benefit, to labour. It fits the limited perspective of an 'under the sun' view that does not move above the horizon of human life to solve the problems of life. It fits a search for meaning in life that does not privilege wisdom but also wants to experience the implications of maddening folly. The phrase 'chasing the wind', used in conjunction with *hebel*, also supports the idea of futility. Even though commentators understand this phrase in a number of different ways,[57] the best understanding is that it is futile to try to catch the wind.[58]

The breakdown of the deed–consequence relationship

Another matter that supports the negative 'under the sun' message of the autobiography of Qohelet and the meaning of *hebel* as futile is how Qohelet understands the deed–consequence relationship. The breakdown of divine retribution is a major theme, as he keeps coming back to it throughout his autobiography (2:15–16, 26; 3:16–21; 6:1–2; 7:15–18; 8:10–14; 9:1–6). The reason that human activity and labour do not achieve a net gain or the desired result is that the deed–consequence relationship does not work, at least not consistently enough to count on it. The righteous and the wise do not receive the promised blessings in life and the fool and the wicked do not receive the expected negative consequences in life. Life should not work like this and so he concludes it is 'futile' (*hebel*) to live a righteous life. Wisdom does not produce what it promises.

[55] Fox 1999: 36; Christiansen 1998: 90. Although it is possible that in a few passages later in the book when Qohelet speaks of the period of youth before the coming of death, *hebel* may have the connotation of 'fleeting' (11:8, 10), even in those passages the point seems to be that the period of youth is futile.
[56] Meek (2013: 241–256) argues that there is an intertextual relationship between *hebel* and the name Abel in Gen. 4 that Qohelet uses to argue that the discontinuity that is experienced in life is the same discontinuity that righteous Abel experienced when he was unjustly murdered by his brother Cain.
[57] See Belcher 2017a: 55–57 for the different ways commentators understand this phrase.
[58] Longman 1998: 81–82. He also appeals to Hos. 12:1.

A summary of the conclusions

Qohelet is part of the wisdom tradition of Israel but he wrestles with how normative wisdom teaching, as represented in Proverbs, matches what he observes in life. He writes a first-person account (1:12 – 12:7) that chronicles his search for meaning. It becomes clear, however, that the foundation for his search is flawed. He operates with an empirical methodology that does not privilege wisdom because he examines both wisdom and folly to see where each will lead. He operates with a limited human horizon that does not use what he knows about God to solve the dilemmas he finds in life. If one starts with an empirical methodology and draws conclusions based on observations apart from a theological foundation, then life will appear to be futile and wisdom will fail to produce what is expected. Thus there is no 'profit' (*yitrôn*) to labour so one may as well enjoy the limited 'portion' (*ḥēleq*) that comes from labour expressed in the calls to enjoyment. This is all one can hope for in a world that does not make sense or meet one's expectations.

The autobiography of Qohelet is an illustration of the dangers of speculative wisdom and how easy it is to move away from a solid foundation as one wrestles with the problems of life. This danger is why someone would present the words of Qohelet to his son (12:12) as an example of how easy it is to fall into the trap of speculative wisdom. The experiences and struggles of life can easily overwhelm people, so that they become disoriented to the true foundation of life. He points his son to the answer in 12:13–14.[59]

[59] For the specific view that Qohelet is Solomon (both a king and a wise man), and that he wrote the first-person account during the period of life when his wives turned his heart away from Yahweh (1 Kgs 11), see Belcher 2017a: 14–29, 51–66.

Chapter Nine

The message of Qohelet

As the hermeneutical basis for the 'under the sun' view was covered in the previous chapter, this chapter will seek to develop a consistent 'under the sun' view, which is foundational to the next chapter that will discuss the theology of the book and how to preach or teach the 'under the sun' view. The following simple outline will be followed:

1. Prologue: exploration of the nature of the world (1:1–11)
2. The search for meaning under the sun (1:12 – 6:9)
3. Human limitations concerning knowledge (6:10 – 10:20)
4. Living with the uncertainty of the future (11:1 – 12:7)

Prologue: exploration of the nature of the world (1:1–11)

Qohelet is presented to the reader in a prologue that is part of the third-person frame (1:1–11; 12:8–14). The purpose of the prologue is not only to introduce Qohelet but to prepare the reader for his message.[1] The superscription (1:1) introduces the one who will be speaking in 1:12 – 12:7. The motto (1:2) is a summary of Qohelet's thought, stated in an emphatic way and meant to be taken as comprehensive. The translation 'utterly senseless' is a superlative that represents the ultimate conclusion of Qohelet concerning life. The key question of the book (1:3) sets out the fundamental problem that Qohelet seeks to answer. It is a question about human labour but includes other human activities associated with life. Qohelet will answer this question (2:10–11) but the prologue ends with a section on the futility of the natural world (1:4–7) and the futility of the human world (1:8–11).

The futility of the natural world (1:4–7)

The cyclical nature of natural events on the earth is emphasized in order to demonstrate the futility of those cyclical processes. Although

---

[1] See the previous chapter, where introductory questions concerning Ecclesiastes were addressed.

the fleeting nature of the generations of humanity in contrast to the permanence of the earth is the focus of 1:4, the whole section contrasts the cyclical movements of activities on the earth with the permanence of the earth. The participles throughout emphasize repeated, continuous activity. The continual rising and setting of the sun is stated in 1:5 with the use of the negative phrase 'it pants toward its place'. Although the word 'pants' can have the positive meaning of longing or desire (Ps. 119:131; Job 7:2),[2] emphasizing that the sun eagerly moves toward its next appearance, the verb also refers to a weary panting (Isa. 42:14; Jer. 2:24).[3] The blowing of the wind as it goes round and round is described in 1:6. The participles stress the continuous round and round nature of the blowing of the wind. Also, the delay of the subject until the end of the verse gives a deliberate, worn out, monotonous sense. The movement of the wind in circles gives the impression of much activity with little accomplishment.[4] The continual flowing of the streams into the sea is described in 1:7. Although Whybray argues that the cyclical movement of the water describes a beneficial phenomenon of the redistribution of the water over the earth,[5] nothing is said about what is accomplished by the flowing of the streams into the sea. What is mentioned is that the continual flowing of the streams into the sea has no impact on the sea because the sea is not full. The activity is futile because it does not produce anything.[6]

The futile activity of the natural world in 1:4–7 is seen when this passage is compared with other OT passages that speak of the purposeful nature of these activities. In Psalm 19:5 the sun goes forth as a strong man running a race, full of vigour, reflecting the glory of God, but in Ecclesiastes 1:5 the sun pants along, tired and weary. In Psalm 104:3–4 God directs the wind as his messenger to accomplish his purposes, but in Ecclesiastes 1:6 the wind goes round and round and round in monotonous repetition with no purpose stated. In Psalm 104:10–11 the rivers are sent forth to give drink to the animals and to cause the grass to grow for the cattle, but in Ecclesiastes 1:7 the rivers do not accomplish anything. Thus Ecclesiastes 1:4–7 is a demonstration of the motto that everything is futile or senseless.

---

[2] Whybray 1989: 41.
[3] The negative view is supported by the LXX ('drags') and the Tg ('crawls').
[4] Longman 1998: 69.
[5] Whybray 1989: 43.
[6] Murphy 1992: 8; Seow 1997: 115.

The futility of the human world (1:8–11)

The first clause in verse 8, 'All things are weary', summarizes what has gone before and anticipates what is coming next in the world of human experience. Three negatives are used to describe the futile actions of speech, seeing and hearing. Human words never achieve their purpose.[7] The seeing of the eye and the hearing of the ear never achieve a final goal or result. Thus 1:8 is a judgment on the empirical possibilities of human knowledge, which are limited and do not achieve their desired result.

Human history comes into view in 1:9–11. The keynote of these verses is that there is nothing new under the sun. It is difficult to give these verses a positive meaning because the emphasis is on the paralysing repetition of the past. The fact that something seems new is due to the faulty faculties of human memory. History is going nowhere and individuals are destined to live lives that never achieve fulfilment.[8] Such a view contrasts with other teaching in the OT where history is understood as controlled by God and moving toward a goal. The possibility of something new is seen in the exhortations to sing a new song (Ps. 96:1), the possibility of a new covenant (Jer. 31:31) and the prospect of new heavens and earth (Isa. 65:17). To say there is nothing new under the sun negates these possibilities. The opening words of Qohelet indicate the direction of his thinking concerning the futility of the things he will examine in the first-person autobiography.

The search for meaning under the sun (1:12 – 6:9)

The search for profit to labour (1:12 – 2:26)

The first-person autobiography begins in 1:12 and the first call to enjoyment comes in 2:24–26. This section is Qohelet's attempt to answer the question of 1:3. Qohelet's initial thoughts in 1:12–18 can be divided into two parallel sections that follow a similar pattern (1:12–15 and 1:16–18). Qohelet makes a statement about himself (1:12; 1:16), a statement about the search itself (1:13; 1:17a), a preliminary conclusion about the search (1:14; 1:17b) and a proverbial saying that supports the conclusion (1:15; 1:18). The concluding

---

[7] Crenshaw 1987: 66.
[8] Longman 1998: 72.

proverb of 1:18 affirms that wisdom and knowledge will not solve the problems of life but only increase a person's vexation and sorrow. This agrees with the previous conclusion that everything under the sun takes on the character of 'futility' (*hebel*) and a chasing after the wind (1:14). There is no hope that this will ever change (1:15).

The focus of Qohelet's search in 2:1–11 is pleasure and the things in life that bring pleasure. The word translated 'pleasure' (*śimḥâ*) can have the connotation 'joy', but its use in 2:1–11 is more in line with the idea of pleasure or enjoyment. Such activities are associated with kingly pursuits and connected to the key question of 1:3 because they are termed 'labour' (2:10–11). Qohelet urges himself to 'experience pleasure' and 'enjoy the good life' as part of his search for meaning. But he can hardly refrain from offering his conclusion that these activities will be *hebel* because they do not really achieve anything of lasting value (2:2). The focus of his investigation is laid out in 2:3: 'giving my body up to wine' and 'grabbing hold of folly'. The mention of wine includes activities that accompany drinking, such as feasting. The mention of 'folly' shows that Qohelet is more than just a connoisseur of fine wine, but is willing to explore activities that are called foolish. His pursuit of these things is tempered with the phrase 'my heart guiding me by wisdom'.[9] He will not get so involved in the investigation of pleasure that he is unable to weigh the significance of what is happening.[10] He will indulge in pleasure without being consumed by it. The fact that Qohelet is willing to examine folly shows that his perspective is not the same as that of the sages in Proverbs, who operate with the doctrine of two ways and seek to avoid folly at all costs.[11]

Qohelet gives an account of his great achievements in his search for meaning (2:4–8). These kinds of achievements bring glory and honour to kings. They include great building activities (houses, gardens and parks), great possessions (servants, flocks and wealth) and entertainment (singers and concubines[12]). He offers a summary of his findings in 2:9–11. His immediate evaluation is that he received enjoyment from all these activities. This enjoyment is called his 'portion' (*ḥēleq*) and people should enjoy this result of their labour. The specific content of this enjoyment will be filled out in the calls to

---

9 Wisdom refers to the methodology of observation, reflection and the drawing of conclusions used by the sages (Ogden and Zogbo 1997: 53).

10 Longman 1998: 89.

11 Bartholomew 2009: 131.

12 For a justification of the translation 'concubine' see Belcher 2017a: 105–106.

enjoyment. Although Qohelet encourages people to enjoy this portion, the results of labour do not attain to the level of 'profit' (*yitrôn*). Qohelet offers his ultimate judgment in 2:11, where he concludes that there is no profit, or lasting benefit, to labour because 'all is senseless and chasing after wind'.

Qohelet examines in 2:12–18 whether wisdom has any advantage over folly. One would think that if meaning were to be found anywhere, it would be found in wisdom as distinguished from folly. The way Qohelet evaluates wisdom and the conclusions that he draws are a paradigm for the way he evaluates many things. Qohelet has observed that wisdom has an advantage over folly just as light has an advantage over darkness. Specifically, wisdom allows people to see where they are going. The fool, on the other hand, goes through life stumbling over the obstacles in life because he walks in darkness. The person with wisdom can see those obstacles in order to avoid them (as in Prov. 22:3). And yet Qohelet also observes that the contrast between wisdom and folly breaks down because death has an impact on the wise and the fool the same way. Qohelet is concerned that there is no lasting remembrance of the wise or the fool after death, a contrast to the teaching of Psalm 112:6 and Proverbs 10:7. But Qohelet is also concerned about the manner of death as he exclaims with some desperation, 'How will the wise die? Like the fool' (2:16). One of the benefits of wisdom is long life (Prov. 3:13–18), but if there is no distinction between the death of the wise and the fool, then death comes to both randomly regardless of how they have lived their lives. Qohelet brings this section to a close with a statement that shows his deep frustration at the way things work in this life under the sun: 'I hated life' (2:17). Although wisdom has a relative advantage over folly, it fails to produce any distinctions between the wise and the fool in the manner of their death. Death relativizes the value of wisdom and makes everything *hebel* and a chasing after wind.

Qohelet next examines the results of labour in his search for meaning under the sun (2:18–23). Some form of the word 'labour' (*'āmāl*) occurs nine times in this section and can refer either to the work itself or the results of the work. Qohelet has already concluded that there is no profit to labour, but there is a portion that should be enjoyed. This portion includes material possessions and property that can be passed on to someone else (2:21). Perhaps meaning can be found in the results of labour. Qohelet wastes no time in giving his conclusion 'Then I hated all the results of my labour' (2:18). Qohelet's negative conclusion is due to the fact that someone works hard all his life and then leaves the results of his labour to someone else who did not work for it. The added problem is that no one can know whether the person who inherits the results of labour will be wise or a fool (2:19). A fool can quickly destroy what someone has worked a lifetime to achieve. Working hard does not seem worth the effort and is given the verdict of 'senseless' (*hebel*). This confirms that there is no profit to labour; not even the portion from labour offers any lasting benefits. The main thing that results from labour is sorrow, vexation and very little rest (2:23).

The first call to enjoyment comes in 2:24–26 after Qohelet has concluded that there is no profit to labour but that there is a portion to enjoy (2:10–11). Even though that portion fails to provide any consolation at death (2:18–23), it is to be enjoyed during this life. The phrase 'there is nothing better than' is not a rousing endorsement or the answer to the search for meaning, but is all one can expect from a world that is characterized by futility. One might as well enjoy the limited benefit that comes from labour because it is all that one can enjoy in this futile life under the sun. But does not the fact that these things come from the hand of God give a more positive evaluation of these things? Qohelet's view of God will become clear in other passages of the book, but there is a glimpse here of his ultimate conclusion concerning God's involvement in the world. Qohelet seems to state in 2:26 the positive, traditional view that God gives wisdom, knowledge and joy to the one who pleases him, but to the sinner gives the work of gathering and collecting to benefit the one who pleases God. This sentiment sounds very much like Proverbs 13:22:

> A good man leaves an inheritance to his children's children,
>   but the sinner's wealth is laid up for the righteous.

The righteous person is rewarded and the sinner ends up being frustrated by having his or her goods given to the righteous. And yet the hope that life might turn out this way is dashed, as Qohelet ends this section with 'This also is senseless and a chasing after wind.' This *hebel* judgment should not be limited to the work of the sinner but includes the whole account of work and the enjoyment of the results of labour. Thus one might as well enjoy the portion from labour because there is no lasting benefit from it in this dark world 'under the sun'.

The search for understanding the role of human beings (3:1–22)

Ecclesiastes 3 is connected to what has gone before in many ways. After the introductory poem, the question concerning profit from labour is asked again (3:9). Also, 3:10 reflects 1:13, 3:14–15 reflects 1:9, and 3:12 and 22 reflect 2:24–26. Thus 3:1–22 carries on the search begun in the first section of the book. And yet there is more of an emphasis on God in this chapter. God is mentioned four times earlier in the book, but in chapter 3 God is mentioned eight times. The question concerning profit to labour is broadened to include the proper role of human beings in relation to God. Does God make any difference to the questions raised and the answers given concerning labour and the results of labour? Although God is more prominent in this section, he does not provide Qohelet with the answers to his questions. Frustration related to labour and its results is still prevalent, and at the end of the chapter, because the future is uncertain, the role of humanity is not settled.

Ecclesiastes 3:1–15 sets forth a poem on time (3:1–8) and then reflects again on the question of labour (3:9–15). The purpose of the poem is to set forth a positive picture of the world in accordance with traditional wisdom teaching. It is a world that is purposeful and understandable so that people can make wise decisions. All the times listed, except for the first pair ('a time to be born and a time to die'), speak of times that require human action to do something. For example, there may be a time to plant but if people do not act at the right time, the opportunity is lost. The poem presents the traditional view that wisdom understands the right time to act (Prov. 10:4–5; 15:23; 20:18; 25:11). When the time is right, human action is required.[13]

Qohelet responds to the poem on time with a question about profit from labour (3:9) followed by an observation about God's works in the world (3:10–11) and two conclusions (3:12–13 and 3:14–15). If Qohelet has already answered the question about profit from labour in 2:11, why does he ask the question again here? The poem on time acknowledges that there are appropriate times for people to take action. Surely in such a world there would be profit to human activity. Qohelet responds to the question of 3:9 with an empirical observation

---

[13] For an analysis of the meaning of the fourteen pairs of opposites in the poem see Belcher 2017a: 138–140.

(3:10–11) concerning the task God has given human beings (see also 1:13). Are human beings able to act at the right time in order to produce profit? The answer is 'no' because it is impossible to act at the right time (3:11). Even though God has made everything appropriate for its time and has put eternity into the hearts of people, the conclusion is that people are not able to understand what God is doing in the world. Certainly God understands how the times work and when it is appropriate to act. Also, God has given people a desire to understand how the world works. The word translated 'eternity' ('ōlām) can mean 'totality', or having a desire to move beyond the fragmentary knowledge of our immediate situation in order to understand the character and purpose of the events of the world.[14] In other words, Qohelet asserts that humans have a desire to see how events fit together so that wise decisions can be made.[15] The problem is that 'people cannot discover the work God does from beginning to end' (3:11b). The desire to understand the world in conjunction with the inability to understand what God is doing in the world leads to frustration. The wisdom teaching of being able to act at the right time does not work. Although Qohelet does not specifically state that there is no profit from labour, there are enough parallels with the previous section (1:12 – 2:26) that such a conclusion is inevitable. Even though God is brought into the picture in a more prominent way, Qohelet's view that there is no profit to labour does not change.

Qohelet draws two conclusions based on his observations (3:12–13 and 3:14–15). Both conclusions are introduced by the verb 'to know', translated 'I perceived'. The first conclusion is another call to enjoyment. There is no profit to human activity because people cannot understand what God is doing in the world, so the best response is to enjoy the limited results that come from labour. The second conclusion does not focus on how people should respond but on why people will never be able to understand God's work in the world. God's work is permanent, unchangeable and beyond human comprehension. The last clause of 3:15 is difficult, but one explanation that fits the context is that God seeks to do things he has already

---

[14] Longman 1998: 121; Bartholomew 2009: 167.

[15] It is unlikely that Qohelet has in view life beyond this life (see the comments on Eccl. 9:10). Qohelet operates with an 'under the sun' perspective that is limited to life in this world. The knowledge of God is not used to solve the problems with which he wrestles.

done.[16] Longman paraphrases it as God makes things happen over and over again.[17] This view reinforces things Qohelet has stated earlier concerning the fact that there is nothing new under the sun, except now it is clear that God is behind the repetitive nature of events in the world.[18]

The fear of God occurs for the first time in Ecclesiastes 3:14. There is a tendency to assume that the fear of God in the autobiography of Qohelet means the same thing as the fear of Yahweh in the book of Proverbs. But if Qohelet does not find any answers to his quest for meaning 'under the sun', and if God is not the answer to his problems, then it is hard to see how the fear of God refers to a reverence and awe of God. Qohelet has already concluded that wisdom fails to live up to its expectations (2:12–17) and so it makes sense that the fear of God is not the beginning point of wisdom. Rather, the fear of God is the intended purpose God wants people to have in the light of the nature of his indiscernible work in the world. If there is no profit to human labour, then people are left in a state of uncertainty when it comes to God's works in the world. This is not the fear of God that leads to wisdom in knowing how to make right decisions, but is a fear that relates to not knowing what God will do or how he will act.

The problem of injustice questions God's role in the world (3:16–22)

Qohelet moves from a discussion of the inability of people to discover what God is doing in the world to the problem of injustice. Injustice is part of the reason that people cannot understand what God is doing because it hinders people from understanding the plan of God. Qohelet sets forth an observation of personal experience in 3:16 ('I observed'), followed by two reflections in 3:17 and 3:18–21 ('I said to myself'), and concludes with a final observation in 3:22 ('I perceived'). The problem that Qohelet observes is the prominence of injustice where one would expect to find justice, such as in the law courts and the city gates.[19] Qohelet's first reflection is a theological statement about God's justice:

[16] Fox 1999: 213–214. See Belcher 2017a: 150–152 for the various options.
[17] Longman 1998: 113.
[18] Fox 1999: 213. He comments that 3:15a uses 1:9a to restate 3:14 to show that what is in view in 3:14–15 is the recurrence of the same class of events. What was not stated in 1:9 becomes clear in 3:15: God is the one who stands behind the repetitive nature of the events of the world.
[19] Ogden and Zogbo 1997: 110.

God will judge the righteous and the wicked
because there is a time for every activity and
for every work too.

Qohelet's second reflection in 3:18–21 is a statement on the relationship between humans and animals: the same fate of death awaits both humans and animals. Both have the same breath and both return to dust at death. The key, however, is that he does not see any distinction between humans and animals at death. He states, 'human beings have no advantage over the animals' and he asks the question 'Who knows whether the human breath of life ascends upward or whether the breath of life of animals descends downward?' Although the question 'Who knows?' in some places of Scripture remains open to possible response for human good (Joel 2:14; Jon. 3:9), this question in Ecclesiastes is a closed question with the implied answer that no one really knows.[20] Thus no one really knows whether there is a difference at death between the spirit of humans and the spirit of animals in terms of their destination. Not only does injustice plague life on this earth; there is no confidence that at death things will be made right.

Qohelet's theological reflection and his anthropological reflection are placed next to each other. It is significant that he does not allow his theological reflection about God's judgment to override the negative anthropological reflection that there is no difference between humans and animals. In other words, he does not resolve the difference between humans and animals by appealing to God's justice, either in this life or the life to come. In fact, 3:19–21 ends with a rhetorical question that is not answered in a positive way because no one really knows if there is a difference between humans and animals at death. The negative anthropological reflection gets the last word over the theological reflection. God is not a solution to the problems Qohelet observes.

The call to enjoyment in 3:22 sets the enjoyment of the present in the context of the uncertainty of the future. Because there is no difference between humans and animals in their death, the best one can do is to 'enjoy his activities'. This limited enjoyment is called a person's 'portion' (*ḥēleq*). Qohelet ends this section with another question that expects a negative answer. No one knows what is coming in the future, so the best option is to enjoy one's activities now.

[20] Crenshaw 1986: 274–288.

The frustration of unfulfilled expectations (4:1 – 6:9)

This section is composed of smaller units dealing with a variety of topics, including how to approach God in worship (5:1–7), an important passage because it deals directly with Qohelet's thoughts about God. It has been understood in both positive and negative ways. Placing this passage in the context of this section will help in understanding what Qohelet is saying about God. Although some interpret the individual units of this section independently of each other,[21] there is a theme that runs throughout this section. Every matter that Qohelet covers falls short of what people would expect. In other words, all the topics lead to the frustration of unfulfilled expectations.

This section can be divided into the following units: political power (4:1–3), labour and its relationships (4:4–12), political power (4:13–16), one's relationship to God (5:1–7), political power (5:8–9) and wealth (5:10 – 6:9). Not only does wealth not satisfy, but also a variety of relationships do not satisfy because they also fail to live up to expectations. Qohelet deals with the major relationships in life and finds them all to fall short of offering satisfaction.

The common subject of 4:4–12 is labour (vv. 4, 6, 8–9). Qohelet identifies envy as the motivation behind labour, characterized as *hebel* and a chasing after wind. Instead of advocating the success of labour, motivated by envy (4:4), or the path of laziness that leads to destruction (4:5), Qohelet presents a way of moderation with a 'better-than' saying in 4:6. Labour may produce results but it comes with hard work so that it is better to have a handful of quietness than two hands full of toil. Labour is also the subject of 4:7–12, with an emphasis on relationships. The lonely miser (4:7–8) has no son or brother; and even though he works all the time, he is never satisfied with the product of his hard work. Loneliness can be overcome by the benefits of companionship (4:9–12). Several situations are described to show that it is better to have someone who can help you than to labour alone. It is significant that there is no *hebel* judgment following the description of the benefits of companionship. In fact, companionship answers several of the problems highlighted in chapter 4. Companionship could bring true comfort in facing oppression (4:1), it could curtail the envy that motivates labour (4:4) and it would broaden the perspective of the lonely labourer (4:7–8). And yet strength in numbers

---

[21] Whybray 1989: 81–91; Longman 1998.

brings only a relative advantage because the fleeting nature of political power shows that mere numbers cannot be counted on as a sure thing (4:13–16).[22]

Passages dealing with political power frame chapter 4 (4:1–3, 13–16), and the subject is also covered immediately after the passage talking about a relationship with God (5:8–9). The shortcomings of political power are emphasized. The oppressive nature of political power is a misuse of power that leaves people suffering with no one to comfort them (4:1–3). Qohelet concludes that death is better than being alive, but that it is even better never to have been born. There is no hope of justice after death held out to the oppressed. To face oppression without the help of companionship is unbearable. The fleeting nature of political power is covered in 4:13–16. Although there are many questions related to this short story,[23] it gives an account of someone who starts from a lowly social position but becomes king through wisdom, and then gathers to himself a large popular following. Popularity obtained by wisdom, however, is not permanent because it is easily lost. Thus the success of wisdom is short-lived because it is not able to secure the throne for very long. Popularity trumps wisdom and popularity is fleeting because people are fickle. The final text dealing with political power (5:8–9)[24] comes right after Qohelet discusses God. This passage covers corruption among government officials who are more concerned about maintaining their own position, and the position of their colleagues, than they are about justice and righteousness. This is a structural problem because more than one official is involved.[25] The best view of 5:9 is that it reinforces the negative view of 5:8. The king himself is part of the corruption, as he benefits from the produce of the fields. The negative view of political power fits with the way political power is presented in the other passages in this section.

Approaching God in worship: reverence or caution? (5:1–7)

Qohelet moves from reflections about life based on his observations to admonitions based on imperatives concerning the proper behaviour

---

[22] Seow 1997: 190; Bartholomew 2009: 190.

[23] For a discussion of the issues and interpretations of this text see Belcher 2017a: 180–187.

[24] The Hebrew text is 5:7–8. V. 8 has been called an 'insuperable crux' (Gordis 1955: 240). For a discussion of the problems and the various interpretations see Belcher 2017a: 202–209.

[25] Provan 2001: 126.

in worship. The main issue in this passage is how one should understand the intent of Qohelet's admonitions. Some argue for a positive
meaning to this passage. For example, one should approach the
temple with caution because of the majesty of God who is in heaven.
Qohelet warns his readers not to badger God with superfluous talk
(similar to Matt. 6:7–8).[26] One should also come ready to obey the
law that comes from the instructions of the priests (there is a reference
to Deut. 23:21–23 in the discussion of vows). The fear of God nails
down the proper attitude of worship. Others argue for a negative
meaning to the passage. Qohelet's God is a distant despot, prayer is
an activity that is useless and the fear of God is expressing the belief
that it is dangerous to approach God (Exod. 19:12).[27]

It is difficult to solve this issue because the tone of Qohelet is not
clear. Also, one's assumptions concerning the rest of the book are a
factor in how one understands this passage. Although the view that
Qohelet's God is a distant despot and that prayer is a useless activity
may be too negative, an argument can be made that the basic attitude
expressed toward God here is caution before God in the matter of
prayer (5:1–3) and vows (5:4–7). Caution before God is expressed in
the first admonition, 'Watch your step whenever you go to the house
of God' (5:1). The point is driven home by a comparison with fools
who lack caution before God, 'for they do not recognize that they are
doing wrong' (5:1). Restraint in speech before God is emphasized in
5:2. It is difficult to listen if one is always talking. The reason one
should be cautious before God is that 'God is in heaven and you are
on the earth'. This could be a positive statement of God's sovereign
majesty or it could be a reference to God's distance from humanity.
The latter seems more likely because Qohelet does not express any
passion for God or confidence in God. The psalms, on the other hand,
are full of passion as the psalmist approaches God with questions,
complaints and pleadings. For example, Psalm 115 expresses God's
transcendence, but the psalmist is also concerned about the attitude
of the nations and how God differs from the idols of the nations.
Great concern is expressed in the question the psalmist asks (Ps.
115:2) and in his exhortation for Israel to trust God (Ps. 115:9–11).
Qohelet's attitude is much more reserved.

The same attitude is expressed in the section on vows (5:4–7).
Scripture is clear that it is a serious matter to make a vow before God

[26] Murphy 1992: 50.
[27] Lauha 1978: 98–99; Loader 1986: 58–69.

159

and not to fulfil it (Deut. 23:21; Prov. 20:25). Qohelet emphasizes the negative side of not paying a vow: 'Why should God be angry with your words and destroy the work of your hands?' (5:6). These verses end with an admonition in the form of an imperative: 'Instead, fear God' (5:7). The reserved attitude of Qohelet toward God agrees with the idea of caution toward a God who gives human beings a grievous task (1:13) and who makes it impossible to understand his work in the world (3:11). Qohelet does not have enough confidence in God to appeal to his character or to his work to help him solve his problems (3:16–21). Just as labour, political power and wealth (see the next section) take on the character of unfulfilled expectations, so God is not a solution to the difficulties of life.

Unfulfilled expectations related to wealth (5:10 – 6:9)

Qohelet expresses the idea that wealth does not satisfy in several ways. First, he specifically states this premise (5:10) and argues that wealth brings with it cares and worries that make it difficult for the wealthy to sleep (5:11–12). Second, an example story (5:13–17) demonstrates the disappointing nature of wealth because it can easily be lost and it is no benefit to a person at death. In fact, the pursuit of wealth can make life miserable (5:17). Third, the call to enjoyment in 5:18–20 highlights that it is God's gift if a person is able to enjoy the 'portion' (ḥēleq) that comes from labour. The reason God gives people the ability to enjoy this gift is also stated: 'For one will not ponder the days of his life because God keeps him occupied with the enjoyment of his heart' (5:20). God's role is emphasized in these verses. God gives a person the few days of his life on earth (5:18), God gives riches and wealth (5:19), God gives the power to enjoy riches and wealth (5:19), and God gives a person the ability to enjoy his portion from labour (5:19). The reason God does all this is to distract a person from pondering the disappointing nature of life on this earth. Although this enjoyment is dependent on God, it is meant to distract people from the futility of life. Fourth, Qohelet sets forth the tragedy of someone to whom God does not give the ability to enjoy the gift of wealth (6:1–9). Qohelet is passionate about this, as he calls it a 'sickening tragedy' (6:2). If there is no profit from labour, then all people have left to enjoy is the portion that comes from labour. If God withholds enjoyment of this portion, there is nothing left in life and it is better never to have lived (6:3).

Human limitations concerning knowledge (6:10 – 10:20)

Ecclesiastes 6:10–12 acts as a transition from the first part of Qohelet's autobiography to the second part. Connections to the first part of the book include the cyclical and determined nature of the world (6:10a and 1:9–10), the nature of humanity (6:10b and 3:11), and the nature of God (6:10c and 3:14–15, 18). The two questions of 6:12 introduce the second part of the book. The first question, 'Who knows what is good?', is addressed in 7:1 – 8:17. The second question, 'Who can tell what will come in the future?', is addressed in 9:1 – 10:20. Qohelet moves from pessimism in the first part of the book to scepticism in the second part. In the first part the main question is whether there is profit to labour. In the second part the main question is 'Who knows?'[28] Qohelet questions the ability of human beings to understand the world in which they live, which is a challenge to the ability and achievement of wisdom.

Who knows what is good? (6:10 – 8:17)

The theme 'Who knows what is good?' dominates 7:1 – 8:17. The question is immediately addressed in 7:1–14, which is composed of proverbial sayings (7:1–12) followed by a conclusion (7:13–14). The word 'good' (*ṭôb*) is a keyword in these proverbs. It occurs eleven times, with several of those occurrences in 'better than' sayings, which reinforce the message that certain things in life have only a relative value.[29] Qohelet has already made the argument that wisdom has only a relative advantage over folly (2:12–17), and that labour has only a relative benefit because there is no profit (2:10–11). The conclusion (7:13–14) also emphasizes that wisdom gives only a relative advantage and that people are not able to find out anything that comes after them. The focus in 7:13 is on the activity of God in general:

> Consider the work of God,
> for who is able to straighten what he has made crooked?

This statement is similar to 1:15 except it is clear that God is the one who has made things crooked. This activity of God prohibits someone

---

[28] Salyer 2001: 326–328.
[29] Ibid. 335. Many of the proverbs in ch. 7 go against normal expectations (for a full discussion see Belcher 2017a: 245–260).

from being able to know 'what is good for mankind' (6:12). The work of God also includes good days and bad days (7:14). There is no guarantee that the wise will experience good in the future; in fact, it is impossible to 'find out anything' that will come in the future. A person should enjoy the good days when they come because the future is uncertain.

A cautious approach to life and God (7:15–18)

This text is an important passage in understanding Qohelet's view. He begins with an observation in 7:15 that explains why no one knows what the future holds. He observes the wicked person who lives long in spite of his wickedness and the righteous person who perishes even though he is righteous. He offers advice based on this observation concerning how people should live (7:16–17). Because the wicked live long lives and the righteous die premature deaths, he advises:

> Do not be very righteous
>   and do not be very wise.
> Why should you ruin yourself?
> Do not be very wicked
>   and do not be a fool.
> Why should you die when it is not your time?

These are very jarring words that seem to deny the doctrine of the two ways taught in Proverbs. Some try to soften the negative meaning of these words by arguing that Qohelet is arguing against self-righteousness and a pretence to wisdom.[30] This makes Qohelet's advice agree with traditional wisdom, with 7:18 understood as exhorting someone to avoid these two extremes in order to live in the fear of God. One of the problems with this view is that the parallel in 7:17 does not have in mind a pretence to being a wicked person or to being a fool. Qohelet's advice is really a warning against the pursuit of wisdom and righteousness because they do not produce the benefits in life that they promise. Qohelet recognizes that the connection between how people live their lives and the consequences they experience is not a strong connection. He can argue that wisdom is better than folly (2:12–13); but wisdom ultimately fails, as the observation of 7:15 shows.[31] Therefore, why pursue righteousness and wisdom if

---

[30] Whybray 1978: 195–197.
[31] Eccl. 2:14–17 also makes the point that wisdom fails.

they do not keep one from ruin (7:16)? Although the wicked may live long lives, Qohelet knows that wickedness and folly can also bring negative consequences into one's life, reflected in the question at the end of 7:17.

In the light of the tenuous nature of life, Qohelet offers what he believes is a good response (7:18). There is a translation question that has an impact on the way one understands this verse. The Hebrew word *'ēt* is either the direct object marker or the preposition 'with'. The direct object marker does not work well in this verse. The translation of the verse with the preposition 'with' would read:

> It is good that you seize the one
>   and that you not let go of the other,
> for the one who fears God
>   will go forth *with* both of them [emphasis added].

The NASB is one of the few translations that use the word 'with'. The implication of this translation is that one who fears God should take hold of both wisdom and foolishness. But it seems impossible that Qohelet would give this advice, so the last clause is paraphrased ('to avoid both extremes') or a different meaning of the preposition is given: 'the one who fears God shall come out *from* both of them'.[32] But the meaning 'from' is not a meaning associated with this preposition, so that it is better to understand Qohelet's advice to be to grab hold of both wisdom and folly. The two things that Qohelet refers to in verse 18 are the two things mentioned in verses 16–17. A person should grab hold of righteousness and wisdom, on the one hand, and also not let go of wickedness and foolishness, on the other hand. Qohelet denies the doctrine of the two ways. Thus the fear of God is not the traditional reverence for God but refers to being cautious before God. This response to God arises out of the incongruity between the destiny of the righteous and the wicked. The righteous die prematurely and the wicked live long lives. God is the one who has made the world crooked in this way (7:13). Thus the best approach is to be cautious before God. The inability to know what God will do in response to righteousness or wickedness makes one hesitant to pursue either with much enthusiasm.[33]

---

[32] The NIV paraphrases the last clause, and the ESV and NKJV use the preposition 'from'.

[33] This view of 7:15–18 is an implication of Qohelet's not privileging wisdom but seeking to examine the results of both wisdom and folly (1:17; 2:2–3).

No one knows what is good (7:19 – 8:17)

The theme that no one really knows what is good for humanity continues. Qohelet searches for the sum of things in 7:19–29. He gives a summary statement in 7:23 that wisdom is not easily accessible. He has tested everything by wisdom and has sought to be wise, but it was far from him. He has also sought to know the wickedness of folly and the foolishness that is madness (7:25). Again, he does not privilege wisdom in his search; in fact, because it is far off and deep (7:23–24), he is not able to access wisdom to help him in his search. He admits he has failed (7:28). Instead of discovering the sum of things, he has found many schemes perpetuated by human beings even though God made the first man upright (7:29).

In chapter 8 Qohelet raises the question whether the wise man is able to give an answer: 'Who is like the wise man? And who knows the explanation of a matter?' (8:1). These questions are answered at the end of the chapter in a negative way. Part of the problem is the arbitrary nature of human government (8:1–9). Wisdom should help someone know how to act before the king (8:3–4) and to determine the proper time for the right action (8:5–8). And yet not even the wise man can succeed in these things. The proper time and the right action are not accessible because of the limitations of human power. Another problem for the wise man is the arbitrary nature of divine government (8:10–17). Here Qohelet examines how God governs the world. He focuses on the relationship between the righteous and the wicked (8:10–15) to see whether he can understand the actions of God in the world. It seems that God's government is arbitrary, because Qohelet observes that the wicked flourish and are praised. This observation leads to his contradictory statements concerning the righteous and the wicked, in the middle of which he asserts the traditional view (8:12b–13). This view is not the ultimate answer to the problem because it is followed by further negative statements that the wicked receive what the righteous deserve and vice versa (8:14). It is also significant that the verb 'know' in 8:12b is a participle. Qohelet uses the perfect aspect of 'know' to state his conclusions based on his observations (1:17; 2:14; 3:12, 14). The participle is used by Qohelet in situations where the knowledge being discussed is not affirmed but is questioned. It is used in the question 'Who knows?' of a fool who does not know what he is doing (5:1), or when a person is ignorant of something (8:7; 9:1; 11:6). The problems of life dominate Qohelet's thinking and get the last word. This struggle leads to another call to enjoyment (8:15) commending that people enjoy the benefits from labour.

Qohelet brings his argument to a close in 8:16–17 with a concluding statement. After laying out the goal and intensity of his search (8:16), he gives his conclusion concerning his observation of 'all the work of God' (8:17). This phrase brings to mind 3:11, where Qohelet concluded that people are not able to find out what God has done from beginning to end. He concludes the same in 8:17 and adds that 'even if the wise man claims to know, he is not able to discover it'. This conclusion answers the question asked in 8:1: no one knows the explanation of a matter; not even a wise man. This also answers the question of 6:12 that no one knows what is good for people during life on the earth. Not even the wise man can understand how life works.

The uncertainty of the future (9:1 – 10:20)

This section of Ecclesiastes takes up the second question of 6:12, 'Who can tell what will be in the future?' There are two major topics covered in this section and both raise the question of the uncertainty of the future. Death clouds the future of life on earth, brings uncertainty into people's lives and ends earthly existence (9:1–12). Qohelet does not offer hope of life after death. The second topic is the great damage that one sinner can do (9:18), which also makes the future uncertain (9:13 – 10:20).

Qohelet describes what it is like to live under the cloud of death (9:1–12). He begins with what seems to be a very positive affirmation, 'the righteous and the wise, and their works, are in the hand of God'. In other places of the OT it would be a comforting thought to be in the hand of God because it speaks of God's power to protect (Ps. 10:12; Isa. 50:2). It is not a comfort, however, to Qohelet. Even though the righteous and the wise are in the hand of God, they cannot be sure whether God's love or hate awaits them in the future.[34] The emphasis in 9:2 is that no matter how people live their lives, they will suffer the same fate as everyone else, a fate that comes from the hand of God. It does not matter whether a person is righteous or wicked, clean or unclean, offers sacrifices or does not offer sacrifices, is good or is a sinner – the same fate of death awaits everyone. How people live their lives has no impact on how they are treated by God. The same final destiny of death awaits everyone. There is no distinction

---

[34] Although some argue that love and hate in 9:1 refer to human activities, it is better to understand them to refer to divine activities. Love and hate in 9:1 do not have a suffix, and the hand of God in the previous clause refers to divine power. In 9:6, where love and hate do refer to human activities, they have suffixes and the context favours a reference to human activities.

based on a moral standard that differentiates the way God treats people. This is the reason people do not know whether God's love or hate awaits them. The living have an advantage over the dead because at least they are conscious, but their consciousness is of death (9:4–6).

Qohelet seems to offer a positive view of life in 9:7–10. This passage has clear connections with the other calls to enjoyment (2:24–26; 3:12, 22; 5:18; 8:15), such as the exhortation to eat, drink and enjoy life.[35] And yet this passage is different from those in a number of ways. The formula 'there is nothing better than' is not used. It is longer and more specific than previous passages. It uses imperatives and emphasizes the festivity of the enjoyment. One should eat 'with pleasure' and drink 'with a merry heart' because 'God has already approved your works'. Eaton calls these verses 'the remedy of faith',[36] and Hubbard asserts that these verses are alive with notes of grace.[37] There are indications, on the other hand, that these verses are a resigned conclusion in the light of the senseless world in which people live. The horizon of death permeates these verses, with 9:10 specifically mentioning Sheol and 9:11–12 picking up on the subject of death from 9:1–6. There is also an emphasis on *hebel* and the phrase 'under the sun', a reminder of the limited earthly perspective of Qohelet. The encouragement for people to enjoy their 'portion' (*ḥēleq*) reminds readers that these activities are the gifts of God that have his approval, but do not reach the level of 'profit' (*yitrôn*). People are encouraged to make use of every opportunity in life in a whole-hearted way: 'Whatever your hand finds to do, do it with your might' (9:10). Although this statement appears to be an enthusiastic endorsement of life and its activities, the urgency for one to make use of every opportunity is that death will end all activity. Qohelet affirms, 'there is no work, or planning, or knowledge, or wisdom in Sheol to which you are going'. In the final analysis this call to enjoyment expresses an urgency to enjoy life while enjoyment is possible.[38] When death comes, all activity ceases (9:10).

Qohelet affirms again in 9:11 that life does not turn out the way one would expect, because the deed–consequence relationship does not work. One would expect that the race would belong to the swift, that the battle would belong to the strong, and that the wise would

[35] Ogden and Zogbo 1997: 329.

[36] Eaton 1983: 127. He also comments that in this section Qohelet comes close to affirming justification by faith.

[37] Hubbard 1991: 201–202. The notes of grace include acceptance by God, the festivity of joy, and the gracious gift of God as a person's portion.

[38] Longman 1998: 229; Crenshaw 1987: 162.

have food, wealth and favour. Wisdom itself is ineffective to bring about the desired results because the wise are vulnerable to the events of time: 'a time of misfortune happens to all of them'. The word 'time' reminds the reader of the poem in 3:1–8, where the appropriate time for different events is presented. But these appropriate times are not discernible to people because no one is able to discover what God is doing in the world. The 'time' of 9:11 is characterized by 'chance' (*pega'*), which may give the impression of a random event without purpose. The term 'chance' may mean 'incident' or 'accident' in the sense that something happens randomly. This does not necessarily rule out the role of God in the events of human life, but since no one knows the time of events, the incidents appear as chance events from a human perspective. The times of calamity appear as random and are the cause of the unexpected outcomes earlier in the verse. Such evil times of misfortune fall on people unexpectedly (9:12). The question about knowledge of the future in 6:12 is answered. No one knows what the future may bring because the deed–consequence relationship does not work. The future includes times of misfortune, including sudden, premature death. This is why people must enjoy life now while the opportunity for enjoyment is available.

Qohelet closes this section by emphasizing the great damage one sinner can do (9:18). He presents an example story (9:13–18) followed by a group of proverbs in chapter 10 that show how something insignificant can cause great damage. Even someone's thoughts can do great harm (10:20). Even though wisdom gives people certain advantages, wisdom ultimately fails. Something small can make wisdom ineffective.

Living with the uncertainty of the future (11:1 – 12:7)

The theme of this section is that people should take action even if the future is uncertain. Qohelet argues this point in a number of ways. He focuses on two broad aspects of life. He encourages people to use their resources in ways that will benefit them and others (11:1–6).[39] Even if the future is uncertain (11:6), people should not hesitate to get involved in activities that may do them good. People should not sit on the limited benefit of labour but should put that benefit to use.

---

[39] For a discussion of the various ways that 11:1–6 has been understood see Belcher 2017a: 364–369.

The uncertainty of the future should not lead to paralysis but should lead to a diversity of activities so that if one activity fails there are other activities that may succeed.

The final section of Qohelet's autobiography (11:7 – 12:7) moves from encouraging people to take action now because the future is uncertain to encouraging young people to make use of every opportunity during the time of youth because the future is full of darkness. Although this section begins with light (11:7–8), the darkness slowly dominates and puts a dampener on the whole section. Qohelet encourages young people to enjoy life as long as they can because the horizon is dark. The advice in 11:9 seems problematic:

> Walk in the ways of your heart
> and in the sight of your eyes
> but know that concerning all these things
> God may bring you to judgment.

This advice seems to contradict Numbers 15:39 and to be in conflict with Proverbs. In Numbers 15:39 the commandments of God are set over against following one's own heart and eyes, a path identified with spiritual whoredom. There is a clear admonition in Proverbs not to follow one's heart and eyes. In Proverbs the time of youth is a time of decision where guidance is needed to help a young person follow the way of wisdom. The son is exhorted to give his heart to the wisdom of his parents and to 'let your eyes' observe the way of wisdom (Prov. 23:26). Qohelet is not advocating that a young person pursue hedonism, for he knows that wickedness can produce negative consequences; but because wisdom brings only a relative advantage, it is not clear where the boundaries lie. He has been willing to pursue both wisdom and folly to see where each leads.

Qohelet also mentions God's judgment as a deterrent (11:9) and that the young person should

> Remember your Creator
> in the days of your youth
> before the days of misfortune come.
> (12:1)

Does the mention of God's judgment and God as Creator put things in proper perspective? There is no evidence that Qohelet has in view the final judgment. The finality of death is mentioned in 9:10. The

168

other warnings in this passage refer to events that will happen in this life. The coming days of darkness refers to difficulties in this life (11:8) as do old age and death (12:1–7). Qohelet does not appeal to a final judgment as a solution to the problems of injustice that he observes on the earth. His thinking is limited to the earthly horizon and the judgment that may come to someone in this life. One can never be certain whether righteousness will be rewarded and wickedness punished. So Qohelet modifies his encouragement of pursuing the desires of the heart by holding out the possibility of divine retribution in this life. The mention of the Creator is also a warning to a young person not to get carried away in the pursuit of one's heart and eyes. The fact that there is a limited time to remember the Creator is important because it implies there is coming a time in the future when life will not be enjoyed and it will be difficult to remember the Creator.[40] The onslaught of the coming darkness of death will be permanent.

The fact that the spirit of human beings returns to God who gave it (12:7) seems more positive than the statement of 3:21, where Qohelet was not sure whether the spirit of human beings went upward and the spirit of an animal downward. The focus of 3:21 is whether there is any distinction between the manner of death and the destiny of humans and animals. Yet both humans and animals possess breath that comes from God (Gen. 2:7; Ps. 104:29). One can affirm that God is the giver of life to both humans and animals and also deny that there is any difference between the two in death.[41] Plus, any positive evaluation of 12:7 has to take into account that it is followed by the motto of the book that all is *hebel* and a chasing after wind. Qohelet ends his autobiography with the difficulties of old age and the darkness of death. The superlative *hebel* statement follows immediately. There is little hope offered for light beyond the darkness of death.

---

[40] Shields 2006: 233. He notes that mentioning the Creator may be no more than a reminder of one's mortality. Life is in God's hands and is beyond our control.

[41] The point is that God is the source of life (Murphy 1992: 120; Gordis 1955: 339). Fox (1999: 332) argues that 12:7 is more pessimistic than 3:21 because 12:7 affirms that the spirit does return to God but that fact does not change anything.

Chapter Ten

The theology of Ecclesiastes

Ecclesiastes consists of a first-person autobiography written by Qohelet (1:12 -- 12:7) and a third-person frame (1:1–11; 12:8–14, with a third-person intrusion in 7:27) added by someone else for the purpose of warning his son against speculative wisdom. This person introduces Qohelet and the theme of the book (1:1–11) and adds the epilogue as an evaluation of the words of Qohelet. Qohelet operates with an under-the-sun approach that limits his analysis to empirical observation as the basis for drawing conclusions about life. He wrestles with whether traditional wisdom can explain what he observes in life, especially the breakdown of the deed–consequence relationship and the prominence of injustice in the world. He does not privilege wisdom but also tests the outcome of folly. It is not surprising that his conclusions concerning the 'futility' of the events of this life (*hebel*) do not line up with traditional wisdom teaching. The result is that when one discusses the theology of Ecclesiastes, one has to discuss the theology of Qohelet and the theology of the book as a whole represented in the epilogue.

Qohelet's view of the works of God

Theology begins with the study of God. Qohelet believes in the existence of God, but what is his view of God? Part of the problem with understanding this question is that he does not refer directly to the nature of God. He does not describe God's character; nor does he offer praise to God for his attributes; rather, he speaks only of God's activity. Thus the nature of God must be determined by investigating God's activity and its impact on human existence.[1] Michel points out that it is difficult to understand Qohelet's view of God precisely because of what he does not say. The meaning of this silence is where the discrepancies in interpretation lie.[2] Qohelet calls God Creator (12:1) and talks about God's activity of judgment.

[1] Estes 1982.
[2] Michel 1990: 35.

Qohelet offers positive statements about God in the calls to enjoyment where certain benefits from labour, such as eating, drinking and enjoying life, are from the hand of God. He offers a theological reflection on the nature of God's judgment (3:17), discusses how to conduct oneself before God in worship (5:1–7), and also talks about the fear of God. Many operate with the assumption that Qohelet's view of God agrees with the view of God in the rest of the OT. A closer examination of God's activity in the world, however, raises major questions concerning Qohelet's view of God. This section examines several aspects of God's activity in the world and the results for people in order to determine more precisely Qohelet's view of God and how people should respond to God. This discussion assumes and builds on the previous two chapters that examined the basis for a negative view of Qohelet's message and the development of that message.

God is active in the world. Twice Qohelet states that God has given people their task in order to occupy them (1:13; 3:10). He also affirms that the enjoyment that comes from labour is from the hand of God (2:24); it is the gift of God (3:13; 5:19), who gives wealth and the power to enjoy it (5:19). God also gives people the days of their life (8:15). Even though the days of life are called senseless (9:9), they come from God. In fact, God has already approved the enjoyment of the limited benefits that come from labour (9:7). God is the subject of the verb 'give' (*nātan*), showing that he is the source of these activities. But how are we to understand these activities given by God?

The 'grievous task' God has given people

Twice Qohelet affirms that God has given people a 'task' to occupy them (1:13; 3:10). This task refers to labour and its results, but also includes normal human activities that people carry out every day of their lives. Qohelet searches all that is done under heaven (1:3) and has seen everything that is done under the sun (1:14). He follows the statement in 3:10 with an assertion that God has made everything appropriate in its time. This refers back to the poem of 3:1–8 that describes a variety of human activities. So the task given people includes a wide variety of normal activities in which they regularly participate.

But what kind of task is it? The adjective used to describe this task is a negative term (*ra'*) that can refer to what is 'evil' or 'burdensome'. The task that God has given people is not evil, so the best understanding is that it is difficult, frustrating or 'grievous'.[3] Qohelet sets out the parameters of his search and then draws a negative preliminary conclusion (1:14–15). Everything done under the sun is characterized as 'futile' or 'senseless' (*hebel*) and a chasing after wind. The difficulty of the situation is further stated with a proverb in 1:15 that the crooked cannot be made straight and what is lacking cannot be counted. This proverb affirms the hopelessness of solving the problems of life encountered by Qohelet. If Qohelet cannot solve them, neither can anyone else overcome the grievous, burdensome nature of the task God has given human beings.

The context in 3:10 is different. Qohelet presents a poem on time that agrees with the traditional view that there are appropriate times for people to act and they should be able to determine the right time to act. He then follows the poem with the key question from 1:3 concerning whether there is any profit from labour. He has already answered this question in 2:11, but does this poem on time change his conclusions? He affirms that God has made everything appropriate in its time and that he has put a sense of eternity (a sense of totality) into the heart of people. This reflects on God's role as Creator in the way he has made the world and the desires he has put into the heart of people. God understands the appropriate nature of the times given in 3:1–8 and has put into the heart of people the desire to understand how the times fit together. People should be able to comprehend the orderly world God has created in order to make proper decisions about life. But Qohelet immediately raises a problem. The desire to understand how the times fit together is hindered by the fact that people are not able to understand the actions of God. The statement in 3:14–15 shows that this situation will not change. In fact, these verses are an allusion to 1:9 ('there is nothing new under the sun'), but what becomes clear is that God is the one who stands behind the repetitive nature of events so that there is nothing new under the sun. The conclusion is that the task God has given people is impossible because of the inability of people to comprehend the nature of God's activity in the world.

God's incomprehensible actions in the world

Qohelet clearly states that people are not able to comprehend the actions of God in the world (3:11). Perhaps all that he means is that

[3] Most English translations prefer the connotation of 'difficult' or 'burdensome'. Longman and Bartholomew translate this word as 'evil'. Longman (1998: 80) argues it fits Qohelet's subtle criticism of God throughout the book, and Bartholomew (2009: 124) contrasts it with the original mandate given to people in Gen. 1 – 2 that was good.

God's actions are mysterious or that because people do not know everything it is hard to understand certain events in this world. Is there a sense in Qohelet's view that even though humans cannot understand the works of God, everything will work out for good? Sadly, this is not his conclusion based on the way he observes events in the world. The incomprehensible nature of the activity of God is part of the reason he concludes that the nature of the world is 'senseless' (*hebel*). There are several reasons why he concludes that God's work is incomprehensible, and these reasons explain the futile nature of life in this world.

The breakdown of divine retribution (the deed–consequence relationship)

After affirming the inability of people to understand God's activity in the world, Qohelet observes that where justice is expected, wickedness is found (3:16). He wrestles with the breakdown of the deed–consequence relationship. This is an observation he comes back to over and over in the book. It greatly bothers him and explains some of his conclusions. It is why people cannot understand the works of God and it makes the future uncertain. The passages that examine this problem include 2:13–17; 2:26; 3:16–22; 7:15–18; 8:10–15; and 9:1–6.

Qohelet argues that there is no difference between the wise person and the fool because they receive the same fate (2:13–17). Although wisdom gives a person a relative advantage over a fool, the same fate of death awaits them both. This destroys the advantage the wise person has over the fool. There is no enduring remembrance of the wise just as there is none for the fool (contra Prov. 10:7). All this leads to Qohelet's exclamation 'So why then have I become very wise?' (2:15). The relative advantage of wisdom is negated because death comes to the wise and the fool in the same way with the same result. Thus he hates life and affirms that all is *hebel* and a chasing after wind (2:17).

Qohelet denies any difference between the sinner and the one who is good before God (2:26). He despairs that labour does not produce any real benefit (2:18–23). This sentiment fits the conclusion he drew in 2:11 that there is no profit to labour. Yet he encourages the enjoyment of the portion that comes from labour (2:24–25). He follows this with a statement that seems to support a traditional view of divine retribution (Prov. 13:22; 28:8): wisdom and knowledge and joy is given to the one who is good, whereas the sinner gathers and collects only to give to the one who is good. Qohelet negates the distinction between the good and the sinner with a concluding *hebel* judgment and that the activity of gathering and collecting is chasing after wind.

Qohelet denies any difference between the destiny of people and animals (3:16–22). After the observation that where one would expect to find justice there is only wickedness, he makes a theological and an anthropological reflection. The theological reflection (3:17) affirms that God will judge the righteous and the wicked because there is a time for every activity (as the poem of 3:1–8 affirms). The anthropological reflection (3:18–21) states that people have no advantage over the animals because the destiny of both is the same. They both have breath, both die the same way, and both end up at the same place (the dust of the ground). No one knows whether the spirit of a human being ends up in a different place than the spirit of the animal. Qohelet does not allow the theological reflection about God's judgment to solve this problem but lets the negative anthropological statement have the last word. The uncertainty of the destiny of people leads to the call to enjoyment. One should enjoy the limited benefit that comes from labour (one's portion) in the light of the uncertainty of the future.

Qohelet denies any difference between the path of the righteous and the path of the wicked (7:15–18). After another observation that the righteous person perishes despite his righteousness and the wicked person prolongs his life in evildoing, he offers his advice that one should not be very righteous or very wicked. The reason for this advice is that both could end up experiencing negative consequences. Righteousness could lead to ruin, and wickedness to an early death. Blessings do not always come to the righteous; and although the wicked may live long, there are perilous consequences that could befall them. So his advice is not to get too involved in either path, a denial of the doctrine of the two ways.

After wrestling with whether people get what they deserve in life, Qohelet denies that there is any difference between the righteous and the wicked (8:10–15). The wicked are treated well (8:10) and because there is a delay in carrying out the sentence against evil, people are encouraged to do evil (8:11). Although Qohelet is aware of traditional wisdom teaching that the wicked and the righteous get what they deserve (8:12b–13), his final statement on this theme is that the righteous receive what the wicked deserve and the wicked receive what the righteous deserve (8:14). This characteristic of life brings a judgment of 'futility' (*hebel*) and a commendation to enjoy life (call to enjoyment). The breakdown of the deed–consequence relationship makes God's work in the world impossible to understand. Not even a wise person can explain it (8:17).

Qohelet denies that being in the hand of God makes any difference to the righteous and the wise (9:1–10). The hand of God refers to his power and protection. But even though the righteous and the wise are in the hand of God, there is no guarantee that they will experience love instead of hate. This uncertainty is because the same fate of death awaits both the righteous and the wicked. In fact, Qohelet emphasizes that a person's character or actions do not make any difference in how he or she is treated. It does not matter if you are the righteous or the wicked, the clean or the unclean, those who sacrifice or those who do not sacrifice, the good or the sinner, the one who swears an oath or the one who does not swear an oath – all are treated the same way and death comes to all in the same way. Death is presented as permanent and final. The dead know nothing, they have no more reward, their memory is forgotten and they will never again have any 'portion' (*ḥēleq*) in anything done under the sun. Qohelet strongly exhorts people to enjoy their portion in life before death. Whatever a person wants to do, it must be done before death because there is no work, planning, knowledge or wisdom after death (9:10).

Several conclusions can be drawn from Qohelet's observations of the breakdown of the deed–consequence relationship. First, there is an explanation as to why it is impossible for people to understand the work of God in the world. The failure of divine retribution is the first topic that Qohelet examines (3:16) after his statement that people cannot discover the work that God does from beginning to end (3:11). He begins chapter 8 by asking whether the wise person knows the explanation of a matter. At the end of the chapter he restates that people are not able to discover the work that God does under the sun before answering the question he raised at the beginning of the chapter: 'if a wise man claims to know, he is not able to discover it'. Because the righteous and the wicked do not receive what they deserve, God's work seems arbitrary and thus it is impossible for people to understand it.

Second, God is not brought into the discussion in order to solve any of the problems with which Qohelet is wrestling. Twice he could have appealed to God to help solve the problem. He makes a theological reflection about God's judgment in 3:17 but it is followed by a pessimistic anthropological reflection in 3:18–21 that gets the last word. This leaves the reader with the negative conclusion that people are no different from animals in their destiny at death. The fact that the righteous, the wise and their deeds are in the hand of God (9:2) does not make any difference in how they are treated or in the results of their death. God is not a solution to these problems.

Third, death brings an end to human existence. Death destroys the contrast between the wise person and the fool (2:15–16), people and animals (3:18–21), and the righteous and the wicked (9:1–2). The fact that these groups experience the same fate destroys the distinctions between them. Death itself is not the problem, but the manner, timing and outcome of death are problems.[4] Concerning the manner and timing of death, the OT distinguishes between a good and a bad death. Balaam exclaims, 'Let me die the death of the upright' (Num. 23:10). This would certainly include long life, as Abraham is described as dying in a good old age, a man full of years (Gen. 25:8).[5] A good death would also include passing on the name of the family through heirs (Job 42:16). The corollary of this perspective is that life is a precious gift from God so that long life is seen as a great blessing from God (Pss 21:4; 61:6; 91:16). There is also a bad death described in the OT that could include an impending violent death, as in the case of Joab or Saul, or a sudden, premature death, as in the case of the wicked.[6] It is premature death that raises the problems related to divine retribution. Life does not turn out the way one expects because evil times of misfortune, particularly death, suddenly overtake people (9:11–12). The blessing of long life and the avoidance of premature death is represented in Proverbs as coming from wisdom (9:11) and the fear of the Lord (10:27; 14:27). Thus the ambiguity of death is not as prominent in Proverbs as it is in Ecclesiastes.[7]

Qohelet has no clear statement of life after death. Death brings an end to participation in the activities of this earthly life. Those who die know nothing and have no more reward because the memory of them is forgotten (9:5). The strongest statement that there is no life after death comes in 9:10, where Qohelet exhorts people to pursue things in this life while the opportunity presents itself because death

---

[4] The subject of death in the OT is complex. The difficult nature of the subject is attributed to the fact that the material is divergent, brief, sporadic and often bound to a particular historical context (Bailey 1971: 22). For further discussions of death and Sheol see Spronk 1986, Alexander 1986, Johnston 2002 and Levenson 2006.

[5] Bailey 1971: 24.

[6] Bailey (ibid.) and Spronk (1986: 311–312) discuss the aspect of premature death in the OT.

[7] Crenshaw 1978: 213.

brings an end to work, thought, knowledge and wisdom. Qohelet does not hold out hope that life after death can help alleviate the problems of this life, or that if someone dies young, there is a life after death that gives consolation to such an unfortunate event. Qohelet never introduces life after death to solve the problem of injustice in this world. He struggles with the fact that the righteous receive what the wicked deserve but never points the righteous to an anticipation of justice in the life to come.

Qohelet's view of God

Several conclusions can be drawn concerning Qohelet's view of God based on his discussion of the failure of divine retribution, the difficulty of understanding God's work in the world, the manner and nature of death, and the fact that God is not a solution to the problems of life.

God as judge

Qohelet affirms that God acts as a judge (3:17; 5:5; 8:12b–13; 11:9), but if there is no life after death then there is no final judgment and his judgments are limited to what happens in this world. The theological reflection that God will judge the righteous and the wicked because there is a time for every matter reflects the poem on time in 3:1–8, where the focus is on events in this life. God will judge the righteous and the wicked in this life by ensuring that each receives what he or she deserves. This reflection does not match up to what Qohelet observes in the world when he sees the righteous suffering and the wicked prospering. The breakdown of the deed–consequence relationship destroys the proper distinctions between the righteous and the wicked and makes it difficult to make sense of the events of life because God seems to act in arbitrary ways. This explains why the nature of God or his judgment is not offered as a solution to the problem of divine retribution. When Qohelet talks about the uncertainty of the future (3:22), he has in view the fact that no one can be sure that anything good will come in the future, even if one is in the hand of God (9:1–2).

The fear of God

The fear of God is a concept that is difficult to define, partly because Qohelet does not give a definition of it and partly because it is dependent on how one understands other ideas in the book. Many assume that it should have the same meaning as in Proverbs. Qohelet uses some form of the fear of God in 3:14, 5:6, 8:12–13 and 7:18. Divine retribution is directly related to it in 5:6, 8:12–13 and 7:18, while 3:14 occurs in a context discussing the work of God. Thus divine retribution, God's role as judge and the incomprehensibility of God's work in the world are important concepts in understanding Qohelet's use of the fear of God.

In order to understand Qohelet's view of the fear of God one must also understand his approach to wisdom, because both are different from what one finds in Proverbs. Qohelet does not privilege wisdom as the starting point of his search. He wants to investigate both wisdom and folly to see what the results are. If wisdom is not Qohelet's starting point, then the fear of God is not his beginning principle. Qohelet calls into question the benefits of wisdom (2:12–17), and the knowledge of God's works is not available to people (3:11). The concepts associated with the fear of Yahweh in Proverbs are questioned by Qohelet. The fear of Yahweh in Proverbs 2:5 is associated with finding the knowledge of God. Qohelet denies that people can understand what God is doing in the world (3:11; 8:1, 17), because his works are incomprehensible. The fear of Yahweh prolongs life (Prov. 10:27) but Qohelet questions whether the life of the righteous is prolonged (8:11–14; 9:1–6). The fear of Yahweh is associated with a strong confidence (Prov. 14:26), but it is hard to be confident in God when one is unsure how he is going to act. A person who is in the hand of God does not even have confidence concerning the future (9:1–6). The fear of God in 7:15–18 arises out of the incongruity between the righteous dying prematurely and the wicked living long lives so that the best approach is to take hold of both righteousness and wickedness. It is hard to pursue either one with much enthusiasm. Thus to fear God is to be cautious before him.[8]

Qohelet uses the name Elohim for God. He does not refer to God as Yahweh. The use of the name Elohim does not necessarily mean that Qohelet has a distant view of God, but in the light of how Qohelet has presented God's involvement in the world, the use of Elohim instead of Yahweh makes sense. The name Yahweh emphasizes the personal nature of God (Gen. 2 – 3) and becomes the covenant name of God in the exodus, where he fought for his people and delivered them from slavery. Yahweh is associated with faithfulness

---

[8] Longman (2015: 13) argues that Qohelet encourages people to be afraid of God and not to draw his attention.

to the covenant promises of God and is very prominent in Proverbs.[9] Qohelet's view of God is a distant God whose works in the world are not understood by people. Thus the fear of God expresses caution before a God who does not always deliver on his promise to bless the righteous and make life difficult for the wicked. God must be approached cautiously because he is a distant God who is unpredictable in how he will treat the wise and the fool (Eccl. 5:1–7). Qohelet does not display any passion toward God or affirm that it is good to be near him or that there is nothing else on earth besides God that he desires (as in Ps. 73:23–28).

Qohelet's view of the world

Even though God is the Creator, the world is a messed up place because human expectations are not met. Qohelet observes over and over again that life does not turn out the way people expect. Neither labour nor wisdom delivers the expected results. There is no profit to labour so that the only enjoyment people have is the limited benefit that comes from labour (the calls to enjoyment). Wisdom has a relative advantage over folly, but it too falls short of what it promises. God does not give security to the righteous or the wise concerning their future. This uncertainty has several results and leads to several conclusions. First, the character of the world is *hebel*, the keyword used by Qohelet to describe his observations concerning what happens in the world. Qohelet does not resolve any of the problems he observes, so *hebel* cannot refer to what is fleeting, but must refer to what is permanent. In the light of the failure of the deed–consequence relationship, *hebel* must refer to the senseless, futile nature of all the things that Qohelet describes.

Second, the *hebel* nature of the world is reflected in Qohelet's view of the processes of creation and the events of history. His opening words presented by the frame narrator (1:1–11) describe the futility of the endless actions of the natural phenomena (1:4–7). There is constant movement but no discernible purpose.[10] The sun 'pants' along tired and weary, unlike the view of the sun as a strong man running a race, full of vigour, reflecting the glory of God (Ps. 19:5). The wind goes round and round in monotonous repetition, unlike the view that God directs the wind to accomplish his purposes (Ps. 104:3–4). The rivers flow into the sea but the sea is not full, unlike

---

9 The name Elohim is used only four times in Proverbs.
10 Crenshaw 1987: 62.

the view of the rivers as going forth to give drink to the animals and to cause the grass to grow for the cattle (Ps. 104:10–11).

The realm of human activity does not achieve its intended purpose, as the mouth, eyes and ears fail in their actions (1:8). Human words are not able to speak meaningfully about the world.[11] Qohelet will emphasize that people are not able to understand the world, not even the wise man (8:17). Qohelet argues that the possibilities of human knowledge are limited and always fall short. Concerning history there is nothing new under the sun (1:9). History is going nowhere and people are destined to live lives that never achieve fulfilment. This view contrasts with other teaching in the OT where history is controlled by God and is moving toward a goal (Gen. 50:20; Prov. 19:21; 21:2). The possibility of something new is seen in the exhortations to sing a new song (Ps. 96:1), the possibility of a new covenant (Jer. 31:31) and the prospect of a new earth and heavens (Isa. 65:17). To say there is nothing new under the sun negates these possibilities and demonstrates an 'under the sun' perspective.

Third, Qohelet recognizes that the flawed nature of people is part of the problem with the world. There are wicked and foolish people who can cause trouble. Something insignificant can cause harm and take away the relative value of wisdom (9:13 – 10:20). One sinner can do great damage (9:18). He also reflects OT teaching about the character of people when he tries to find an explanation of things (7:19–29). He argues that wisdom may have great value (7:19) but is easily undermined by sin (7:20–22). Wisdom itself is ineffective and escapes Qohelet's ability to discover it (7:23–24). After examining both wisdom and folly and the scheme of things, he concludes that he has not been able to provide an answer to life's questions. What he has found is that God has made people upright, but they have sought out many schemes. This discovery agrees with Genesis 1 – 3 and the early history of humanity before the flood (Gen. 6:5). Qohelet cannot find any women of worth and could find only one man.[12] If there are no worthy women, then the positive statements about women in Proverbs are called into question (Prov. 18:22; 31:10).

[11] Murphy 1992: 8.
[12] There is some discussion whether Qohelet is a misogynist because of what he says about women in this passage. Those who argue that 7:26 refers to women in general view Qohelet as negative toward all women (Longman 1998: 204), but those who see a particular type of woman in view (Enns 2011: 87), or argue that it is a composite image of Lady Folly (Seow 1997: 272 and Bartholomew 2009: 267), tend to deny that Qohelet is a misogynist. Qohelet is also very negative toward men, so that both men and women are viewed negatively. He does encourage the enjoyment of one's wife in 9:9.

Qohelet's message and New Testament teaching

Qohelet's dark 'under the sun' view is a true assessment of the fallen world apart from God's redeeming love. It is a picture of the hopelessness of the world, which is fallen and cursed. The word *hebel* is translated by the LXX with the word *mataiotēs*, used in Romans 8:20 to describe the subjection of creation to futility. The creation groans as it waits to be set free from the bondage of decay. The futility to which creation has been corrupted can be overcome. Creation itself is eagerly awaiting freedom from bondage, just as the sons of God, although groaning inwardly, are eagerly awaiting the redemption of their bodies (Rom. 8:18–25). Futility, however, will not have the last word because Jesus has taken upon himself our sin and the futility of life.[13] He has redeemed us from the curse of the law (Gal. 3:13), so that our lives change from frustrating futility to having a purpose (Rom. 8:28). The power of the new creation is seen in the resurrection of Jesus from the dead. The believer's perspective is no longer limited to this earthly life, for we are able to see the glory of the new earth and heavens. The frustration of life that Qohelet documents so well is still part of what believers struggle with because we live in a fallen world, but even in the darkness of this life the light of Christ shines.

Preaching or teaching the book of Ecclesiastes

Preaching or teaching Ecclesiastes is difficult, and perhaps even more so if one takes an 'under the sun' approach. The benefit is that Qohelet deconstructs many activities in which people find security. The difficulty is that people cannot be left in the dark with no real answers to their problems week in and week out. Once the negative work of deconstruction is presented, an 'above the sun' view that provides answers should be given. This move can be accomplished by going to the last few verses of the epilogue (12:13–14), by examining other OT scriptures or by showing how the NT handles the topic.[14] There are many ways an above-the-sun connection can be made. Some examples have already been given and a couple more will be given here.

Qohelet was able to pursue all the pleasures of life, including those that come with folly (2:1–11), and concludes that there was no profit to them. He had it all at his fingertips and could not find meaning in

[13] Longman 1998: 39–40.
[14] See Belcher 2017a. Examples of how to do this are scattered throughout the commentary under the title 'Homiletical Implications'.

any of his activities. Jesus, on the other hand, had it all but gave it all up to enter this sinful world to deliver people from the bondage of sin and the attitude that having it all in this life brings fulfilment. As followers of Jesus, who will one day have it all when Jesus returns, we must be willing to give it all up now for the sake of Christ's kingdom and his glory.

Qohelet emphasizes the difficult nature of labour. Work is hard in every respect because it involves both physical exertion and mental anguish. People work long and hard and then are frustrated because their efforts do not pay off (2:18–23). Qohelet agrees that there is a curse of sin on work (Gen. 3:17–19),[15] but does not stress that work is a divine vocation (Gen. 1:26–28; 2:15). The 'above the sun' view would affirm that labour is hard and frustrating but there is a broader principle at work (Rom. 8:28). The drudgery and futility of work is overcome by seeing work as a divine vocation redeemed by Christ. In the light of the resurrection of Christ, Paul asserts that there is profit to labour: 'be steadfast, immovable, always abounding in the work of the Lord, knowing that in the Lord your labour is not in vain' (1 Cor. 15:58).

Wisdom can be very beneficial but it does not take much to hinder the advantages of wisdom (9:13 – 10:20). One sinner can do great damage (9:18). A small grain of sand that ends up in the wrong place can be harmful. A broader perspective understands that God is able to work out his purposes in the difficult things in life. He is able to use the weak and small things to accomplish his purposes (Ps. 8:2). The one who is the wisdom of God appeared to be weak and was despised, but through his resurrection guaranteed that God's wisdom would triumph. Although Satan has great power and can do great damage on the earth, just 'one little word shall fell him'.[16] The future is not uncertain because of foolishness or wickedness, but is certain because of the power and victory of Christ.

The theological message of Ecclesiastes (12:8–14)

There are several questions concerning the origin, function and purpose of the epilogue of Ecclesiastes (12:8–14).[17] The answers to these questions are related to whether one understands the message of Qohelet as positive or negative and whether the ending of the book

---

[15] Anderson 1998: 99–113.

[16] This is a line from the hymn 'A Mighty Fortress Is Our God'.

[17] For a review of the different positions see Boda 2013: 257–282 and Belcher 2017a: 407–413.

agrees with Qohelet's viewpoint. These verses shift from first to third person, a shift that signals a new speaker, who comments on the work of Qohelet.[18] The use of 'my son' gives these verses a didactic tone.[19] Although 'my son' is common in Proverbs, it is not found in Ecclesiastes apart from the epilogue. A wise man presents the words of Qohelet as instruction and warning to his son concerning the danger of speculative wisdom.

The epilogue can be divided into two sections. The work of Qohelet is described and evaluated in 12:9–11, and an instructional warning is given in 12:12–14 that emphasizes what is most important to know in order to avoid speculative wisdom.[20] Qohelet is involved in activities associated with wisdom, such as teaching people knowledge and collecting, evaluating and arranging proverbs. He is called 'a wise man' (*ḥākām*) because he did work that a wise man would do. Some English versions translate this as Qohelet was 'wise' (NIV, ESV), a translation that could lead people to a positive evaluation of his work. And yet not every wise man is wise. Jeremiah refers to a group of wise men, along with other officials (Jer. 8:9; 18:18), who were not wise because they had rejected the word of Yahweh and Jeremiah as a prophet. The word *ḥākām* can refer to someone in an official position and is not necessarily an evaluation of whether that person has true wisdom.

Qohelet also 'sought to find words of delight and to write words of truth correctly' (v. 10).[21] This translation states that Qohelet sought to do two things, but it does not comment on whether he was successful. Many of Qohelet's words are difficult, jarring and full of frustration. He is also clear that he did not attain wisdom (7:23) and that his attempt to find the explanation of things failed (7:28). In fact, he concludes that not even a wise man can understand these matters (8:1, 17). The metaphor of a shepherd is also used to evaluate the words of Qohelet and other wise men. Some commentators see two metaphors in verse 11. The goads express something painful and the

---

[18] Among others, Longman 1998: 274; Gordis 1955: 341; Seow 1997: 391.

[19] Fox 1999: 363.

[20] The verses that describe the work of Qohelet (12:9–11) use the indicative, and the verses that are instruction and warning (12:12–14) use the imperative (Hubbard 1991: 247).

[21] This is my own translation and is also found in the NASB; for a justification of it see Belcher 2017a: 415. The other way to translate the second clause of v. 10 is to assert something that Qohelet accomplished, such as 'uprightly he wrote words of truth' (ESV) or 'what he wrote was upright and true' (NIV). Based on Qohelet's starting point, his empirical methodology, and his limited 'under the sun' view, one could argue that Qohelet's conclusions were truthful based on his starting point and the method he used in his search (see Longman 2017: 40–41, who also comes to this conclusion).

nails express something positive, perhaps tent spikes firmly driven into the ground signifying strength.[22] But the verse is a chiasm that can be translated, 'the words of the wise men are like goads and like nails firmly fixed are the owners of the collection'. The chiasm supports one metaphor, not two. Goads were nails firmly fixed on the end of a stick used to prod cattle to get them to move.[23] The painful aspect of wisdom sayings is emphasized. The shepherd is not a reference to God as the source of the sayings but continues the metaphor of goads used by shepherds.[24]

The final section of the epilogue (12:12–14) gives a warning against speculative wisdom and points the son to what is most important as the foundation for life. The warning highlights the difficult nature of a wise man's work that consists in much study and the making of many books, activities that can be consuming (12:12). This is especially true of Qohelet, who operates with an empirical methodology, does not privilege wisdom in his search and is confined to a limited, earthly horizon under the sun. There comes a point where endless searching and wearying study must give way to something else described in 12:13–14.

The real foundation of wisdom comes at the end of the book. There are two imperatives followed by two motive clauses giving the reasons why the imperatives should be heeded. The first imperative is 'fear God', and the second is 'keep his commandments'. Qohelet does not refer to God's commandments in his search for meaning 'under the sun'. This added dimension of God's law shows that the fear of God in the epilogue agrees with the meaning of this idea in Proverbs, where the fear of God is the first principle of wisdom. The first motive clause, 'for this concerns every person', shows that everyone should be concerned with the fear of God and the keeping of his commandments as the most important things in life.[25] The next motive clause emphasizes the idea that everyone is responsible to fear God and keep his commands, 'for God will bring every deed into judgment, including every hidden thing, whether good or evil'. The judgment of God mentioned here is different from the arbitrary judgment discussed by Qohelet, because this judgment is certain and comprehensive. The mention of 'hidden' things brings into view judgment after death. No

[22] Murphy 1992: 125; Bartholomew 2009: 360.

[23] Fox 1999: 354–355; Longman 1998: 280.

[24] Fox 1999: 355–356. He points out that when God is referred to as 'shepherd', it refers to his capacity as keeper and protector, which is not relevant here.

[25] Murphy 1992: 123; Fox 1999: 349; and others.

matter how much someone is struggling in life, the most important response is to fear God and keep his commandments.

The purpose of the book of Ecclesiastes

Why would an orthodox wise man present a sceptical work to his son if he were unhappy with its contents?[26] Would it not be better to let such a work recede into the oblivion of history by not commenting on it? Such a view ignores the real dangers of speculative wisdom, a wisdom removed from its proper foundation. The reason someone would present the struggles of Qohelet and then offer a simple explanation (12:13–14) is that this struggle is common in the OT. Trying to understand the prosperity of the wicked or the suffering of the righteous is not an isolated problem. Jeremiah and Habakkuk wrestle with it, the discussion of Job and his friends centres around it and certain psalms explore it (37; 49; 73). When the problems of life begin to dominate people's thinking, they can lose the very foundation of wisdom in the difficulty of trying to explain life's problems.

The struggle of the psalmist in Psalm 73 is a microcosm of Qohelet's struggle and shows how easy it is to move away from the proper foundation of wisdom. It begins with a theological affirmation that God is good to Israel and to the pure in heart, but then the psalmist acknowledges that he almost stumbled because of the prosperity of the wicked (vv. 2–3). He describes the security and prosperity of the wicked (vv. 3–12) and then lays out some of the implications of his struggle (vv. 13–17). He wonders if it has been useless to live a life of purity before God (v. 13). He talks about the anguish of his struggle and that it is a wearisome task trying to understand this problem (v. 16). He clearly states that had he continued down this path and taught such things he would have betrayed God's people (v. 15). The danger of speculative, doubting wisdom is that the difficult problems of life so dominate a person's thinking that he moves away from the foundation of wisdom. The change in the psalmist's perspective comes when he goes into the temple and sees the true end of the wicked. In Ecclesiastes 12:13–14 we are pointed back to the true foundation of wisdom. The book of Ecclesiastes sets forth Qohelet's 'under the sun' struggle to show the danger of speculative, doubting wisdom and to remind God's people of the true foundation of wisdom: a reverent trust in God and his revelation.

[26] Eaton 1983: 40–41.

True wisdom is not limited to the horizon of this world. On 12 April 2001 Sarah Ann Longstreet left her home in the morning to attend high school, but never made it because she was killed in a motor car accident. She was young, talented, a strong believer in Jesus Christ, with her whole life in front of her, and yet in one instant was gone. Qohelet would have seen this event as a grievous burden because how Miss Longstreet lived made no difference to how long she lived or how she died. Her parents saw things differently. Here is a portion of her obituary:

> While most would call the car accident that took Sarah's life a 'tragedy' the family knows that it was the case of God calling one of his children home. Certainly unexpected, but an indication that Sarah's work on earth was complete. For those who read of Sarah's accident and feel that a young life has been cut short, the Longstreets believe that Sarah would want them to know what the Bible says, 'for me to live is Christ and to die is gain'. And she would challenge you to consider where you will spend eternity.[27]

The Longstreets were able to place the loss of their child within a world view that included the sovereignty of a loving God, who is working out his purposes for their lives even in the difficulties of life. This is true wisdom.

---

[27] *The Charlotte Observer*, Charlotte, North Carolina, USA, April 2001.

Chapter Eleven

Jesus and wisdom

The relationship between Jesus and wisdom can be approached from a variety of angles. This chapter will start from the basic consideration of Jesus as a wisdom teacher and then move into deeper discussions of his relationship to wisdom in his person and work.

Wisdom in the teaching of Jesus

The teaching ministry of Jesus exhibits the characteristics of a wisdom teacher so that it is appropriate to call him a sage. In other words, Jesus was a wise man. Whether or not the term 'sage' is the most all-encompassing and satisfying term to apply to Jesus,[1] there is abundant evidence that he is a person of wisdom. To identify Jesus as a sage does not take away from his other roles as prophet, priest and king.[2] The fact that Jesus uses parables and proverbs shows his connection to wisdom, but this should not be set over against his authority as a prophet.[3] Jesus does not need to use the prophetic phrase 'Thus saith the Lord', because of his own inherent authority. He speaks in the first person in offering the true understanding of the law of God (Matt. 5:21–22) and in affirming the certainty of his words (John 1:51). The people recognize that he speaks on his own authority and not on the authority of other rabbis. Jesus' approach is so different that they are astonished at his teaching (Matt. 7:28–29).

Jesus' use of proverbs

Seventy per cent of Jesus' teaching is in some form of wisdom utterance.[4] It includes the use of parables, proverbs and riddles. Although Jesus' use of parables is an interesting study, a lot has been written on his parables,[5] but not much has been written on Jesus'

---

[1] Witherington 1994: 201.
[2] For a discussion of these roles see Belcher 2016b.
[3] Witherington 1994: 155. He makes this distinction but does not draw any implications from it.
[4] Ibid. 156.
[5] For a few examples see Kistemaker 2002; Snodgrass 2008; Blomberg 2012.

use of proverbial sayings. Proverbs are prominent in the book of Proverbs and in two chapters of Ecclesiastes. But how do they function in the teaching of Jesus?

A common use of proverbs, some would even say the normal use, is to uphold the norms, rituals, beliefs and institutions of society.[6] The book of Proverbs uses proverbs to encourage the pursuit of wisdom and the benefits it brings. Wisdom in Proverbs is rooted in the fear of Yahweh (Prov. 1:7) and the instructions of Proverbs 1 – 9 lay a religious foundation for understanding the individual proverbial sayings that begin in Proverbs 10. So the proverbs in Proverbs support the religious understanding of life based on God's revelation (see chapters 3 – 4). The proverbs are used to exhort the son to pursue the path of wisdom. They show the benefits of pursuing that path and the negative consequences for walking in the way of foolishness.

Proverbs are used differently in Ecclesiastes, more specifically in the first-person autobiography of Qohelet. Proverbs are used to argue that there is a relative advantage of wisdom over folly, but wisdom fails to meet one's expectations and to provide the answers one is seeking. The collection of proverbs in Ecclesiastes 7:1–12 seeks to answer the question 'What is good?' A high concentration of 'better than' sayings (a comparative use of good) shows that some things are better than others,[7] but ultimately these better things have only relative value, a characteristic that also describes wisdom (Eccl. 2:12–17). Ecclesiastes 7 begins with two proverbs that produce discord. The first proverb in 7:1a, 'Better is a good name than good oil', states that a good reputation is better than expensive ointment, a thought in line with Proverbs 22:1. But the second proverb in 7:1b, 'the day of death is better than the day of one's birth', produces tension with the first proverb because normally the day of death is not considered better than the day of birth. This view is usually expressed by someone who is experiencing suffering (Job 3; Jer. 20). If death is all that awaits people, then what is the value of life and a good reputation?[8]

The proverbs in Ecclesiastes 10:1–20 occur in the context of the argument that a little folly can destroy the benefits of wisdom (9:13 – 10:20). The first proverb makes the point that just as something as small as a dead fly can ruin perfume, so a little folly can destroy the

---

[6] Witherington 1994: 157.
[7] Many of the proverbs in 7:1–12 sound positive, but in the context of ch. 7 are teaching that wisdom has only a relative advantage.
[8] Bartholomew 2009: 246.

value of wisdom.[9] The difficulty a fool runs into is highlighted in verses 2–3 and 12–15 to illustrate the principle that one sinner can destroy the good associated with wisdom (9:18). Although wisdom can help a person avoid some of the difficulties of life (10:8–10), the success of wisdom is dependent on acting at the right time. The wrong timing can cause great damage, as illustrated by the failure of the snake charmer (10:11). Even something hidden, like a person's thoughts, can cause problems (10:20). The proverbs in Ecclesiastes do not support traditional wisdom teaching but are used to question wisdom and show its failures.

How does Jesus use proverbs in his teaching? Some argue that Jesus uses proverbs to question the wisdom teaching of the OT in the same way that Qohelet uses proverbs to question the wisdom teaching of Proverbs.[10] Both Qohelet and Jesus stress certain given dimensions of experience against received traditions.[11] Many of Jesus' proverbs emphasize that people should not worry about their life but should trust God (Matt. 6:25–26; Luke 12:22–23). This teaching is different from the teaching of Proverbs that stresses human responsibility (6:6–8).[12] There are no proverbs in Jesus' teaching urging the fear of God, stressing hard work, using stereotypes like the sluggard or encouraging character building.[13] Rather, the life associated with wisdom must be given up for the sake of God's kingdom. Jesus uses paradox to nullify the present state of things to prepare people to hear the announcement of new life (Matt. 6:24; 10:16). This new life is a counter-order of transcendence announced as the arrival of God's rule.[14]

The Beatitudes: a kingdom lifestyle

The only way to answer these questions is to examine some of the proverbs and related wisdom sayings that Jesus uses in his teaching.[15] Matthew's Gospel has been called a Gospel of wisdom, with the

---

[9] Ibid. 321.

[10] Witherington 1994: 163–164; Williams 1981: 10. Williams comments that Jesus protests against the doctrine of retribution in the sense that he opposes the ancient wisdom conviction that there is a reward for righteousness in this world.

[11] Williams 1981: 69. He compares Qohelet's and Jesus' use of proverbs and sees both similarities and dissimilarities between them, but both use proverbs to undermine or nullify the present order of things.

[12] Williams 1981: 47–56.

[13] Witherington 1994: 162.

[14] Williams 1981: 57–61.

[15] Perdue (1986) gives a list of the different types of wisdom sayings that Jesus uses.

Sermon on the Mount expressing wisdom ideas.[16] A beatitude in the OT is typically one line containing the word *'ašrê* bound to a noun or pronoun, followed by a relative clause (Pss 1:1; 2:12; Prov. 3:13; Eccl. 10:17). Jesus' beatitudes in the Sermon on the Mount (Matt. 5:2–12; Luke 6:20–23) use the word *makarios*, which is bound to a description of the character or state of the person, followed by a clause that gives a reason for that state.[17] Two of the beatitudes in Matthew 5 give the same reason for the blessing, 'for theirs is the kingdom of heaven' (5:3, 10). These two beatitudes promise this reward to emphasize that everything between the two is included in the theme of the kingdom.[18] The Beatitudes describe people who belong to the kingdom of heaven, teach about the lifestyle of the kingdom and emphasize the benefits that come to those who are part of the kingdom.[19]

Most English translations render *makarios* as 'blessed', but Pennington has recently expressed concern that such a translation confuses the differences between *'ašrê/makarios* and *bārak/eulogeō*.[20] The Hebrew word *bārak* is frequently used with God as the subject referring to the bestowal of divine favour. Such a person is empowered or favoured as the recipient of blessing from the Lord, and is thus 'blessed'. The word *'ašrê* is an exclamatory description of the state of happiness or privilege observed by someone else. It is human descriptive speech that generally describes people in a certain state rather than actions. Thus these two words, and their Greek counterparts, are not synonymous and should not be translated the same way. Pennington suggests the translation 'flourishing' for *'ašrê/makarios* because it accurately describes the state of well-being and happiness experienced by a person who is called *'ašrê/makarios*.[21] Pennington recognizes, however, that both *bārak* and *'ašrê* can refer to a state or condition so that God's divine action of blessing and the resulting state are related, but they should be kept separate when discussing the meaning of these words and when translating them. Thus

---

[16] Witherington 1994: 335, 356. He draws a lot of connections between Matthew and the Wisdom of Solomon, particularly the idea of a king seeking wisdom. General associations can be drawn between Jesus' teaching in Matthew and wisdom without arguing that the source of Matthew's ideas is the Wisdom of Solomon.

[17] Hendriksen 1973: 265; for a discussion of the form of the beatitude in different periods of history see Guelich 1982: 63–65.

[18] Carson 1987: 16. He calls the Beatitudes 'The Norms of the Kingdom'.

[19] Ferguson 1987: 10.

[20] The two Hebrew words are regularly translated with the corresponding Greek word.

[21] Pennington 2017: 47–49.

bārak/*eulogeō* should be translated as 'blessed' and '*ašrê*/*makarios* as 'flourishing'. But if '*ašrê* 'refers to true happiness and flourishing within the gracious covenant God has given',[22] it is a bit artificial to make too much of a distinction between these two words. There are times in the Psalms when '*ašrê* is a result of divine action. For example, in Psalm 32:2 a person is in a state of '*ašrê* because God does not count his iniquity against him. In Psalm 65:4 the one God chooses to bring near to dwell in his house is the one called '*ašrê*. Thus in some cases God's actions are directly related to people being able to experience 'well-being' ('*ašrê*). In Matthew 13:16 those who are *makarios* are given the ability to know the secrets of the kingdom of heaven (13:11).[23] In Matthew 16:17 Simon is *makarios* because the Father in heaven revealed to Peter that Jesus is the Christ, the son of the living God.[24] The use of the word *makarios* is not limited to people but also applies to God (1 Tim. 1:11; 6:15).[25] There is benefit in talking about the differences between '*ašrê*/*makarios* and *bārak*/*eulogeō*, and how such differences might have an impact on translation,[26] but there is also overlap between the two word groups. Thus the translation 'blessed' works well as expressing both the benefit of someone being the recipient of God's blessing but also the condition or state in which such a blessing results.

Those who are blessed include the poor in spirit, the ones who mourn, the meek, the ones who hunger and thirst after righteousness, the merciful, the pure in heart, the peacemakers and the ones persecuted for righteousness' sake. The poor in spirit recognize their spiritual bankruptcy as being unworthy before God. It is the deepest form of repentance, showing complete dependence on the Lord.[27]

---

[22] Ibid. 44.

[23] Pennington (ibid. 56) states that the whole point of the explanation is that some are given this and others are not, and those who see and hear experience full and true life because they align with Jesus' teaching.

[24] Pennington (ibid.) separates *makarios* from the giving of this revelation by the Father and limits the state of flourishing to Peter's ability to see who Jesus is. But the reason Peter is *makarios* is 'because' (*hoti*) the Father in heaven has revealed this to Peter (Matt. 16:17).

[25] Carson 2010: 9.161.

[26] There are many very good insights in Pennington 2017. He also describes well the difficulty of trying to find an appropriate word to translate *makarios*. The translation 'flourishing' seems a bit awkward. The word 'happy' is too superficial because for many people happiness is a feeling related to the outward circumstances of life. The word 'truly happy' or 'divinely happy' (Ferguson 1987: 13) might work better, but in the light of the discussion above 'blessed' is still a good word.

[27] Carson 1987: 17. The following descriptions of the blessed depend on Carson and Ferguson.

Such a response receives the kingdom of God. The next three beatitudes (vv. 4–6) describe further the characteristics of those who are part of the kingdom. If the first beatitude describes unworthiness before God, then mourning is grief over sin, meekness is a submission to God and a proper attitude of our relationship to others, and a hunger and thirst after righteousness is a strong desire for a relationship with God and to live rightly before him. The next three beatitudes (vv. 7–9) describe the kind of life that results from poverty of spirit. The merciful respond with kindness to those who are miserable, the pure in heart are undivided in their devotion to God, and the peacemakers are those who live in peace and seek peace with others. The final two beatitudes focus on persecution as a result of living for God.[28] Those who are persecuted for righteousness' sake are blessed as members of God's kingdom and should rejoice because their reward in heaven is great.

There is a correlation in many of the beatitudes between the character of the blessed with what they will receive.[29] The mourners will be comforted, those who hunger and thirst for righteousness will be filled, the merciful will receive mercy, the pure in heart will see God, and the peacemakers will be called the sons of God. These benefits are a reflection of the character of the God of the kingdom of which they are members. The life of the blessed is similar to those in Proverbs who fear Yahweh. They have a reverence for God so that they are willing to submit everything to his authority. They turn away from evil because they fear Yahweh instead of being wise in their own eyes (Prov. 3:7), are steadfast in righteousness (Prov. 11:19), do not forsake steadfast love (Prov. 3:3), are blameless (Prov. 11:5; Job 1:1) and make peace with their enemies (Prov. 16:7). The phrase 'steadfast love' (*ḥesed*) stresses mercy that arises from faithfulness, and 'blameless' (*tām*) expresses a wholeness of life that avoids hypocrisy, much like the description of the pure in heart.

Jesus' teaching and the teaching of Proverbs

Jesus' teaching centres on the kingdom of God. The character of the kingdom has an impact on the life of a follower of Jesus and explains some of the differences with the OT. The basic character of God's

---

[28] See Pennington 2017: 116–117 for a discussion of whether there are eight or nine beatitudes. He argues for nine based on the many sets of three in the Sermon and that the ninth beatitude (Matt. 5:11) is an expansion of the eighth, a custom common in ancient literature.

[29] Carson 1987: 17.

kingdom is a spiritual kingdom that is present now, but has not yet come in its fullness.[30] The material blessings promised in the OT are not negated, but will not be fully experienced until the fullness of the kingdom comes in Jesus' second coming. As the kingdom of God moves out into the world, there will be opposition to it that will have an impact on the lives of believers. Jesus even calls blessed those who are persecuted for righteousness' sake and those who are reviled by others because of him.[31] The response to persecution is to rejoice because there is a reward in heaven. Trouble for a believer is not a sign of God's displeasure but is a blessing associated with following Jesus. The promise that the meek will inherit the earth (Ps. 37) is expanded from a focus on the land as Israel's inheritance to the earth as the believer's inheritance (Rom. 4:13), culminating in the new heavens and earth. The one who feared Yahweh sought God's wisdom in Proverbs, but the one who is poor in spirit will seek Jesus as the wisdom of God. The kingdom of God established by Jesus has an impact on his use of proverbs.

The topics in the Sermon on the Mount after the Beatitudes are very similar to the topics addressed in the early chapters of Proverbs after the introduction of wisdom. Table 2 shows the connections.[32]

Table 2: A comparison of topics in Proverbs and
the Sermon on the Mount

Topics addressed	Proverbs	Sermon on the Mount
The narrow path	Prov. 2:1–22	Matt. 7:13–14
Keep the commandments	Prov. 3:1	Matt. 5:17–20
Use of material goods	Prov. 3:8–9	Matt. 6:19–21
God's wisdom in nature	Prov. 3:19–20	Matt. 6:25–34
Sexual purity	Prov. 5:1–23	Matt. 5:27–32
Guard one's speech	Prov. 6:1–3	Matt. 5:33–37
Be active	Prov. 6:4–6	Matt. 5:16

The teaching in Proverbs overlaps with many of the topics that Jesus addresses. The Beatitudes describe a person who exhibits the same characteristics as one in Proverbs who fears Yahweh. The topic 'Be active' in Matthew emphasizes living in such a way that others see

---

[30] For discussions of the nature of the kingdom see Carson 1987: 11–15; Ladd 1959; and Ridderbos 1962.

[31] Pennington (2017: 153–156) discusses the paradoxical nature of suffering in relationship to human 'flourishing' (*makarios*).

[32] This list follows Witherington 1994: 356 with some minor adaptations.

your good works, an antidote to laziness (Prov. 13:4; 19:15). Even though there is overlap in the subject matter addressed, how does Jesus teach on these topics in the light of the kingdom of God?

Life is transformed when the kingdom becomes a priority. Jesus warns against anxiety concerning the basic needs of life (Matt. 6:25–34). People should not worry about what they will eat, drink or wear because God will provide what they need. The birds and flowers are given as an example. Birds do not sow or reap but God feeds them. Lilies do not spin but God clothes them. People are more valuable than birds or flowers. If God takes care of the birds and flowers, he will take care of his own. Worry does not contribute anything positive to life because God knows what his people need. The proper response is to seek first the kingdom of God and his righteousness, and God will supply everything that is needed. This teaching ends with the proverb 'Therefore do not be anxious about tomorrow, for tomorrow will be anxious for itself. Sufficient for the day is its own trouble' (6:34). Jesus' teaching sounds different from the emphasis in Proverbs on planning and taking responsibility. But Proverbs does not treat planning and responsibility as if they are opposed to trust in the Lord (Prov. 3:5–6). There are proverbs that emphasize that human planning may come to nothing apart from God's purposes (Prov. 16:9; 19:21; 21:30–31). In Luke's Gospel Jesus follows teaching about anxiety concerning the provisions of life with two parables that emphasize the necessity of planning and responsibility (Luke 12:35–48). He ends the second parable with the proverb 'Everyone to whom much was given, of him much will be required, and from him to whom they entrusted much, they will demand the more' (12:48). The disciples of Jesus must be faithful and responsible while they await the coming of Jesus. Both trust and responsibility are important.

The teaching of the two ways was central in Proverbs and Jesus also taught it. The conclusion of the Sermon on the Mount begins with a proverb about two gates, two ways, two travellers and two destinations. He encourages people to enter by the narrow gate that leads to life, even though its way is hard and few find it. Many, on the other hand, enter the wide gate that is easy and leads to destruction (7:13–14). The two paths are not ends in themselves, but have eternal significance beyond themselves. Thus the narrow way ends in life (7:14), good fruit (7:17), entrance into the kingdom of heaven (7:21) and stability (7:25). The broad way ends in destruction (7:13), bad fruit and fire (7:19), exclusion from the kingdom (7:23) and ruin

(7:27).[33] The way of following Jesus is a way of blessing, but it is a difficult way that goes against the way most people live and so brings opposition (Matt. 5:10–12).[34] Jesus has announced the kingdom of God and is clear on the cost of entering the kingdom.

There are many reasons why it is difficult to follow Jesus and some of them he expresses in proverbs. There is opposition to Jesus in his own home town because he is too familiar to the residents. Even though at first they speak well of him, they begin to reflect that Jesus is well known to them as the son of Joseph. Their familiarity leads to indifference and scepticism.[35] How can he fulfil Isaiah 61 to set at liberty those who are oppressed? Perceiving their scepticism, Jesus put into their mouths the proverb 'Physician, heal yourself' (Luke 4:23).[36] This is a statement challenging Jesus to prove himself and to do in his home town of Nazareth what they heard he has done in Capernaum. Jesus does not comply with the request and gives an example of OT prophets who ministered outside the bounds of Israel. These examples anger the people, so they try to kill him.

People rejected both John the Baptist and Jesus by not taking seriously their ministries. After speaking of the important role of John the Baptist, Jesus shows how the people act like children in their evaluation of their respective ministries. Children sit in the market-places and call out to their playmates:

> We played the flute for you, and you did not dance;
> we sang a dirge, and you did not mourn.
>
> (Matt. 11:17)

The people were not satisfied with either Jesus or John's ministries, even though they were the opposite of each other. John ministered in the barren wilderness apart from the abundant necessities of life and they said he had a demon. Jesus ministered among the people, eating and drinking, and they called him a glutton and a drunkard. They were like children in the marketplace who were not satisfied.[37]

---

[33] Carson 1987: 130.

[34] Carson (ibid. 130–133) reflects on the implication that the majority follow the broad way.

[35] Geldenhuys 1977: 168.

[36] Edwards (2015: 140) calls this a general proverb, widespread in Judaism, which pertains to the rejection of prophets and sages.

[37] Ridderbos 1987: 220–221.

Jesus concludes with another proverb, 'Yet wisdom is justified by her deeds' (11:19). The ministries of both John the Baptist and Jesus are vindicated by their results. True wisdom is found in following them and not by indifference to them. In context the deeds refer to the lifestyles of John and Jesus, which are acknowledged as coming from wisdom.[38] The parallel passage in Luke 7:35 ends with 'Yet wisdom is justified by all her children.' This proverb is similar to the proverb in Matthew, for Luke focuses on the lifestyles of John and Jesus as wisdom's children.[39] If John and Jesus represent wisdom in the way they live, then those who reject them are rejecting wisdom.

Jesus uses proverbs to distinguish the righteous from the wicked. When Jesus is accused of casting out demons by the prince of demons, he utters the proverb 'Either make the tree good and its fruit good, or make the tree bad and its fruit bad, for a tree is known by its fruit' (Matt. 12:33). A good tree cannot produce bad fruit so the tree and its fruit must be considered good or bad.[40] The fruit gives evidence of what kind of tree it is. Jesus then identifies the evil of the Pharisees by calling them a brood of vipers. They cannot speak good things about Jesus because they are evil. Jesus identifies the characteristics of the wicked just as Proverbs does.

Jesus also calls people to follow him, such as Matthew the tax collector (Matt. 9:9). When a Pharisee saw that tax collectors and sinners were eating with Jesus, he asked his disciples why Jesus ate with such people. Jesus responds with a proverb: 'Those who are well have no need of a physician, but those who are sick' (Matt. 9:12). He follows this up with 'I came not to call the righteous, but sinners' (v. 13). Jesus speaks against the self-righteousness of the Pharisees and emphasizes that he came to call sinners. By following Jesus sinners can become righteous.

Jesus gives wisdom to those who follow him. He calls twelve disciples and sends them out to proclaim the kingdom and to minister to the people (Matt. 10:1–15). Jesus warns them of the opposition they will face; in fact, they will be defenceless, like sheep among wolves. He instructs them how to respond: 'be wise as serpents and innocent as doves' (10:16). They need to be shrewd in their analysis

---

[38] Carson 2010: 9.314. The connection between the deeds and lifestyles of John and Jesus is that wisdom is concerned with right living.

[39] Ibid. Wisdom's children is a reference to John, Jesus and all God's messengers and is not a reference to the crowds.

[40] Hendriksen 1973: 530.

of situations and people in order to make good decisions,[41] and they need to be genuine in their motives and behaviour.[42] They will be flogged in their synagogues and be dragged before governors and kings to bear witness, but will be given wisdom concerning what to say (Luke 21:15). Stephen, the first martyr of the early church, was given wisdom and the Spirit in his disputes with the Jews (Acts 6:10). Family members will deliver family members to death and they will be hated by all. Having wisdom as followers of Jesus does not keep them from suffering persecution that may cause physical, emotional and financial harm. A clear connection exists between following Jesus and persecution, so that the expectation of those who follow Jesus is that there will be suffering. The relationship between wisdom and blessing is not severed, but a follower of Jesus understands that there will be spiritual blessing in persecution and that the fullness of blessing will not be received until the fullness of the kingdom comes. Instead of struggling with this kind of suffering, as Qohelet did, the disciples of Jesus rejoice that they are counted worthy to suffer for Jesus (Acts 5:41).

The proverbs of Jesus: the radical reorientation of life

Does Jesus' use of proverbs support or reject the status quo? Sometimes Jesus seems to support the status quo, as when he tells people, 'Render to Caesar the things that are Caesar's, and to God the things that are God's' (Mark 12:17). Jesus is responding to a question from the Herodians about whether it is lawful to pay taxes to Caesar. They are trying to trap him by forcing him to answer a question that can get him into trouble no matter how he answers. If he answers that the people do not have to pay taxes, then the Herodians will use that information against him with the Roman government. If he answers they have to pay taxes to Rome, then the people may reject him. Jesus' response points out that they are under the authority of the Roman government and have accepted this by using Roman money with Caesar's likeness and inscription on it. It is only appropriate that they give back to Caesar what is due him and to God what is due him. Jesus avoids the trap and indicates that the kingdom of God will not be tied up with the civil government (John 18:36).[43] The coming of

[41] Ibid. 461. He notes that this involves '*insight* into the nature of one's surroundings, both personal and material, *circumspection, sanctified common sense, wisdom* to do the right thing at the right time and place and in the right manner . . .' (emphases original).
[42] Ridderbos 1987: 201.
[43] Lane 1974: 424.

the kingdom transforms a person's life and relationships to other institutions.

The transformation that comes from a person's relationship to Jesus is brought out in other proverbs. Followers of Jesus must make a total commitment of self-denial. The reason self-denial is important is expressed by 'For whoever would save his life will lose it, but whoever loses his life for my sake and the gospel's will save it' (Mark 8:35). This is a paradoxical statement that goes against the way of the world because in the world people normally get ahead in life by seeking to save their life. Followers of Jesus must lose their life in order to save it. In other words, they must be willing to give up everything that is important to follow Jesus. Putting Jesus first reorients all of life around him. People normally seek to be first, but those who follow Jesus must seek to be last of all and a servant of all (Mark 9:35). Following Jesus is subversive of the status quo in the sense that what was important before is now not very important.

After a rich young man walks away from Jesus because of the former's many possessions (Mark 10:17–22), Jesus teaches his disciples how difficult it is for those who have wealth to enter the kingdom. The disciples are amazed at these words. Jesus emphasizes this teaching with a 'how much more' proverb: 'It is easier for a camel to go through the eye of a needle than for a rich person to enter the kingdom of God' (Mark 10:25). The disciples are 'exceedingly astonished' at this saying and ask Jesus, 'Then who can be saved?' (v. 26). Jesus uses a proverb to show that the temptations that come with wealth can keep people from following him. People trust in their wealth rather than in God. Jesus affirms the impossibility of someone with wealth entering the kingdom when he says it is easier for a camel to go through the eye of a needle. Whatever picture lies behind this state-ment,[44] it stresses the impossibility of something actually taking place. This explains the disciples' question about who can be saved and Jesus' answer that 'With man it is impossible, but not with God. For all things are possible with God' (Mark 10:27). God has the power to transform a person's relationship to wealth. At first this teaching may seem to go against the teaching in Proverbs that wealth is a great blessing.[45] But Proverbs does not view wealth as an absolute good;

---

[44] Witherington (1994: 166, n. 80) agrees with Lane (1974: 369) that attempts to whittle off the hard edge of this saying by talking about some needle-gate in Jerusalem should be resisted.

[45] Witherington (1994: 164) states that this proverb reflects an order that goes counter to traditional wisdom.

rather, it is something that has relative value as expressed in the 'better than' sayings (16:8; 17:1). Proverbs also states that wisdom is more valuable than riches (3:13–15), and Jesus states that becoming a member of the kingdom of God by following him is more valuable than wealth. The transformation of a person's orientation to life is brought out in Peter's follow-up statement 'we have left everything and followed you' (Mark 10:28). Jesus' response is that the normal relationships in life are changed when a person follows Jesus. Natural family relationships are still important (Matt. 19:5–6), but the family is expanded to include other followers of Jesus, who act as brothers, sisters and mothers. Financial help is also available along with the fact of persecution and in the age to come eternal life. The impact of following Jesus is expressed in the proverb 'But many who are first will be last, and the last first' (Mark 10:31). The kingdom of God rearranges people's priorities when they put Jesus first.

Jesus' use of proverbs is dependent on his mission to proclaim and establish the kingdom of God. The proverbial sayings of Jesus must be understood in relationship to the character of the kingdom as submission to the rule of God embodied in the person and work of Jesus. They must also be understood in the light of the urgency of the moment of decision that comes with the kingdom. Entering the kingdom must be a person's highest priority. This parallels the emphasis in Proverbs of seeking wisdom and getting wisdom at all costs, except now it is seeking Jesus and following him at all costs. Jesus' teaching does not stand against the wisdom in Proverbs, but highlights aspects of response because of the radical nature of the kingdom. One must seek first the kingdom with the assurance that everything else a person needs will be provided by God. This commitment leads to a life of faith and trust without worry about the details of life. Trust, however, does not take away the need for planning and acting responsibly in earthly matters.

A person who follows Jesus recognizes the spiritual nature of the kingdom and that it is here now but will not come in its fullness until Jesus comes again. This perspective has an impact on how people perceive their earthly life. Material blessings may be experienced in this life, but wealth is not the most important pursuit of a believer. Following Jesus is more important, and following Jesus can bring persecution that may have an impact on a believer's financial situation. A follower of Jesus must be willing to give up material blessings with the realization that the fullness of blessings that will be received when Jesus comes will be greater than anything experienced in this life.

Wisdom and the person of Christ

The humanity of Jesus

One of the main purposes of Proverbs is to teach young people the benefits of wisdom so that they will choose the path of wisdom and avoid the path of foolishness. The young person who follows wisdom 'will find favour and good success in the sight of God and man' (Prov. 3:4). Jesus is described in the same way early in his life before the age of twelve: 'And the child grew and became strong, filled with wisdom. And the favour of God was upon him' (Luke 2:40). Jesus developed physically, intellectually and spiritually.[46] At the age of twelve Jesus went to the Feast of Passover in Jerusalem with his parents. When they left the city, Jesus stayed behind in the temple, sitting among the teachers and asking them questions (Luke 2:46–47). All who heard him were amazed at his understanding and questions. Even at the age of twelve Jesus' wisdom was evident for all to see. His parents, who had been looking for him, were also astonished and expressed concern that Jesus had stayed behind: 'Son, why have you treated us so?' (v. 48). Jesus' answer expresses surprise that they did not know where to find him: 'Did you not know that I must be in my Father's house?' (v. 49). Jesus is already aware of a divine mission upon his life that arises from a special relationship he has with 'my Father'.[47] And yet his relationship with his heavenly Father does not take away his responsibility to submit to his earthly parents (v. 51). Jesus' early life is summarized in the statement 'And Jesus increased in wisdom and in stature and in favour with God and man' (v. 52). Here is an example of what it looks like for a young person to pursue the way of God's wisdom.

Jesus demonstrated wisdom in a number of ways in his ministry. He used wisdom forms in his teaching. The way he taught generated responses of astonishment from the people. He did not teach like other rabbis but taught as one who had authority (Matt. 7:28–29). Other teachers based their authority on what others said by quoting them, but Jesus did not appeal to any outside authority to verify his words.[48] When the scribes and Pharisees ask Jesus for a sign, he

---

[46] For further description of Jesus' development see Hendriksen 1978: 179–180.

[47] Ibid. 186.

[48] Ridderbos 1987: 157. Carson (Carson 2010: 9.232) summarizes well the uniqueness of Jesus' authority when he states, 'he speaks in the first person and claims that his teaching fulfills the OT, that he determines who enters the messianic kingdom, that as the Divine Judge he pronounces banishment, that the true heirs of the kingdom will be persecuted for their allegiance to him, and that he alone fully knows the will of his Father'.

warns them that at the judgment the Queen of the South will rise up to condemn their generation. She came from the ends of the earth to hear the wisdom of Solomon, but someone greater than Solomon is here (Matt. 12:42). Solomon was the wisest man of the OT but Jesus has more wisdom than Solomon. Jesus' generation is squandering a great opportunity in their rejection of him. The Queen of the South had to travel a long way to hear Solomon, but Jesus is near the people. The Queen gave gifts to Solomon, but the people of Jesus' day do not bring him gifts. The Queen showed more wisdom than the foolish of Jesus' day who reject him. Even the people who grew up with Jesus were astonished at his teaching and asked, 'Where did this man get this wisdom and these mighty works?' (Matt. 13:54). They took offence at him and did not believe.

One passage brings together Jesus as the Wisdom of God and his status as God himself. Jesus pronounces 'woe' on the lawyers who load people with burdens hard to bear and build the tombs of the prophets, whom their fathers killed. They are complicit in what their fathers have done because they consent to it. Jesus charges his generation with the blood of all the prophets. In commenting on the source of the ministry of the prophets he states, 'Therefore also the Wisdom of God said, "I will send them prophets and apostles, some of whom they will kill and persecute"' (Luke 11:49). The Wisdom of God here could be a reference to God the Father because the prophets in view are OT prophets. God did send the prophets to his people. The parallel passage, however, has Jesus saying, 'I send you prophets and wise men and scribes . . .' (Matt. 23:34). A comparison of these passages shows that Jesus is the Wisdom of God and has the authority to send prophets. No wonder people marvel at his teaching and works. One greater than Solomon is here, even God in the flesh.

The deity of Jesus

How does the divinity of Jesus relate to the wisdom of God? What is the source of the NT statements about Jesus' divinity? Some argue for a wisdom Christology that goes back to early Jewish Christianity reflected in some of the earliest Christological statements about Jesus, particularly the Christological hymn fragments (Phil. 2:6–11; Col. 1:15–20; 1 Tim. 3:16; Heb. 1:2–4; John 1:1–5, 9–14). Three primary sources used for the Christological hymns are the earliest Christian preaching about the life of Jesus, the Christological use of the psalms, and earlier Jewish discussions about personified or hypostasized wisdom. Many argue that the dominant source is the Jewish reflection on personified wisdom. These hymns offer the first reflection on what it might mean to say that the pre-existent Redeemer became a human being.[49] Others express caution in giving personified wisdom too much explanatory value to the doctrine of Christ because Jesus is not just an attribute of God but is a distinct person.[50] This discussion goes back to Proverbs 8 and it is important how one defines the role of Wisdom in that passage. Is Wisdom a hypostasis? Is Wisdom a personification, and if so, what does Wisdom personify? Is Wisdom a major source for understanding the person of Jesus?

John 1: Jesus as the Word of God
There are limits to what can be accomplished here. A full-blown exposition of the following texts will not be attempted, but the focus will be on what is taught about the person of Christ and whether the source of that teaching can be identified. The prologue of John's Gospel (1:1–18) affirms many things about the Son. He is called the 'Word' (*logos*) who existed before the creation of the world. He was already in existence with God 'in the beginning' and, in fact, he was God (1:1–2). He was God's agent in the creation of the world as 'All things were made through him' (1:3). He is light and life (1:4); but when the true light came into the world, that light was rejected by many. The Word took on human flesh and dwelt among God's people, who saw his glory (1:14). Several things are important concerning John's description of the Son. First, he is called the 'Word' (*logos*). Second, the use of 'in the beginning' has associations with the creation account (Gen. 1:1) where God creates by the power of his word. The word of God is prominent in the OT and is used to describe God's powerful activity in creation (Gen. 1; Ps. 33:6), revelation (Jer. 1:4; Isa. 9:8; Ezek. 33:7) and deliverance (Ps. 107:20; Isa. 55:1).[51] Third, the Word was an agent in the work of creation, bringing all things into existence. Fourth, the source of life is the Word, who is also the light of human beings. Life is the dynamic power of human existence that radiates light which others can see.[52] Fifth, the light comes into the world and is rejected (1:10–11). Finally, the Word became flesh to dwell among his people, which resulted in a demonstration of his glory.

[49] Witherington 1994: 249–254.
[50] Ebert 2011: 5.
[51] Carson 1991: 115.
[52] Carson (ibid. 119) comments that 'The self-existing life of the Word was so dispensed at creation that it became the light of the human race.'

There are associations between John's discussion of the pre-existence of Jesus and the creation account of Genesis 1. God speaks and things come into existence. The power of God's word in John 1:1 is identified as the Son as the agent of creation. The use of 'Word' (*logos*) and not 'Wisdom' (*sophia*) is significant if there was a wisdom Christology in early Jewish Christianity. John could have used wisdom but he bypassed it to associate the Son with creation. But there are other ideas expressed in John 1 that are not clearly articulated in Genesis 1. The fact that the Word was with God speaks of a relationship between the Word and God before the creation of the world. The rejection of the light obviously occurs at a time much later than creation. The incarnation of the Word and his glory that accompanies Jesus' life on earth manifests God's presence with his people. It is possible that these ideas reflect the role of Wisdom in Proverbs 8, but not in a direct way, as if John is associating Jesus with a hypostasis of Wisdom that develops into a wisdom Christology.[53] The personification of Lady Wisdom in Proverbs 8 allows for connections to be made with Jesus while at the same time recognizing significant differences between Lady Wisdom and Jesus. If Wisdom is only the personification of an attribute of God, then there are fewer reasons to see associations with Jesus.[54] If Wisdom is the personification of the revelation of God (see chapter 2), then other associations with Jesus, who is the final revelation of God, are possible. Wisdom was with God during creation and is presented as an agent in creation as God 'by wisdom' founded the earth (Prov. 3:19). Wisdom is also rejected when she calls to the simple and fools to follow her (Prov. 1:20–33). Although there is a rich heritage in the OT of God's presence with his people in the tabernacle and temple, 'glory' (*kābôd*) is also associated with wisdom (Prov. 8:18).[55] John may be drawing on common ideas in the OT without a direct dependence on a wisdom

[53] The development of wisdom in Second Temple Judaism is important as a general background to the NT use of wisdom. E.g. Witherington (1994: 285) highlights that in the Wisdom of Solomon 7.27 Wisdom is the effulgence of eternal light and the very life breath of God. Some, however, make too much of these developments as if the NT authors are dependent on Second Temple Judaism for how they explain OT concepts. The NT authors are more likely to interact directly with the OT because it was their authoritative Scripture. Wisdom was also associated with life (Prov. 3:13–16) and light (Prov. 6:23) in the OT. Second Temple Judaism should not be used to determine what is possible for the NT authors to affirm.
[54] Ebert 2011: 22.
[55] The ESV translates this word as 'honour'.

Christology.[56] Associations between Jesus and wisdom are not a problem as long as one recognizes differences between Jesus and the personification of wisdom.

Colossians 1:15–20: Christ the wisdom of God
Although there would be great benefit in examining the other hymns that speak about Christ's pre-existence (Phil. 2:5–11; 1 Tim. 3:16; Heb. 1:2–4),[57] Colossians 1:15–20 is a key text in discussing the person of Jesus and his relationship to wisdom.[58] Paul identifies Christ as the one 'in whom are hidden all the treasures of wisdom and knowledge' (2:3). Paul writes Colossians to address false teaching that has led the Colossians away from the gospel and orthodox views of Christ. This false teaching appears to combine Graeco-Roman philosophy with Jewish regulations that lead people to assert the centrality of issues other than Christ and the gospel.[59] Paul writes Colossians to address the problem of false teaching so that the church will not be deluded by it. Part of Paul's response is to set forth the proper view of Christ, who is not only the Wisdom of God but is God, 'For in him the whole fullness of deity dwells bodily' (2:9). A key passage in the book that discusses Christ as God's wisdom is 1:15–20.

Paul proclaims the supremacy of Christ over creation (1:15–16) and over the new creation of Christ's body the church (1:18–20). The centre of the poem (1:17) asserts that Christ holds all things together as the sustainer and the unifying principle of the universe (Heb. 1:3).[60] Christ is the creator and sustainer of the universe, he is the

[56] Carson (1991: 116) points out that the determining factor in John's use of *logos* may not be this or that background but the church's experience of Jesus Christ. Background information is important, but in order to determine what John means by *logos* we must listen to John himself.
[57] These are the texts discussed by Witherington in his chapter on early Christological hymns. He connects the Servant concept in Phil. 2:5–11 with wisdom in Sirach and the Wisdom of Solomon and the idea of 'being seen by angels' in 1 Tim. 3:16 as an allusion to the sapiential material in *1 Enoch* 42. Many ideas associated with wisdom are in Heb. 1:2–4, including Christ as the agent of creation, temporal pre-existence and the Redeemer sitting down by the right hand of God (Wis. 9.4). Although Witherington recognizes the OT connections, the associations with wisdom overshadow the clear OT connections.
[58] Moo (2008: 108–110) discusses whether Paul is using traditional material, like a hymn, to explain the distinctive syntax of this passage, or whether Paul himself could have composed it. He concludes that it is difficult to decide.
[59] For a brief discussion of the false teaching in Colossians see Carson and Moo 2005: 523–524 and Gladd 2016: 305–306. For an extensive analysis of this question see Moo 2008: 46–60.
[60] For discussions of the structure of Col. 1:15–20 see Ebert 2011: 89–90 and Garland 1998: 85–86.

redeemer of his people, and the one who will reconcile all things to himself. In discussing Christ's relationship to creation, Paul states the following about Christ (1:15–16):

1. He is the image of the invisible God.
2. [He is] the firstborn of all creation.
3. He is the creator of all things (all things were created in him, through him, and for him).

Christ also is before all things and upholds all things (1:17). In discussing Christ's relationship to his body, the church, Paul states the following about Christ (1:18–21):

1. He is the head of the body, the church.
2. He is the beginning.
3. He is the firstborn from the dead.
4. In him all the fullness of God dwells.
5. He will reconcile all things to himself.

What is the source of Paul's statements about Christ? Some argue for a heavy dependence on the Wisdom of Solomon by listing parallels between Colossians and phrases from the Wisdom of Solomon.[61] For example, Wisdom 7.26 calls Wisdom 'a spotless mirror of the working of God, and an image of his goodness', which is supposed to parallel the statement of Christ as the image of the invisible God (Col. 1:15a). In Wisdom 6.22 the course of Wisdom is traced 'from the beginning of creation', which is supposed to parallel 'firstborn of all creation' (Col. 1:15b). In Wisdom 7.24 she pervades and penetrates all things (Col. 1:16–17) and Wisdom 7.29 comments on her priority and superiority (Col. 1:17–18). Others refer to Sirach 1.4 and 24.9, where Wisdom is said to be created before all things. Dunn argues that Christ is praised in Colossians 1:15–20 in language commonly used in Hellenistic Judaism to refer to Wisdom. In discussing the idea of 'firstborn' he argues that the antecedent for this term is obviously Proverbs 8:22, and in a footnote comments that the use of this term in Psalm 89:27 (LXX 88:28) is less relevant.[62] But it is hard to argue for

---

[61] Wink 1990: 235, cited by Witherington 1994: 266–267. Witherington is more cautious when he states that 'the composer of this hymn is not simply transferring what was once said of Wisdom to Christ, for there are various small emendations or additions along the way'.

[62] Dunn 1996: 89–90.

a direct dependence of Paul on these Wisdom texts because of the difference between what Paul says about Christ and what these texts say about Wisdom.[63] Sirach develops the concept of Wisdom in Proverbs 8 but also identifies Wisdom with Israel's covenant law (Sir. 24.23).[64] The author of the Wisdom of Solomon sought to harmonize Jewish wisdom tradition with the concepts of Greek philosophy. Wisdom is presented as a supernatural entity (a hypostasis) that occupies an intermediary role between God and creation.[65] Such a move puts at risk the claims of Jewish monotheism by allowing them to be read within the context of a pantheistic cosmology and anthropology.[66]

Paul's assertions about Christ are on a different level. There may be general associations between what is said about Wisdom and what is said about Christ, but the subject is not Wisdom herself but the Son of God in whose person and work God's wisdom is found.[67] The personification of Wisdom in Proverbs 8 allows general similarities with Christ to be made, but Christ is very different from personified Wisdom. He is the image of the invisible God, an exact representation of God[68] and not just an image of God's goodness (Wis. 7.26).[69] The very nature and being of God have been perfectly revealed in him.[70] Christ is also the firstborn of all creation, not as the one who was first created, but as the one who is superior over everything else. Although Wisdom exists before creation, Wisdom is not superior over creation. Paul's thought reflects Psalm 89:27 where the promise is to make David the firstborn, the highest of the kings of the earth.[71] The

[63] McDonough 2009: 78–82. He examines the key texts in the Wisdom of Solomon and does not believe they provide a 'creating and saving' Wisdom which became the basis for the NT portrait of Christ. He argues that the role of Christ as the agent of creation developed from OT creation texts within a 'messianic matrix' of interpretation.

[64] Perdue 1977: 190, 193.

[65] Winston 1979: 34.

[66] Jobes 2000: 235.

[67] Ebert 2011: 93.

[68] Garland 1998: 86–87. He comments that an image of something was not considered as something distinct from the object it represented, but it has a share in the reality that it reveals.

[69] Moo (2008: 118) sees the possibility of a word/wisdom tradition as a possible background to Paul's comments about Christ in this passage, especially connections between Philo and Gen. 1, with the concept of image. In discussing that Christ is the one through whom all things were created, he comments that although it is likely that Christ's relationship to creation owes something to a word/wisdom tradition (including Prov. 8), it does not depend on that tradition (123–124).

[70] Bruce 1957: 193.

[71] Moo 2008: 119.

reason Christ is supreme over creation is given in verse 16, where all things are created 'in him', 'through him' and 'for him'. The first preposition 'in' (*en*) maintains Christ as 'the location from whom all came into being and in whom all creation is contained'.[72] The preposition 'through' (*dia*) expresses that he is the agent of creation, the one through whom all things came into existence. The preposition 'for' (*eis*) signifies that he is the goal of creation.[73] Christ is also before all things and all things hold together in him (1:17). He is the controlling principle of all creation.[74] He maintains all things so that there is a unity of purpose in creation and history. Everything is held together by Christ, who is orchestrating all things.[75] All of God's purposes for the universe are accomplished through Christ and for Christ. Wisdom, on the other hand, is used by God to create the world, but not in the same way that Christ is the Creator. Nowhere is it claimed that all things were created in her or for her (Col. 1:16), or that all things hold together in her (Col. 1:17). According to Wisdom 1.7 the Spirit of the Lord, not Wisdom, has filled the world and holds all things together. Christ is God's agent in creation, revelation and redemption, and all of God's purposes for the universe are accomplished through him.[76]

Paul then speaks about Christ as lord over God's new order, the church, where reconciliation takes place (1:18–20). He shows how Christ has the pre-eminent place in creation and in the new creation. Christ is the head of his body as its unifying source and authority. As head of the church Christ causes the church to live and grow. He also exercises authority over the church so that his body is not dependent on anything or anyone else.[77] Christ is the beginning of the new creation, who as the firstborn of the dead conquered death that he might have the first place in everything. Christ deserves that place because all the fullness of God dwells in him.[78] Christ ascended into heaven in his full humanity and deity, where he rules the world

[72] Garland 1998: 88, citing House 1992: 182. Moo (2008: 121) cautions that the 'in Christ' language of Paul may just be making the general point that all of God's creative work took place 'in terms of' or 'in reference to' Christ.

[73] Ebert 2011: 97.

[74] Garland 1998: 89. He comments that Christ keeps the cosmos from becoming a chaos.

[75] Hendriksen 1964: 74–75.

[76] Garland 1998: 84–85.

[77] Hendriksen 1964: 76–77.

[78] Moo (2008: 133) states that a word/wisdom background is not helpful in explaining the 'fullness' language; rather, such language can be explained better by OT descriptions of God's 'dwelling' in the temple.

on behalf of his church and where he will reconcile all things to himself by bringing everything under his authority.[79] Paul moves from creation to consummation and shows that every part of creation will be touched by Christ's reconciling work on the cross. The destinies of creation and the church are bound together. The universal supremacy of Christ matches the universality of the gospel and assures believers of the sufficiency of Christ.[80]

Wisdom and the work of Christ

Paul used wisdom terms to refer to the message that he preached in Corinth, a message centred on the word of the cross, Jesus Christ and him crucified. Paul calls Christ the wisdom of God (1 Cor. 1:24, 30). Many argue for a connection to the Jewish Wisdom tradition that developed from Proverbs 8, Sirach 24.3–22 and the Wisdom of Solomon 6.1 – 10.21 (esp. 7.12, 22; 8.4–5; 9.1–9).[81] Barrett comments on 1 Corinthians 1:30 on the use of wisdom:

> [wisdom] . . . now appears with a new meaning. In Jewish speculation . . . the more or less personified figure of Wisdom had come to occupy a place of increasing importance as a mediator between God and men, both in creation, and in communicating knowledge and salvation. Wisdom was thus a term that lay ready at hand for Christological purposes, and Paul uses it, sometimes directly, as here, and sometimes by appropriating to Christ functions and predicates which in Judaism had been ascribed to Wisdom . . . Christ crucified himself becomes the personal figure of Wisdom, God's agent in creation . . . but especially . . . God's means of restoring men to himself.[82]

Barrett associates Wisdom not only with creation but also with the work of Christ in salvation, even identifying Christ crucified with the personal figure of Wisdom. Witherington sees a counter-order of Wisdom behind Paul's discussion in 1 Corinthians 1 – 4 that is indebted to the closing sections of Job. He sees a hidden Wisdom in

[79] Moo (2008: 130) comments that 'Christ rules the church with the purpose of bringing all things ultimately within the scope of that rule'.
[80] Garland 1998: 81, 90–91.
[81] Fee 2000: 252. He comments that the wisdom background to Paul's works has become prominent in the study of Pauline theology.
[82] Barrett 1968: 59–60.

Job 28 revealed only by God or God's agent. Paul's statement in 1 Corinthians 2:10–11 is drawn from Elihu's words in Job 32:8 because they both speak of the breath of God within a person giving understanding. Both Paul and Elihu are unusual mouthpieces that proclaim a revelatory wisdom. The message they convey is meant to be a rebuke of arrogant human wisdom. There are two kinds of wisdom: a revelatory wisdom, revealed by God and not discoverable by people, and a wisdom that can be discovered by examining creation as found in Proverbs. Paul's discussion of wisdom is thus a critique of the wisdom of Proverbs.[83]

There are several problems in associating Paul's argument in 1 Corinthians 1 – 4 with Jewish Wisdom theology. First, the one clear point where Wisdom and Christ intersect is the matter of pre-existence, particularly Wisdom's role in creation.[84] It is a stretch to identify the work of salvation of the incarnate Christ, as expressed in the phrase 'Christ crucified', with the personal figure of Wisdom.[85] Second, Paul uses 'wisdom' because he is responding to the Corinthians' view of wisdom that takes away from the message of the gospel.[86] Third, there is no hidden wisdom in Job 28 that is different from the wisdom discovered by interacting with God's creation in Proverbs. The 'hidden' wisdom in Job 28 is not a reference to wisdom in general but to specific questions concerning the reasons for suffering that were debated in Job. The answer to Job's suffering is not a wisdom that can be discovered through the normal channels of wisdom but must come from God himself. Elihu's wisdom was not able to answer Job's questions (see chapter 7).

Paul responds to the divisions of the church by emphasizing the message of the gospel (1:10–17). He highlights three things in 1:18 – 2:5: the foolishness of the message of Christ (1:18–25), the foolishness of the people of Christ (1:26–31) and the foolishness of the method of preaching Christ (2:1–5). God's wisdom appears foolish to the world but it is God's way of saving sinners. The message of Christ crucified is not foolish to those who are being saved but is the power of God because Christ delivers sinners from sin and death.

[83] Witherington 1994: 304–305, 309, 313.

[84] Fee 2000: 252.

[85] Jobes (2000: 238) makes this point in relation to feminist theologians who do not find in the literature of Hellenistic Judaism any role for Wisdom-Sophia in atonement. In fact, Sophia Christology destroys the heart of the gospel, for they see no need for atonement.

[86] Fee 2000: 256.

Paul refers to the OT to prove his point that God destroys the wisdom of the wise. He quotes Isaiah 29:14 and alludes to Isaiah's prophecy in the questions he asks (1:19–20). The questions show that neither the wise, nor Jews trained in Jewish religion, nor Greek philosophers have wisdom. The world is not able to discover God through their wisdom but only through the folly of the message of Christ preached. The world's wisdom and the cross stand in absolute contradiction to each other.[87] The problem with the Jews is that they demand a sign. They will not believe in Jesus unless he becomes a miracle worker at their command.[88] Greeks seek their own wisdom, but Paul preaches Christ crucified, a problem for both Jews and Greeks. To the Jews a crucified Messiah is accursed, and to the Greeks a person crucified is a criminal slave. And yet a crucified Christ is the wisdom of God because he is God's way of confounding the wisdom of the world by saving sinners.

If the message of the cross is foolishness to the world, it follows that the people of the cross and the method of preaching the cross will be foolishness to the world. Paul asks the Corinthians to consider that not many of them were wise or powerful according to the world's standards. God chooses the foolish and weak to shame the strong so that no one can boast before God. Christ Jesus became to us wisdom from God so that in him we receive wisdom. We who are called by God understand the wisdom of God in the message of Christ crucified and in our own calling. Righteousness, sanctification and redemption are given to us by God so that we have nothing to boast about. Paul's ministry in Corinth exemplified a method of simply preaching Christ crucified. Paul did not preach with lofty speech or wisdom.[89] He came in weakness and in fear and much trembling, solely dependent on the power of the Spirit who changes people's lives. The power and wisdom of Christ is demonstrated in the message of Christ, the people of Christ and the method of preaching Christ. The teaching of Christ, the power of Christ and the work of Christ all exhibit God's wisdom in its fullness and glory.

---

[87] Fee 1987: 74.

[88] Kistemaker 1993: 59.

[89] Ciampa and Rosner (2010: 87) comment that 'the problem with preaching the gospel with *wisdom and eloquence* is that it represents a mismatch between message and medium' (emphasis original).

Bibliography

Alden, R. L. (1993), *Job*, NAC, Nashville: Broadman & Holman.

Alexander, T. D. (1986), 'The Old Testament View of Life After Death', *Them* 11.2: 41–46.

——— (1987), 'Psalms and the Afterlife', *IBS* 9: 6–11.

Alter, R. (1985), *The Art of Biblical Poetry*, New York: Basic.

Andersen, F. I. (1974), *Job: An Introduction and Commentary*, TOTC, Leicester: Inter-Varsity Press; Downers Grove: InterVarsity Press.

Anderson, W. H. U. (1998), 'The Curse of Work in Qohelet: An Exposé of Genesis 3:17–19 in Ecclesiastes', *EvQ* 70.2: 99–113.

Archer Jr, G. L. (1974), *A Survey of Old Testament Introduction*, Chicago: Moody.

Arnold, B. T., and J. H. Choi (2003), *A Guide to Biblical Hebrew Syntax*, Cambridge: Cambridge University Press.

Ash, C. (2014), *Job*, PTW, Wheaton: Crossway.

Atkinson, D. (1996), *The Message of Proverbs*, BST, Leicester: Inter-Varsity Press; Downers Grove: InterVarsity Press.

Bailey, L. R. (1971), 'Death as a Theological Problem in the Old Testament', *Pastoral Psychology* 22: 20–32.

——— (1979), *Biblical Perspectives on Death*, Philadephia: Fortress.

Baker, D. W. (1997), 'רעע (*rʿʿ*)', in *NIDOTTE* 3: 1154.

Baldwin, J. G. (1978), *Daniel*, TOTC, Leicester: Inter-Varsity Press; Downers Grove: InterVarsity Press.

Barrett, C. K. (1968), *The First Epistle to the Corinthians*, New York: Harper & Row.

Bartholomew, C. G. (1998), *Reading Ecclesiastes: Old Testament Exegesis and Hermeneutical Theory*, Rome: Editrice Pontificio Istituto Biblico.

——— (2009), *Ecclesiastes*, Grand Rapids: Baker.

——— (2016), 'Old Testament Wisdom Today', in D. G. Firth and L. Wilson (eds.), *Interpreting Old Testament Wisdom Literature*, Downers Grove: InterVarsity Press; Nottingham: Apollos, 3–36.

Bartholomew, C. G., and R. P. O'Dowd (2011), *Old Testament Wisdom Literature*, Downers Grove: InterVarsity Press; Nottingham: Apollos.

Barton, G. A. (1993), *The Book of Ecclesiastes*, ICC, Edinburgh: T&T Clark.

Belcher Jr, R. P. (2006), *The Messiah and the Psalms*, Fearn, Ross-shire: Christian Focus.

—— (2008), 'Suffering', in *DOTWPW*, 775–781.

—— (2016a), 'Job', in M. Van Pelt (ed.), *A Biblical-Theological Introduction to the Old Testament*, Wheaton: Crossway, 357–372.

—— (2016b), *Prophet, Priest, and King: The Roles of Christ in the Bible and Our Roles Today*, Phillipsburg: P&R.

—— (2017a), *Ecclesiastes: A Mentor Commentary*, Fearn, Ross-shire, Christian Focus.

—— (2017b), *Job: The Mystery of Suffering and God's Sovereignty*, Fearn, Ross-shire: Christian Focus.

Blomberg, C. L. (2012), *Interpreting the Parables*, 2nd ed., Downers Grove: IVP Academic; Nottingham: Apollos.

Boda, M. J. (2013), 'Speaking into the Silence: The Epilogue of Ecclesiastes', in M. J. Boda, T. Longman III and C. G. Rata (eds.), *The Words of the Wise Are Like Goads: Engaging Qohelet in the 21st Century*, Winona Lake: Eisenbrauns, 257–282.

Bollhagen, J. (2011), *Ecclesiastes*, Concordia Commentary, St. Louis: Concordia.

Boström, L. (2016), 'Retribution and Wisdom Literature', in D. G. Firth and L. Wilson (eds.), *Interpreting Old Testament Wisdom Literature*, Downers Grove: InterVarsity Press; Nottingham: Apollos, 134–154.

Brenner, A. (1989), 'Job the Pious? The Characterization of Job in the Narrative Framework of the Book', *JSOT* 43: 37–52.

Brown, W. P. (2000), *Ecclesiastes*, Louisville: John Knox.

—— (2014), *Wisdom's Wonder: Character, Creation, and Crisis in the Bible's Wisdom Literature*, Grand Rapids: Eerdmans.

Bruce, F. F. (1957), *A Commentary on the Epistle to the Colossians*, NICNT, Grand Rapids: Eerdmans.

Brueggemann, W. A. (1972), *In Man We Trust: The Neglected Side of Biblical Faith*, Richmond, Va.: John Knox.

Carson, D. A. (1987), *Jesus' Sermon on the Mount and His Confrontation with the World*, Grand Rapids: Baker.

—— (1990), *How Long, O Lord? Reflections on Evil and Suffering*, Grand Rapids: Baker; Leicester: Inter-Varsity Press.

—— (1991), *The Gospel According to John*, PNTC, Grand Rapids: Eerdmans; Leicester: Apollos.

——— (2010), 'Matthew', in T. Longman III and D. E. Garland (eds.), EBC, vol. 9, rev. ed., Grand Rapids: Zondervan, 23–670.

Carson, D. A., and D. J. Moo (2005), *An Introduction to the New Testament*, 2nd ed., Grand Rapids: Zondervan.

Childs, B. S. (1979), *Introduction to the Old Testament Scripture*, Philadelphia: Fortress.

Christiansen, E. S. (1998), *A Time to Tell: Narrative Strategies in Ecclesiastes*, Sheffield: Sheffield Academic Press.

Ciampa, R. E., and B. S. Rosner (2007), in G. K. Beale and D. A. Carson (eds.), *Commentary on the New Testament Use of the Old Testament*, Grand Rapids: Baker; Nottingham: Apollos, 695–752.

——— (2010), *The First Letter to the Corinthians*, Grand Rapids: Eerdmans; Nottingham: Apollos.

Clarke, R. (2016), 'Seeking Wisdom in the Song of Songs', in D. G. Firth and L. Wilson (eds.), *Interpreting Old Testament Wisdom Literature*, Downers Grove: InterVarsity Press; Nottingham: Apollos, 100–114.

Clements, R. E. (1992), *Wisdom in Theology*, Grand Rapids: Eerdmans.

——— (1995), 'Wisdom and Old Testament Theology', in J. Day, R. P. Gordon and H. G. M. Williamson (eds.), *Wisdom in Israel: Essays in Honour of J. A. Emerson*, Cambridge: Cambridge University Press, 269–286.

Clines, D. J. A. (1982), 'The Arguments of Job's Three Friends', in D. J. A. Clines, D. M. Gunn and A. J. Hauser (eds.), *Art and Meaning: Rhetoric in Biblical Literature*, Sheffield: JSOT, 199–214.

——— (1989), *Job 1–20*, WBC, Dallas: Word.

——— (2004), 'Job's Fifth Friend: An Ethical Critique of the Book of Job', *BI* 12: 233–250.

——— (2006), *Job 21–37*, WBC, Nashville: Thomas Nelson.

——— (2011), *Job 38–42*, WBC, Nashville: Thomas Nelson.

Cole (née Cady), S., M. Ronan and H. Taussig (2016), *Wisdom's Feast: Sophia in Study and Celebration*, Berkeley: Apocryphile.

Cook, J. A. (2013), 'The Verb in Qohelet', in M. J. Boda, T. Longman III and C. G. Rata (eds.), *The Words of the Wise Are Like Goads: Engaging Qohelet in the 21st Century*, Winona Lake: Eisenbrauns, 309–342.

Craigie, P. C. (1983), *Psalms 1–50*, WBC, Waco: Word.

Crenshaw, J. L. (1974), 'The Eternal Gospel (Ecclesiastes 3:11)', in J. L. Crenshaw and J. T. Willis (eds.), *Essays in Old Testament Ethics*, New York: KTAV, 23–55.

———— (1976), 'Prologomenon', in H. M. Orlinsky (ed.), *Studies in Ancient Israelite Wisdom*, New York: KTAV, 1–35.

———— (1978), 'The Shadow of Death in Qoheleth', in J. G. Gammie, W. A. Brueggemann, W. L. Humphreys and J. M. Ward (eds.), *Israelite Wisdom: Theological and Literary Essays in Honor of Samuel Terrien*, Missoula: Scholars Press, 205–216.

———— (1981), *Old Testament Wisdom: An Introduction*, Atlanta: John Knox.

———— (1985), 'Education in Ancient Israel', *JBL* 104: 601–615.

———— (1986), 'The Expression *mî yôdea'* in the Hebrew Bible', *VT* 36: 274–288.

———— (1987), *Ecclesiastes*, OTL, Philadelphia: Westminster.

———— (1989), 'Poverty and Punishment in the Book of Proverbs', *QR* 9: 30–43.

———— (1990), 'The Sage in Proverbs', in J. G. Gammie and L. G. Perdue, *The Sage in Israel and the Ancient Near East*, Winona Lake: Eisenbrauns, 205–216.

———— (1995), 'Method in Determining Wisdom Influence upon "Historical" Literature', in *Urgent Advice and Probing Questions: Collected Writings on Old Testament Wisdom*, Macon: Mercer University Press, 312–325.

———— (1998), *Education in Ancient Israel: Across the Deadening Silence*, New York: Doubleday.

Currid, J. D. (1997), *Ancient Egypt and the Old Testament*, Grand Rapids: Baker.

Curtis, J. B. (1979), 'On Job's Response to Yahweh', *JBL* 98: 497–511.

Davies, J. A. (2011), 'Discerning Between God and Evil: Solomon as a New Adam in 1 Kings', *WTJ* 73: 39–57.

Day, J. (1985), *God's Conflict with the Dragon and the Sea*, Cambridge: Cambridge University Press.

Day, J., R. P. Gordon and H. G. M. Williamson (eds.) (1995), *Wisdom in Ancient Israel: Essays in Honour of J. A. Emerson*, Cambridge: Cambridge University Press.

Delitzsch, F. (1978a), *Job*, in C. F. Keil and F. Delitzsch, *Commentary on the Old Testament in Ten Volumes*, vol. 4, Grand Rapids: Eerdmans.

———— (1978b), *Proverbs, Ecclesiastes, Song of Solomon*, in C. F. Keil and F. Delitzsch, *Commentary on the Old Testament in Ten Volumes*, vol. 6, Grand Rapids: Eerdmans.

Dell, K. J. (2010), 'Does God Behave Unethically in the Book of Job?', in K. J. Dell (ed.), *Ethical and Unethical in the Old*

Testament: God and Humans in Dialogue, New York: T&T Clark, 170–186.

——— (2017), *Job: An Introduction and Study Guide: Where Shall Wisdom Be Found?*, New York: T&T Clark.

Dunn, J. D. G. (1996), *The Epistles to the Colossians and to Philemon: A Commentary on the Greek Text*, NIGTC, Grand Rapids: Eerdmans.

Eaton, M. A. (1983), *Ecclesiastes*, TOTC, Downers Grove: InterVarsity Press.

Ebert IV, D. J. (2011), *Wisdom Christology: How Jesus Becomes God's Wisdom for Us*, Phillipsburg: P&R.

Edwards, J. R. (2015), *The Gospel According to Luke*, PNTC, Grand Rapids: Eerdmans; Nottingham: Apollos.

Eichrodt, W. (1967), *Theology of the Old Testament*, 2 vols., London: SCM.

Emerson, M. Y. (2017), 'The Role of Proverbs 8: Eternal Generation and Hermeneutics Ancient and Modern', in F. Sanders and S. Swain (eds.), *Retrieving Eternal Generation*, Grand Rapids: Zondervan, 44–66.

Enns, P. (2011), *Ecclesiastes*, THOTC, Grand Rapids: Eerdmans.

Estes, D. J. (1997), *Hear My Son: Teaching and Learning in Proverbs 1 – 9*, NSBT, Leicester: Apollos; Downers Grove: InterVarsity Press.

——— (2010), 'What Makes the Strange Woman of Proverbs 1–9 Strange?', in K. J. Dell (ed.), *Ethical and Unethical in the Old Testament: God and Humans in Dialogue*, New York: T&T Clark, 151–169.

Estes, H. B. (1982), 'God Is in Heaven: An Investigation of the Concept of God in the Book of Ecclesiastes', ThD diss., New Orleans Baptist Theological Seminary.

Farmer, K. A. (1991), *Proverbs & Ecclesiastes: Who Knows What Is Good?*, ITC, Grand Rapids: Eerdmans.

Fee, G. D. (1987), *The First Epistle to the Corinthians*, NICNT, Grand Rapids: Eerdmans.

——— (2000), 'Wisdom Christology in Paul: A Dissenting View', in J. I. Packer and S. K. Soderlund (eds.), *The Way of Wisdom*, Grand Rapids: Zondervan, 251–279.

Ferguson, S. B. (1987), *The Sermon on the Mount: Kingdom Life in a Fallen World*, Carlisle: Banner of Truth Trust.

Fiorenza, E. S. (1994), *Jesus: Miriam's Child, Sophia's Prophet: Critical Issues in Feminist Christology*, New York: Continuum.

Firth, D. G., and L. Wilson (eds.) (2016), *Interpreting Old Testament Wisdom Literature*, Downers Grove: InterVarsity Press; Nottingham: Apollos.

Fisher, M. C. (1980), 'נער (*n'r*)', in *TWOT* 2: 585–586.

Fohrer, G. (1968), *Introduction to the Old Testament*, Nashville: Abingdon.

Fox, M. V. (1977), 'Frame-Narrative and Composition in the Book of Qohelet', *HUCA* 48: 83–106.

——— (1999), *A Time to Tear Down and a Time to Build Up: A Rereading of Ecclesiastes*, Grand Rapids: Eerdmans.

——— (2000), *Proverbs 1–9*, AB, New York: Doubleday.

——— (2009), *Proverbs 10–31*, AB, New York: Doubleday.

——— (2012), 'Behemoth and Leviathan', *Bib* 93: 261–267.

——— (2013), 'God's Answer and Job's Response', *Bib* 94.1: 1–23.

Frame, J. M. (2013), *Systematic Theology: An Introduction to Christian Belief*, Phillipsburg: P&R.

Fredericks, D. C. (1988), *Qohelet's Language: Re-evaluating Its Nature and Date*, Lewiston: Edwin Mellon.

——— (1993), *Coping with Transience*, Sheffield: JSOT Press.

Fredericks, D. C., and D. J. Estes (2010), *Ecclesiastes & The Song of Songs*, Nottingham: Apollos; Downers Grove: InterVarsity Press.

Fretheim, T. E. (1997), 'חנן (*ḥnn*)', in *NIDOTTE* 2: 203–206.

Fyall, R. S. (1995), *How Does God Treat His Friends?* Fearn, Ross-shire: Christian Focus.

——— (2002), *Now My Eyes Have Seen You: Images of Creation and Evil in the Book of Job*, Leicester: Apollos; Downers Grove: InterVarsity Press.

Garland, D. E. (1998), *Colossians/Philemon*, NIVAC, Grand Rapids: Zondervan.

Garrett, D. A. (1993), *Proverbs, Ecclesiastes, Song of Songs*, NAC, Nashville: Broadman.

Geldenhuys, N. (1977), *Commentary on the Gospel of Luke*, NICNT, Grand Rapids, Eerdmans.

Gladd, B. (2016), 'Colossians', in M. J. Kruger (ed.), *A Biblical-Theological Introduction to the New Testament: The Gospel Realized*, Wheaton: Crossway, 61–92.

Goldberg, L. (1980), 'חכם (*ḥākam*)', in *TWOT* 1: 282–284.

Goldingay, J. E. (1989), *Daniel*, WBC, Dallas: Word.

——— (2006), *Psalms 1–41*, Grand Rapids: Baker.

Gordis, R. (1955), *Koheleth – The Man and His World*, New York: Schocken.

———— (1965), *The Book of God and Man*, Chicago: University of Chicago Press.

Green, W. H. (1999), *Conflict and Triumph*, Carlisle: Banner of Truth Trust.

Greenspoon, L. J. (1981), 'The Origin of the Idea of the Resurrection', in B. Halpern and J. D. Levenson (eds.), *Traditions in Transformation: Turning Points in Biblical Faith*, Winona Lake: Eisenbrauns, 247–321.

Grogan, G. W. (2008), *Psalms*, THOTC, Grand Rapids: Eerdmans.

Guelich, R. A. (1982), *The Sermon on the Mount: A Foundation for Understanding*, Waco: Word.

Habel, N. C. (1985), *The Book of Job*, OTL, Philadelphia: Westminster.

Hadley, J. M. (1995), 'Wisdom and the Goddess', in J. Day, R. P. Gordon and H. G. M. Williamson (eds.), *Wisdom in Ancient Israel*, Cambridge: Cambridge University Press, 234–243.

Hamilton Jr, J. M. (2014), *With the Clouds of Heaven: The Book of Daniel in Biblical Theology*, NSBT, Nottingham: Apollos; Downers Grove: InterVarsity Press.

Hamilton, V. (1997), 'נער (*na'ar*)', in *NIDOTTE* 3: 124–127.

Hartley, J. E. (1988), *The Book of Job*, NICOT, Grand Rapids: Eerdmans.

———— (1994), 'From Lament to Oath: A Study of Progression in the Speeches of Job', in W. A. M. Beuken (ed.), *The Book of Job*, Leuven: Leuven University Press, 79–100.

Hayes, J. H., and F. Prussner (1985), *Old Testament Theology: Its History and Development*, Atlanta: John Knox.

Hendriksen, W. (1964), *Exposition of Colossians and Philemon*, NTC, Grand Rapids: Baker.

———— (1973), *Exposition of the Gospel According to Matthew*, NTC, Grand Rapids: Baker.

———— (1978), *Exposition of the Gospel According to Luke*, NTC, Grand Rapids: Baker.

Hengstenberg, E. W. (1960), *A Commentary on Ecclesiastes*, Evansville: Sovereign Grace.

Hermission, H.-J. (1978), 'Observations on the Creation Theology in Wisdom', in J. G. Gammie, W. A. Brueggemann, W. L. Humphreys and J. M. Ward (eds.), *Israelite Wisdom: Theological and Literary Essays in Honor of Samuel Terrien*, Missoula: Scholars Press, 43–57.

Holmstedt, R. (2013), 'The Grammar of הבל and ש in Qohelet', in M. J. Boda, T. Longman III and C. G. Rata (eds.), *The Words of the Wise Are Like Goads: Engaging Qohelet in the 21st Century*, Winona Lake: Eisenbrauns, 283–307.

Hopkins, D. D., and M. S. Koppel (2010), *Grounded in the Living Word: The Old Testament and Pastoral Care Practice*, Grand Rapids: Eerdmans.

House, H. W. (1992), 'The Doctrine of Christ in Colossians', *BSac* 149: 180–192.

Hubbard, D. A. (1966), 'The Wisdom Movement and Israel's Covenant Faith', *TynB* 17: 3–33.

———— (1989), *Proverbs*, Communicator's Commentary, Dallas: Word.

———— (1991), *Ecclesiastes, Song of Solomon*, Dallas: Word.

Isaksson, B. (1987), *Studies in the Language of Qoheleth*, Stockholm: Almqvist & Wiksell International.

Jobes, K. H. (2000), 'Sophia Christology: The Way of Wisdom?', in J. I. Packer and S. K. Soderlund (eds.), *The Way of Wisdom*, Grand Rapids: Zondervan, 226–250.

Johnston, P. S. (2002), *Shades of Sheol*, Leicester: Apollos; Downers Grove: InterVarsity Press.

Jones, D. W., and R. S. Woodbridge (2011), *Health, Wealth, and Happiness: Has the Prosperity Gospel Overshadowed the Gospel of Christ?*, Grand Rapids: Kregel.

Jones, H. R. (2007), *A Study Commentary on Job*, Darlington: Evangelical Press.

Kaiser Jr, W. C. (1978), *Ecclesiastes: Total Life*, Everyman's Bible Commentary, Chicago: Moody Bible Institute.

———— (1988), 'The Old Testament Promise of Material Blessings and the Contemporary Believer', *TJ* 9 NS: 151–170.

———— (2013), *Coping with Change – Ecclesiastes*, Fearn, Ross-shire: Christian Focus.

Kidner, D. (1964), *Proverbs: An Introduction and Commentary*, TOTC, London: Tyndale; Downers Grove: InterVarsity Press.

———— (1985), *An Introduction to Wisdom Literature: The Wisdom of Proverbs, Job & Ecclesiastes*, Leicester: Inter-Varsity Press; Downers Grove: InterVarsity Press.

Kistemaker, S. J. (1993), *Exposition of the First Epistle to the Corinthians*, Grand Rapids: Baker.

———— (2002), *The Parables: Understanding the Stories Jesus Told*, Grand Rapids: Baker.

Kitchen, J. A. (2006), *Proverbs: A Mentor Commentary*, Fearn, Ross-shire: Christian Focus.

Kitchen, K. A. (1977), 'Proverbs and Wisdom Books of the Ancient Near East: The Factual History of a Literary Form', *TynB* 28: 69–114.

—— (2008), 'Proverbs 2: Ancient Near Eastern Background', in T. Longman III and P. Enns (eds.), *DOTWPW*, 552–566.

Klein, W. W., C. L. Blomberg and R. L. Hubbard Jr (1993), *Introduction to Biblical Interpretation*, Dallas: Word.

Kline, M. G. (1972), *The Structure of Biblical Authority*, Grand Rapids: Eerdmans.

Knierim, R. P. (1995), *The Task of Old Testament Theology: Method and Cases*, Grand Rapids: Eerdmans.

Koch, K. (1955), 'Gibt es ein Vergeltungsdogma im Alten Testament?', *ZTK* 52: 1–42.

—— (1983), 'Is There a Doctrine of Retribution in the Old Testament?', in J. L. Crenshaw (ed.), *Theodicy of the Old Testament*, Philadelphia: Fortress, 57–87.

Koh, Y. V. (2006), *Royal Autobiography in the Book of Qoheleth*, Berlin: de Gruyter.

Konkel, A. H. (2006), 'Job', in P. Comfort (ed.), *Cornerstone Biblical Commentary*, vol. 6, Carol Stream: Tyndale.

Koptak, P. E. (2003), *Proverbs*, NIVAC, Grand Rapids: Zondervan.

Kraus, H.-J. (1993), *Psalms 1–59: A Continental Commentary*, Minneapolis: Fortress.

Krüger, T. (2004), *Kohelet*, Hermeneia, Minneapolis: Fortress.

Kushner, H. S. (1981), *When Bad Things Happen to Good People*, New York: Avon.

Kynes, W. (2012), *My Psalm Has Turned into Weeping: Job's Dialogue with the Psalms*, Berlin: de Gruyter.

—— (2015), 'The Modern Scholarly Wisdom Tradition and the Threat of Pan-Sapientialism: A Case Report', in M. R. Sneed (ed.), *Was There a Wisdom Tradition? New Prospects in Israelite Wisdom Studies*, Atlanta: SBL Press, 11–38.

—— (forthcoming), *An Obituary for 'Wisdom Literature'*, Oxford: Oxford University Press.

Ladd, G. E. (1959), *The Gospel of the Kingdom*, Grand Rapids: Eerdmans.

Lane, W. L. (1974), *The Gospel According to Mark*, NICNT, Grand Rapids: Eerdmans.

Lauha, A. (1978), *Kohelet*, BKAT, Neukirchen-Vluyn: Neukirchener Verlag.

Levenson, J. D. (2006), *Resurrection and the Restoration of Israel: The Ultimate Victory of the God of Life*, London: Yale University Press.

Lo, A. (2003), *Job 28 as Rhetoric*, Atlanta: Society of Biblical Literature.

Loader, J. A. (1986), *Ecclesiastes: A Practical Commentary*, Text and Interpretation, Grand Rapids: Eerdmans.

Longman III, T. (1991), *Fictional Akkadian Autobiography*, Winona Lake: Eisenbrauns.

——— (1998), *The Book of Ecclesiastes*, NICOT, Grand Rapids: Eerdmans.

——— (2006), *Proverbs*, Grand Rapids: Baker.

——— (2012), *Job*, Grand Rapids: Baker.

——— (2015), 'The "Fear of God" in the Book of Ecclesiastes', *BBR* 25.1: 13–21.

——— (2017), *The Fear of the Lord Is Wisdom: A Theological Introduction to Wisdom in Israel*, Grand Rapids: Baker.

Luc, A. (1997), 'ערם (*'rm*)', in *NIDOTTE* 3: 539–541.

Lucas, E. C. (2013), *Exploring the Old Testament: The Psalms and Wisdom Literature*, Downers Grove: InterVarsity Press.

——— (2015), *Proverbs*, THOTC, Grand Rapids: Eerdmans.

——— (2016), 'The Book of Proverbs: Some Current Issues', in D. G. Firth and L. Wilson (eds.), *Interpreting Old Testament Wisdom Literature*, Downers Grove: InterVarsity Press; Nottingham: Apollos, 37–59.

McCabe, R. (1997), 'Elihu's Contribution to the Thought of the Book of Job', *DBSJ* 2: 47–80.

McDonough, S. M. (2009), *Christ as Creator: Origins of a New Testament Doctrine*, Oxford: Oxford University Press.

McKane, W. (1970), *Proverbs: A New Approach*, OTL, Philadelphia: Westminster.

Mays, J. L. (1994), *Psalms*, Interpretation, Louisville: John Knox.

Meek, R. L. (2013), 'The Meaning of הבל in Qohelet: An Intertextual Suggestion', in M. J. Boda, T. Longman III and C. G. Rata (eds.), *The Words of the Wise Are Like Goads: Engaging Qohelet in the 21st Century*, Winona Lake: Eisenbrauns, 241–256.

Michel, D. (1990), 'Gott bei Kohelet', *BK* 45: 32–36.

Moo, D. J. (2008), *The Letters to the Colossians and to Philemon*, PNTC, Grand Rapids: Eerdmans.

Murphy, R. E. (1969), 'The Interpretation of Old Testament Wisdom Literature', *Int* 23: 289–301.

—— (1975), 'Wisdom and Yahwism', in J. W. Flanagan and A. W. Robinson (eds.), *No Famine in the Land*, Missoula: Scholars Press, 117–126.

—— (1992), *Ecclesiastes*, WBC, Dallas: Word.

—— (1998), *Proverbs*, WBC, Nashville: Thomas Nelson.

—— (2002), *The Tree of Life: An Exploration of Biblical Wisdom Literature*, Grand Rapids: Eerdmans.

Murray, J. (1997), 'Common Grace', in *Select Lectures in Systematic Theology, Collected Writings of John Murray*, 4 vols., Carlisle: Banner of Truth Trust, 2: 93–122.

Newell, R. L. (1992), 'Job: Repentant or Rebellious?', in R. B. Zuck (ed.), *Sitting with Job*, Grand Rapids: Eerdmans, 441–456.

Newsom, C. A. (2003), *The Book of Job: A Context of Moral Imaginations*, Oxford: Oxford University Press.

—— (2014), *Daniel: A Commentary*, OTL, Louisville: Westminster John Knox.

—— (2015), 'The Book of Job', in *NIB* 3: 17–270.

Oblath, M. (1999), 'Job's Advocate: A Tempting Suggestion', *BBR* 9: 189–201.

O'Dowd, R. P. (2013), 'Epistemology in Ecclesiastes: Remembering What It Means to Be Human', in M. J. Boda, T. Longman III and C. G. Rata (eds.), *The Words of the Wise Are Like Goads: Engaging Qohelet in the 21st Century*, Winona Lake: Eisenbrauns, 195–218.

Ogden, G. S. (2007), *Qoheleth*, 2nd ed., Sheffield: JSOT Press.

Ogden, G. S., and L. Zogbo (1997), *A Handbook on Ecclesiastes*, New York: United Bible Societies.

Pennington, J. T. (2017), *The Sermon on the Mount and Human Flourishing: A Theological Commentary*, Grand Rapids: Baker Academic.

Perdue, L. G. (1977), *Wisdom and Cult: A Critical Analysis of the Views of the Cult in the Wisdom Literatures of Israel and the Ancient Near East*, Missoula: Scholars Press.

—— (1986), 'The Wisdom Sayings of Jesus', *Forum* 2: 3–35.

—— (1994a), *The Collapse of History: Reconstructing Old Testament Theology*, Minneapolis: Fortress.

—— (1994b), *Wisdom and Creation: The Theology of Wisdom Literature*, Nashville: Abingdon.

—— (2007), *Wisdom Literature: A Theological History*, Louisville: Westminster John Knox.

Preuss, H. D. (1972), 'Das Gottesbild der älteren Weisheit Israels', in *Studies in the Religion of Ancient Israel*, VTSup 23, Leiden: Brill, 117–145.

——— (1987), *Einführing in die alttestamentliche Weisheitsliteratur*, Stuttgart: Kohlhammer.

Provan, I. (2001), *Ecclesiastes/Song of Songs*, NIVAC, Grand Rapids: Zondervan.

Rad, G. von (1962), *Old Testament Theology*, 2 vols., New York: Harper & Row.

——— (1968), 'The Theological Problem of the Old Testament Doctrine of Creation', in *The Problem of the Hexateuch and Other Essays*, New York: McGraw-Hill, 131–143.

——— (1972), *Wisdom in Israel*, New York: Harper & Row.

Reventlow, H. G. (1985), *Problems of Old Testament Theology in the Twentieth Century*, Philadelphia: Fortress.

Ridderbos, H. N. (1962), *The Coming of the Kingdom*, Philadelphia: P&R.

——— (1987), *Matthew*, Grand Rapids: Zondervan.

Robertson, D. A. (1973), 'The Book of Job: A Literary Study', *Soundings* 56: 446–469.

Robertson, O. P. (2017), *The Christ of Wisdom: A Redemptive-Historical Exploration of the Wisdom Books of the Old Testament*, Phillipsburg: P&R.

Rodd, C. S. (1990), *The Book of Job*, Narrative Commentaries, Philadelphia: Trinity Press International.

Ross, A. P. (2008), 'Proverbs', in T. Longman III and D. E. Garland (eds.), EBC, rev. ed., 13 vols., Grand Rapids: Zondervan, 6: 21–252.

Rowley, H. H. (1980), *The Book of Job*, rev. ed., Grand Rapids: Eerdmans.

Ruffle, J. (1977), 'The Teaching of Amenemope and Its Connection with the Book of Proverbs', *TynB* 28: 29–68.

Salyer, G. D. (2001), *Vain Rhetoric: Private Insight and Public Debate in Ecclesiastes*, Sheffield: Sheffield Academic Press.

Schmid, H. H. (1966), *Wesen und Geschichte der Weisheit*, Berlin: Alfred Töpelmann.

——— (1984), 'Creation, Righteousness, and Salvation: "Creation Theology" as the Broad Horizon of Biblical Theology', in B. W. Anderson (ed.), *Creation in the Old Testament*, Philadelphia: Fortress, 102–108.

Schoors, A. (2004), *The Preacher Sought to Find Pleasing Words: A Study of the Language of Qoheleth: Part II: Vocabulary*, Leuven: Peeters.

Schroer, S. (2000), *Wisdom Has Built Her House: Studies on the Figure of Sophia in the Bible*, Collegeville: Liturgical Press.

Schultz, R. L. (1997), 'Unity or Diversity in Wisdom Theology? A Canonical and Covenantal Perspective', *TynB* 48.2: 271–306.

Schwab, G. M. (2009), 'The Book of Proverbs', in P. W. Comfort (ed.), *Cornerstone Biblical Commentary*, Carol Stream: Tyndale House, 7: 451–669.

Scott, R. B. Y. (April 1960), 'Wisdom in Creation: The *'Amôn* of Proverbs VIII 30', *VT* 10.2: 213–223.

———— (March 1961), 'Priesthood, Prophecy, Wisdom, and the Knowledge of God', *JBL* 80: 1–15.

———— (1965), *Proverbs, Ecclesiastes*, AB, New York: Doubleday.

———— (1970), 'The Study of Wisdom Literature', *Int* 24.1: 20–45.

———— (1976), 'Solomon and the Beginnings of Wisdom in Israel', in J. L. Crenshaw (ed.), *Studies in Ancient Israelite Wisdom*, New York: KTAV, 84–101.

Seow, C. L. (1995), 'Qohelet's Autobiography', in A. B. Beck, A. H. Bartelt, P. R. Raabe and C. A. Franke (eds.), *Fortunate the Eyes That See: Essays in Honor of David Noel Freedman in Celebration of His Seventieth Birthday*, Grand Rapids: Eerdmans, 275–287.

———— (1997), *Ecclesiastes*, AB, New York: Doubleday.

———— (2013), *Job 1–21*, Grand Rapids, Eerdmans.

Shields, M. A. (2006), *The End of Wisdom: A Reappraisal of the Historical and Canonical Function of Ecclesiastes*, Winona Lake: Eisenbrauns.

———— (2013), 'Qohelet and Royal Autobiography', in M. J. Boda, T. Longman III and C. G. Rata (eds.), *The Words of the Wise Are Like Goads: Engaging Qohelet in the 21st Century*, Winona Lake: Eisenbrauns, 117–136.

Smick, E. B. (2010), 'Job', in T. Longman III and D. Garland (eds.), EBC, vol. 4, rev. ed., Grand Rapids: Zondervan, 677–921.

Sneed, M. R. (2015), '"Grasping After the Wind": The Elusive Attempt to Define and Delimit Wisdom', in M. R. Sneed (ed.), *Was There a Wisdom Tradition? New Prospects in Israelite Wisdom Studies*, Atlanta: SBL Press, 39–68.

Snodgrass, K. (2008), *Stories with Intent: A Comprehensive Guide to the Parables of Jesus*, Grand Rapids: Eerdmans.

Spencer, A. B. (1995), *The Goddess Revival*, Grand Rapids: Baker.

Spronk, K. (1986), *Beatific Afterlife in Ancient Israel and in the Ancient Near East*, Neukirchen-Vluyn: Neukirchener Verlag.

Steel, A. (2001), 'Could Behemoth Have Been a Dinosaur?', *TJ* 15.2: 42–45.

Steinmann, A. E. (2009), *Proverbs*, Concordia Commentaries, St. Louis: Concordia.

Stocks, S. P. (2016), '"Children Listen to Me": The Voicing of Wisdom in the Psalms', in D. G. Firth and L. Wilson (eds.), *Interpreting Old Testament Wisdom Literature*, Downers Grove: InterVarsity Press; Nottingham: Apollos, 194–204.

Stuart, D. (2009), *Old Testament Exegesis*, 4th ed., Louisville: Westminster John Knox.

Talbert, L. (2007), *Beyond Suffering: Discovering the Message of Job*, Greenville: Bob Jones University.

VanDrunen, D. (2014), *Divine Covenants and Moral Order: A Biblical Theology of Natural Law*, Grand Rapids: Eerdmans.

VanGemeren, W. A. (2008), 'Psalms', in T. Longman III and D. E. Garland (eds.), EBC, rev. ed., 12 vols., Grand Rapids: Zondervan, 5: 22–1011.

——— (2016), 'Proverbs', in M. V. Van Pelt (ed.), *A Biblical-Theological Introduction to the Old Testament: The Gospel Promised*, Wheaton: Crossway, 373–398.

Van Leeuwen, R. C. (1988), *Context and Meaning in Proverbs 25–27*, SBLDS 96, Atlanta: Scholars Press.

——— (1992), 'Wealth and Poverty: System and Contradiction in Proverbs', *HS* 33: 25–36.

——— (2001), 'Psalm 8:5 and Job 7:17–18: A Mistaken Scholarly Commonplace?', in P. M. M. Daviau, J. W. Wevers and M. Weigl (eds.), *The World of the Aramaeans I: Biblical Studies in Honour of Paul-Eugene Dion*, Sheffield: Sheffield Academic Press, 205–215.

——— (2015), 'The Book of Proverbs', in *NIB* 3: 749–946.

Vawter, B. (1980), 'Prov 8:22: Wisdom and Creation', *JBL* 99.2: 205–216.

Waltke, B. K. (2004), *The Book of Proverbs: Chapters 1–15*, NICOT, Grand Rapids: Zondervan.

——— (2005), *The Book of Proverbs: Chapters 15–31*, NICOT, Grand Rapids: Zondervan.

Waltke, B. K., and M. O'Connor (1990), *An Introduction to Biblical Hebrew Syntax*, Winona Lake: Eisenbrauns.

Waltke, B. K., with C. Yu (2007), *An Old Testament Theology: An Exegetical, Canonical, and Thematic Approach*, Grand Rapids: Zondervan.

Walton, J. H. (2008), 'Retribution', in *DOTWPW*, 647–655.

—— (2012), *Job*, NIVAC, Grand Rapids: Zondervan.
Walton, J. H., and T. Longman III (2015), *How to Read the Book of Job*, Downers Grove: InterVarsity Press.
Weeks, S. (1999), 'Wisdom in the Old Testament', in S. C. Barton (ed.), *Where Shall Wisdom Be Found? Wisdom in the Bible, Church and the Contemporary World*, Edinburgh: T&T Clark, 19–30.
Westermann, C. (1977), *The Structure of the Book of Job: A Form-Critical Analysis*, Philadelphia: Fortress.
Whybray, R. N. (1978), 'Qoheleth the Immoralist? (Qoh 7:16–17)', in J. G. Gammie, W. A. Brueggemann, W. L. Humphreys and J. M. Ward (eds.), *Israelite Wisdom: Theological and Literary Essays in Honor of Samuel Terrien*, Missoula: Scholars Press, 191–204.
—— (1982), 'Qoheleth, Preacher of Joy?', *JSOT* 23: 87–98.
—— (1989), *Ecclesiastes*, NCBC, Grand Rapids: Eerdmans.
—— (1994), *Proverbs*, NCBC, Grand Rapids: Eerdmans.
—— (1996), *Reading the Psalms as a Book*, Sheffield: JSOT Press.
—— (1998), *Job*, Sheffield: Sheffield Academic Press.
Williams, J. G. (1981), *Those Who Ponder Proverbs: Aphoristic Thinking and Biblical Literature*, Sheffield: Almond.
Wilson, G. H. (2007), *Job*, NIBC, Peabody: Hendrickson.
Wilson, L. (2015), *Job*, THOTC, Grand Rapids: Eerdmans.
—— (2016), 'Job as a Problematic Book', in D. G. Firth and L. Wilson (eds.), *Interpreting Old Testament Wisdom Literature*, Downers Grove: InterVarsity Press; Nottingham: Apollos, 60–80.
—— (2017), *Proverbs: An Introduction and Commentary*, TOTC, London: Inter-Varsity Press; Downers Grove: InterVarsity Press.
Wink, W. (1990), 'The Hymn of the Cosmic Christ', in R. T. Fortna and B. R. Gaventa (eds.), *The Conversation Continues: Studies in Paul and John in Honor of J. L. Martyn*, Nashville: Abingdon, 235–244.
Winston, D. (1979), *The Wisdom of Solomon*, AB, Garden City: Doubleday.
Witherington III, B. (1994), *Jesus the Sage: The Pilgrimage of Wisdom*, Minneapolis: Fortress.
Wolters, A. (2001), *The Song of the Valiant Woman: Studies in the Interpretation of Proverbs 31.10–31*, Carlisle: Paternoster.
Wright, G. E. (1952), *God Who Acts: Biblical Theology as Recital*, London: SCM.
Young, E. J. (1952), *An Introduction to the Old Testament*, Grand Rapids: Eerdmans.

Young, I. (1993), *Diversity in Pre-Exilic Hebrew*, Tübingen: J. C. B. Mohr (Paul Siebeck).

Young, I., Robert Rezetko and Martin Ehrensväd (2008), *Linguistic Dating of Biblical Texts*, 2 vols., Tübingen: J. C. B. Mohr (Paul Siebeck).

Zimmerli, W. (1964), 'The Place and Limit of Wisdom in the Framework of Old Testament Theology', *SJT* 17: 146–158.

——— (1976a), 'Concerning the Structure of Old Testament Wisdom', in J. L. Crenshaw (ed.), *Studies in Ancient Israelite Wisdom*, New York: KTAV, 175–199.

——— (1976b), 'The Place and Limit of Wisdom in the Framework of the Old Testament Theology', in J. L. Crenshaw (ed.), *Studies in Ancient Israelite Wisdom*, New York: KTAV, 314–328.

Index of authors

Index of Scripture references

240

241

Titles in this series:

An index of Scripture references for all the volumes may be found at
http://www.thegospelcoalition.org/resources/nsbt

Finding the Textbook You Need

The IVP Academic Textbook Selector
is an online tool for instantly finding the IVP books
suitable for over 250 courses across 24 disciplines.

---

ivpacademic.com